THE FORTUNE SELLERS

The Big Business of Buying and Selling Predictions

William A. Sherden

JOHN WILEY & SONS, INC.

New York • Chichester • Weinheim • Brisbane • Singapore • Toronto

To my father, Arthur F. Sherden, who could not have predicted the good fortune that has blessed his life.

This text is printed on acid-free paper.

Copyright © 1998 by William A. Sherden.
Published by John Wiley & Sons, Inc.

All rights reserved. Published simultaneously in Canada.

Library of Congress Cataloging-in-Publication Data:

Sherden, William A.
  The fortune sellers: the big business of buying and selling predictions / William A. Sherden.
      p.   cm.
  Includes index.
  ISBN 0-471-18178-1 (cloth: alk. paper)
    1. Forecasting.   2. Forecasting—History.   I. Title.
CB158.S456   1998
003'.2—dc21   97-15012

Printed in the United States of America

10 9 8 7 6 5 4 3 2 1

Preface

On a daily basis, we are showered with all types of predictions: tomorrow will be unseasonably warm; next winter will experience record snowfall; the economy will stall next quarter; a deep recession is imminent by year end; the stock market will experience a technical correction; invest in biotech stocks; the aging of the population will bankrupt social security; burgeoning world population will lead to massive famine; global warming will raise sea levels three feet; artificial intelligence will transform society; robotics will antiquate manual labor; declining values will cause increased violence; nations will splinter during the post–cold war era; Microsoft will dominate information technology.

Of these sixteen types of forecast, only two—one-day-ahead weather forecasts and the aging of the population—can be counted on; the rest are about as reliable as the fifty-fifty odds in flipping a coin. And only one of the sixteen—short-term weather forecasts—has any scientific foundation. The rest are typically based on conjecture, unproved theory, and the mere extrapolation of past trends—something no more sophisticated than what a child could do with a ruler (or perhaps a protractor). It makes one wonder. At least it did me. The idea for *The Fortune Sellers* dates back to 1985, when I was providing inflation forecasts as an expert witness at an administrative rate hearing. In preparing my testimony, I analyzed the accuracy of inflation projections generated by different forecasting methods, including the simplest of all projection methods: that tomorrow's inflation will be the same as today's. Economists call this simple projection the "naive forecast." I also included in my analysis forecasts published by leading economic forecasting firms. I was surprised to find that the naive forecast proved to be the most accurate projection method. I was *astonished* to discover that the naive

forecast also beat the forecasts of the prestigious economic forecasting firms equipped with their Ph.D.s from leading universities and
thousand-equation computer models.

When I discussed this finding with one of my colleagues, he claimed
that the same thing was true for weather forecasting: anyone could beat
professional weather forecasters by merely assuming that tomorrow's
weather will be just like today's. The fact that the naive forecast could
outperform highly educated professionals in *both* weather and economic
forecasting seemed more than a coincidence. What if, I pondered, all
the experts whose forecasts we take as gospel were no better than just
flipping a coin or making naive guesses? That would mean that all the
money paid to such experts was a pure waste; worse still, the cost of
faulty decisions predicated on erroneous forecasts would be unimaginably high.

In 1995, I started in earnest to research these issues of forecasting skill
and reliability and the role that forecasts play in our society. Right away,
I was confronted with the issue of scope. The subject of prediction is
enormously broad and multifaceted, including numerous forecasting
practices based on everything from science to the occult. Ultimately I
decided to focus on the seven established forecasting professions and
practices that are most widely used by individuals and organizations to
plan for the future: meteorology, economics, investments, technology
assessment, demography, futurology, and organizational planning. As it
turned out, these seven established areas of prediction contained plenty
enough mythology and baloney without the inclusion of such fallacious—albeit lucrative—practices as astrology, divination, and fortune-
telling.

In exploring each of these seven forecasting fields, I found that similar themes emerged again and again. Forecasters in each field encounter
the same challenges and make the same mistakes in their attempts to predict the future. The application of hard scientific principles is notice-
ably lacking in all but a few areas of forecasting. Even the psychological
reasons that people believe experts' predictions are the same: believers
mistake chance events for feats of amazing forecast accuracy and find—
or look for—validation for their existing beliefs. In the end, my "hypothesis" that the future cannot be predicted was borne out by my
analysis of all the various experts' attempts to do so.

But I also have discovered that there are in fact actions we *can* take to thrive in an uncertain future, whose foundations are in age-old advice as well as in more recent biological metaphors. These are discussed at the end of each chapter and in the last two chapters of the book as well.

The future, in fact, is a subject rich in intellectual history, literature, and debate. Prophecy has pervaded intellectual thought for thousands of years, dating back to such ancient works as the Judeo-Christian Bible. In *The Fortune Sellers,* I explore the historical roots of the seven forecasting professions and discuss some of the leading intellectuals from the eighteenth and nineteenth centuries whose ideas have helped to shape modern thinking, including the great prophets of social progress like John Stuart Mill and Karl Marx; Malthus and his dismal outlook for human populations; and the masters of economic theory, Adam Smith and John Maynard Keynes. Much of the prophetic intellectual thinking has been expressed in literature ranging from Jules Verne's nineteenth-century optimistic vision of future space travel to H. G. Wells's early twentieth-century apocalyptic depiction of a global nuclear war, and from Edward Bellamy's utopian prediction of a gentle and egalitarian society in the the year 2000 to George Orwell's frightening vision of techno-totalitarianism in 1984.

The currently popular concepts of chaos and complexity, which explain both the uncertainty in life and the inability to predict the future, also have historical roots. Though popularized in 1987 by James Gleick's book, *Chaos: Making a New Science,* the notion of chaos as a natural phenomenon dates back to 1900, when French mathematician Louis Bachelier found chaos hidden within Isaac Newton's deterministic laws of nature. Also popularized in the late 1980s by the Sante Fe Institute, an independent think tank established in 1984 to explore complex systems, the concept of complex systems originates with Adam Smith's eighteenth-century explanation of how economies self-organize and Karl Popper's mid-twentieth century thesis that social systems are inherently unpredictable.

Although most of my research for *The Fortune Sellers* involved debunking false prophecy and assertions of forecasting skill, I found considerable support for my thesis in the highly original and clear-thinking concepts of a number of current authors, researchers, academics, and scientists. I include in this list Massachusetts Institute of Technology's Professor Edward Lorenz, for proclaiming that long-range weather forecasting was doomed; Sante Fe Institute's W. Brian Arthur and Harvard's Wassily Leontif, for their fresh challenges to established economic theory; Nathan Keyfitz from Harvard, for highlighting the limitations of prediction in his field of demographics; Burton Malkiel from Princeton, for his extensive case against the predictability of the stock market; University of Chicago's James March, for his exposé on the unpredictability of organizational behavior and the irrationality of decision making; Henry Mintzberg from McGill University, for his explanations on why organizational planning has severe limitations; and Peter Drucker, for his voice of reason on all matters of leadership in regard to dealing with an uncertain future.

WILLIAM A. SHERDEN

Boston, Massachusetts
September 1997

Acknowledgments

There are many people to thank for their help in preparing this book. The first is Andrea Pedolsky from the Altair Literary Agency, who has variously served as my agent and/or editor throughout the two-and-a-half-year cycle of developing a book proposal, finding a publisher, and finally completing the manuscript for *The Fortune Sellers*. Without her enthusiasm for the project and continual encouragement, I would neither have started this project nor continued writing chapters during the many months before a book publishing contract was actually secured.

I thank the people I interviewed, in person and by telephone, who shared their views on the state of prediction in their fields of expertise, including (in order by chapter): meteorologists James Lee and Steven Zubric at the National Weather Service and Mark DeMaria and Frank Lapore at the National Hurricane Center; Steven Durlauf, professor of economics at the University of Wisconsin and head of the economics program at the Sante Fe Institute; John Bogle, chairman of the mutual fund Vanguard, and John McDonald, professor of finance at Stanford University; Ed Ayres, editorial director at the Worldwatch Institute; and Francis Lee, a retired and distinguished professor from the Massachusetts Institute of Technology.

I also thank Alan Lawson, professor of history at Boston College, for our many friendly chats over the past ten years regarding diverse topics addressed by *The Fortune Sellers*. I thank Stephen Frankle for his scholarly attention to detail in editing drafts of this book and Marilyn Vogel for her research assistance. Finally, I thank my wife, Molly Sherden, for her legal assistance in reviewing the book contract and, more important, supporting me through the many months of researching and writing.

W.A.S.

Contents

1

The Second Oldest Profession

W hat will the future bring? The question expresses the terrible uncertainty we live in, an uncertainty that we would pay dearly to resolve. Isaac Asimov, the famous writer of futuristic fiction, observed, "If I were asked to guess what people are generally most insecure about, I would say it is the content of the future. We worry about it constantly."

The desire to know the future is a deep human psychic need. It lies at the foundation of virtually every religion created since our earliest days as conscious thinkers. Pope John Paul II notes that people are drawn to religion to answer the really big questions—for example, "What is the ultimate ineffable mystery which is the origin and destiny of our existence?"

The desire to know the future also has great allure because of the material benefits one can accrue. Making instant millions on Wall Street would be a piece of cake if you knew whether the economy was going to expand or contract at a particular time or which technologies were going to become commercial successes. If you knew that a spate of unusually bad earthquakes or hurricanes was going to strike, you could short-sell property insurers for a handsome gain. You could make a killing in the commodities market if you could predict the climate for next year's growing season.

Though the title of "second oldest profession" usually goes to lawyers and consultants, prognosticators are the rightful owners. Our earliest written records, from 5,000 years ago, show that forecasting was widely practiced in the ancient world in the form of divination, the art of telling the future by seeing patterns and clues in everything from animal entrails to celestial patterns. No doubt these ancient seers had power and material wealth. Isaac Asimov wrote in his book *Future Days,* "Such was the eagerness of people to believe these 'augurs' that they had great power and could usually count on being well supported by a grateful, or fearful, public."[1]

The Oracle of Delphi has been the most successful prediction business in history. The Oracle prophesied for ancient rulers from about 700 B.C. to A.D. 300, pronouncing on such important matters of state as whether to wage war or to form strategic alliances. The Oracle's success is clearly evident from the vast architectural investment that we can still see today at Delphi *and* its longevity as a prediction business. It is rare for anything, let alone a business enterprise, to last a thousand years.

Today the predicting business is a multibillion-dollar industry providing employment to hundreds of thousands of people (see Figure 1.1). They work in diverse professions ranging from Ph.D.-intensive scientific fields, to basic white-collar positions, to the purveyors of the paranormal. Mind you, when it comes to foretelling the future, it is sometimes hard to distinguish science from paranormal, and professional from amateur, because the track records are often so similar.

Not surprisingly, the largest group of forecasting professionals are those most closely associated with making money: investment advisers. According to the Securities Industry Association (SIA), a whopping half-million people are licensed by the National Association of Securities Dealers to advise clients on buying securities. They come from all walks of life, and about 200,000 of them actively make a living advising you and me on how to invest our money.

The SIA estimates that, of these 200,000 investment advisers, nearly half are stockbrokers working at securities firms. In fact, almost everyone working in the $71 billion securities industry is involved in projecting the future of investments. The industry employs a large number of "strategists" who project where the overall market is headed and analysts who predict which stocks to buy and sell. Thousands of invest-

Economics	Weather
Federal Reserve banks	National Weather Service
Council of Economic Advisors	National Climate Center
Congressional Budget Office	National Hurricane Center
National Bureau of Economic Research	The armed services' weather forecasters
World Bank	Private-sector weather forecasting firms
National Bureau of Economic Research	Corporations dependent on the weather
U.S. Department of Commerce	University meteorological departments
Private-sector forecasting firms	Radio
University economic departments	Television (e.g., the Weather Channel)
Industry forecasting services	Daily newspaper forecasts
(numerous)	Almanacs (*The Old Farmer's Almanac*)
Publications (magazines and	
newsletters)	**Population**

Financial services	Bureau of the Census
	World Bank
Institutional money management firms	Food and Agriculture Organization
Mutual fund companies	World Population Organization
Stock brokerage firms	University population centers
Investment research firms	Advocacy groups (ZPG)
Investment publications	Think tanks (Worldwatch)
Lending institutions	
Property/casualty and life insurers	**Futurists**

Technology	Self-proclaimed futurists
	Futurist societies
Office of Technology Assessment	Think tanks (Rand Company)
Congressional Research Service	Authors
Research and data service firms	Magazines, newsletters
Technology consultants	Daily newspapers
Magazines and newsletters	

Business planning	Fortune-telling
Department of Commerce	Personal services
Information services companies	Conventional newspaper horoscopes
Consulting firms	Tabloids

Figure 1.1   Overview of the prediction industry.

ment analysts work for investment research firms, whose days are spent cranking out newsletters and research reports.

The Securities and Exchange Commission (SEC) has licensed about 10,000 money management firms. These outfits make up a $50 billion industry that includes everything from major financial institutions like Prudential and Citicorp to thousands of small investment boutiques. According to the Employee Benefit Research and Investment Company Institutes, these tens of thousands of money managers provide investment predicting advice in managing $7.5 trillion in pension, endowment, and mutual funds.

There are 172,000 loan officers predicting whether you will default on your business loan, mortgage, or credit card, and 15,000 actuaries busily crunch statistics about when you are likely to die, be disabled, wreck your car, or suffer damage from a hurricane or an earthquake.

The *Statistical Abstract of the United States* reports 148,000 people purporting to be economists—whatever that means. There is no professional credentialing for economists. Whether employed by government agencies, corporations, economic consulting firms, or academia, economists generally forecast the impacts of proposed policies and programs on the economy and its industrial sectors.

The Bureau of Labor Statistics counts 208,000 people who call themselves consultants, which no doubt includes a sizable segment of those without "real" jobs in industry. Although consultants work on a variety of assignments, much of their work is prediction oriented. The typical consulting assignment involves advising clients on how future trends will affect their businesses—usually not a pretty picture—and then proposing new courses of action to ward off these coming adversities.

Weather forecasting is approximately a $5 billion business employing 6,000 schooled meteorologists and a large number of forecasters, whom those meteorologists consider to be "paraprofessionals." The federal government employs about two-thirds of the meteorologists, mostly at the National Weather Service but also in the armed services (weather has always been a major factor in warfare). The other third work for the hundred or so private forecasting firms or for industries—transportation, for instance—that are severely affected by weather.

The World Future Society boasts a membership of 30,000 "futurists" who predict how we will live in the future, what our society will be like, what the long-term threats are to our nation, how technology will change the workplace, and other big-picture issues. Businesses rely on futurists to keep pace with emerging lifestyles in developing new products and marketing messages. Businesses, for example, might develop new snack foods to fulfill the emerging needs of the couch potatoes of the future.

Additionally, there are numerous futurist types employed throughout government in such organizations as the CIA and the National Security Council. Then of course there are the "beltway bandits": the independent think tanks that advise government agencies in making policy decisions that will affect the future of society and government.

A look at the prediction industry would not be complete without the news media, which flood us every day with forecasts of all types. Daily newspapers contain predictions about the weather, economy, stock market, politics, society, science, and geopolitical trends and events. Many routinely include horoscopes. Much of the editorial page is speculation. The *National Inquirer,* the number-one-selling newspaper in the United States, thrives on prophecy.

THE REIGN OF ERROR

Each year the prediction industry showers us with $200 billion in (mostly erroneous) information. The forecasting track records for all types of experts are universally poor, whether we consider scientifically oriented professionals, such as economists, demographers, meteorologists, and seismologists, or psychic and astrological forecasters whose names are household words.

In fact, these experts whose advice we pay handsomely for *routinely* fail to predict the major events that shape our world, or even the major turning points—the transitions from status quo to something new— whether it be the economy, stock market, weather, or new technologies. Recent events that caught the forecasters by total surprise include the 1987 stock market crash and its subsequent rapid recovery to record heights; the entry of women into the workforce in massive numbers; the fall of communist Eastern Europe; the Gulf War; the decisive Republican victory in 1994 congressional elections; all recessions, including the crash of 1929 and recent, smaller blips in the financial markets; the use of lasers to transmit telephone messages (even though the phone company's researchers at Bell Labs invented it); and the floods in the Mississippi River valley in the summer of 1993 and those that plagued California during the winter of 1995.

How could all our experts miss calling the fall of communist East Berlin? With all our massive investment in foreign intelligence and our aggressive news media, how did such a momentous event elude them? Why wasn't it predicted months ahead—or even the day before?

No doubt you could name an expert or two who predicted some big, surprising event. But . . . did they really? It is very hard to distinguish a long-shot direct hit from pure chance. The laws of probability dictate that if thousands of forecasters make thousands of predictions, someone at some time is bound to make a spectacular direct hit. Typically, these lucky few enjoy their fifteen minutes of fame before sinking back into the ranks of mediocrity as they revert to meting out egregiously wrong forecasts.

A prime example is the stock market guru Elaine Garzarelli, who is said to have predicted the 1987 stock market crash—the worst since the Great Depression. At no time before or after this famous forecast has she ever made any similar long-shot forecasts that proved to be true. In fact, her long-term stock prediction track record is rather poor, judging from the performance of a mutual fund she ran for seven years. During this time, her fund increased 38 percent while the Standard &Poor's 500 Index increased 62 percent. Her employer at the time finally shut down the fund in August 1994.

FUTURE IMPERFECT

Even with all the advances in science and technology that are available to them, the experts are not getting any better at prediction. In some respects, we are hardly better off than the Romans or Greeks, who read animal entrails to make major decisions regarding the future.

How can the experts get it so wrong? The prediction industry attracts some of the best and brightest minds, in addition to enlisting the latest technology. The answer is that the experts are trying to do the impossible. Until recently, scientists viewed the world as an orderly place governed by immutable laws of nature. Once uncovered, it was believed, these laws would enable scientists to determine the future by extrapolating from historical patterns and cycles. This approach worked well for Sir Isaac Newton; once he discovered the mathematics of gravity, he was able to predict the motions of our planets. Since then, scientists have continued to apply the same formula: more laws, more patterns, more predictions.

This line of thinking, called *determinism,* is based on the belief that future events unfold following rules and patterns that determine their course. Dr. Ravi Batra, a recognized economist from Southern Methodist University and a best-selling author of economic prophecy, illustrates his deterministic thinking this way: "History follows a certain pattern, which is observable and which can be used to forecast the future course of events."[2]

Current science is proving this deterministic view of the world to be naive. The theories of chaos and complexity are revealing the future as fundamentally unpredictable. This applies to our economy, the stock market, commodity prices, the weather, animal populations (humans included), and many other phenomena. There are no clear historical patterns that carve well-marked trails into the future. History does not repeat itself. The future remains mostly unknowable.

That we cannot predict the future has been known to better minds for many years. After an unsuccessful stint as a futurist, Winston Churchill complained that the future was one damn thing after another. Benjamin Franklin quipped that the only things certain in life are death and taxes; this, however, did not dissuade him from doing a little prophesying on his own under a pen name in his *Poor Richard's Almanac.* Being shrewd, he no doubt knew that prophecy was a lucrative business. Peter Drucker wrote in his seminal business book, *Management,* "Forecasting is not a respectable human activity and not worthwhile beyond the shortest of periods."[3]

The chaotic path that the future takes is captured especially well in the old verse, "But for a nail the shoe was lost, but for a shoe the horse was lost, but for a horse the soldier was lost, but for a soldier the war was lost, but for a war the kingdom was lost." This verse perfectly describes the tumultuous events that led to the unpredicted fall of East Germany. But for a 100,000 intrepid protesters, a few East German generals disobeying orders to attack them, and Soviet premier Gorbachev's refusal to intercede—unlike his predecessors in similar circumstances in Hungary, Czechoslovakia, and Poland—the crown jewel of the iron curtain for fifty years toppled, hastening the fall of the rest of communist Eastern Europe. So many quirks of fate emerged from the complex geopolitical system that the experts failed to predict this momentous event.

Although chaos and complexity theories alone are sufficient to doom prediction, there are other barriers that obscure our view of the future, such as "situational bias": the phenomenon by which our thinking is so obscured by present conditions and trends that we cannot begin to see the future. For example, for many months following the stock market crash of 1987, economists and market analysts continued to put forth gloomy forecasts even while the economy and the stock market were on their way to record highs. Similarly, after the harsh winter of 1994, meteorologists generally predicted a cold spring and late summer. The weather ended up being unusually warm and pleasant. I. F. Clarke, a historian of future thinking, characterized situational bias well, as follows:

> Traditional beliefs, professional attitudes, customary roles, inherited symbols, sectional and national interests—these make it extraordinarily difficult for all but the most original of minds to break away from patterns of thought and go voyaging on the unknown seas of the future. In consequence it is a rare forecast that makes any allowance for the essential waywardness of human affairs and does not insist on a strict continuity between the self-evident present and the evidential future."[4]

This rain of forecast error has a far greater cost than the approximately $200 billion that consumers and businesses spend on predictions. Individuals, businesses, and governments bear significant financial risk when they use faulty forecasts to make important decisions. As individuals, we pay a large psychological cost when doom-and-gloom predictions gives us needless anxiety. Then there is the cost of just plain being duped.

VOODOO ECONOMICS

Banking on faulty predictions is hazardous business. Yet there are few significant decisions made by governments, businesses, and individuals that are not accompanied by some type of forecast.

Governments continually make major decisions based on faulty forecasts, with disastrous effects that businesses and individuals pay for in higher taxes, increased inflation, and other ways. Reaganomics, for example, was a costly strategy based on a failed economic prediction that a massive tax cut would so stimulate the economy that total tax receipts would increase, thus enabling the administration to spend like crazy on national defense while still balancing the federal budget. George Bush aptly called this idea "voodoo economics." By the time the Reagan administration left office eight years later, it had converted the $1 trillion deficit it inherited from President Carter into a $3 trillion deficit.

Businesses are similarly vulnerable to faulty forecasts, especially when making long-term investments. One hapless executive I know invested heavily in building a new plant for refining copper ore, on advice from a leading economic consulting firm that predicted a substantial increase in copper prices over the long term. At the time, the decision was perfectly logical, except for one small detail: The prices for copper and other commodities fluctuate randomly. Unfortunately, copper prices plunged, making the new plant a financial disaster.

Decision makers in business and government also rely on faulty technology forecasts, to great cost. In the 1980s, for example, a number of leading corporations wasted hundreds of millions of dollars developing videotext technology for home shopping services that experts said would be the wave of the future. The technology failed to win customers, and the videotext ventures folded.

Ten years ago, one CEO bet his company on developing a product for home banking, based on a leading consultant's prediction that home banking would follow in the wake of ATMs and become the next wave in high-tech banking. Home banking failed to catch on, and his firm when bankrupt. Even now, home banking remains an unproved concept with minimal customer interest; only 1 percent of Personal Computer users claim to have ever used some form of home banking services.

Any farmer who bets his ranch on weather forecasts going out more than one or two days could just as well use a roulette wheel. For all our high-tech investment in satellites, radar, supercomputers, and computer models, meteorologists have gained little save for improvements in forecasting weather over the next twenty-four to forty-eight hours. The real gains have mostly been in observing—as opposed to predicting—the weather: knowing what is happening now rather than trying to figure out what will happen in the future.

Nevertheless, many organizations involved in farming, construction, transportation, fishing, commodities, and even the armed services rely on long-term forecasts for the coming month, season, and year. These forecasts are prepared by the National Weather Service or one of the many private forecasters, or drawn from *The Old Farmer's Almanac*.

Finally, there is the voodoo economics of the forecasting business. I have long had a curious question about forecasters : If they are so smart, why aren't they incredibly rich? Though generally a well-heeled lot, forecasters do not in fact rank among the world's richest people. The answer, of course, is that the predictors would quickly go broke gambling on their fallacious forecasts. Instead, they make their money selling advice to others on how *they* should spend *their* money. Although the experts do not get rich quickly, they are in a much safer business because their clients take all the risk.

EVE OF DESTRUCTION

Faulty predictions also have a nonmonetary cost: needless anxiety. We are continually inundated with doom-and-gloom predictions because sensationalism sells. Every segment of the prediction industry has its purveyors of imminent disaster, telling us we are going to go broke, starve, freeze or fry, drown, or suffer countless other horrors. Although these predictions of doom prove to be false, they add a new layer of exploitive and irresponsible fear and stress to our already pressured lives. Shock therapy as fiction is entertaining; when sold as scientific fact, it breeds needless anxiety.

Dreadful forecasts abound in every medium, from seemingly authoritative articles in the legitimate press and front-page stories in tabloids, experts' newsletters, to many best-selling books such as *The Great Depression of 1990, The Population Bomb,* and *Future Shock.*

The Great Depression of 1990 is a perfect example of the literature that predicts the imminent demise of our economy. Written by Ravi Batra, the book warns that we are "moving toward the greatest worldwide depression in history, in which millions of people will suffer catastrophic financial reversals . . . a disaster of the same severity [as the Great Depression], if not greater, is already in the making. It will occur in 1990 and plague the world through at least 1996."[5]

Batra tells us that he is not out to exploit the reader: "I have written this book not to scare you, but to warn you of the impending cataclysm. The evidence I will present . . . is overwhelming, and can be ignored only at your own peril. . . . I am an economist, trained in scientific analysis, not a sensationalist or a Jeremiah . . . [but] unless we take immediate remedial action the price we will have to pay in the 1990s is catastrophic."[6]

Like a gun-toting survivalist, Batra's advice to businesses and individuals is the economic equivalent to building bomb shelters and hoarding food and weapons: avoid long-term investments—"You shouldn't begin projects that will pay off in the 1990s"—and diversify business by pursuing repair-oriented services—"which has a better survival chance in a depression than many other businesses."

If you adopted his remedy, however, you would have been worse off than the predicted disease, since few businesses could endure such corporate chemotherapy. The way I interpret this is that he tells us to do nothing to grow our businesses for ten years. At least he was consistent: if we followed his advice and made nothing new, there would be quite a business opportunity in fixing up all our antiquated stuff.

Paul Ehrlich is a professor of demography at Stanford University and the author of several best-selling books, including *The Population Bomb,* published in 1968. In *The Population Bomb,* Ehrlich predicts that by the 1990s, war and pestilence, and possibly famine, would do us in. He told us to expect that "500 million deaths—one out of every seven people— is not inconceivable." He predicts that a "killer smog" in Los Angeles will bump off 90,000 people; that the polar ice caps will melt and raise the ocean levels by twenty feet, killing many more; and that a nuclear war will finish us off by making the northern two-thirds of the earth uninhabitable. Finally, "The most intelligent creatures ultimately surviving this period are cockroaches." Scary stuff.

Ehrlich does offer a ray of hope: "Pope Pius XIII, yielding to pressure from enlightened Catholics, announces that all good Catholics have a responsibility to drastically restrict their reproductive activities. He gives his blessing to abortion and all methods of contraception."[7]

Boston Globe columnist Jeff Jacoby called Ehrlich "the nation's most shameless fear monger . . . [who has] been richly rewarded for his almost perfect record of getting things wrong."[8] In fact, though famine exists in parts of the world, our ability to grow food today has *outstripped* population growth; on average, humans are better nourished today than ever before.

After writing his bestseller, *Future Shock,* in 1970, Alvin Toffler became the icon of futurology, and today he remains highly influential within the futurist movement. Recently, he is reported to have influence with the Speaker of the House, Newt Gingrich.

In *Future Shock,* Toffler told us that by the 1990s, we were going to experience psychological meltdown. We would fail to keep up with the escalating pace of change and the ephemeral nature of our relationships and institutions. Toffler told us, "In the three short decades between now and the twenty-first century, millions of ordinary, psychologically normal people will face an abrupt collision with the future."[9] We were to suffer "the shattering stress and disorientation that we induce in individuals by subjecting them to too much change in too short a time." We were to have "disposable spouses" and short-lived relationships. We were to succumb to the "the disease of change" and become psychologically disturbed strangers in the strange land of accelerating change.

The central theme of Toffler's prediction proved to be . . . wrong. People today are *not* shocked by change, and in some cases they are embracing it with surprising ease. Perhaps the clearest example is the growing popularity of personal computers that give people a window on the world. The Internet and commercial network services provide all kinds of information (good and not so good), and interpersonal contact through electronic mail, various discussion groups, and message boards. Internet's user base doubles every year and links millions of people around the world. What Toffler failed to see was the ease with which anyone today can easily access advanced technology and how electronic linkages can bring people together in unforeseen ways. The only thing shocking about the future is thinking about how we ever got along without these high-tech tools.

These forecasts of our death were, of course, exaggerations. The doomsday predictions in each of these three popular books proved to contain hardly even an ounce of truth. In fact, the only difference between books like *Future Shock* and Aldous Huxley's *Brave New World* is that the former have been mistakenly sold as nonfiction. The selling of doomsday predictions is a huge business. Doomsday books sell in the millions, enriching authors and publishers, and they help sell television time and newspapers.

THE LAST OF THE TOOTH FAIRIES

Our belief in these everyday prophecies is the adult version of childhood belief in the Tooth Fairy or the Easter Bunny. So long as we believe in experts' ability to foretell the future, we go about planning and directing our lives according to false information and fictitious premises. Our belief in prophecy today is little better than the primitive superstitions of a thousand years ago.

We pay billions of dollars to acquire information that is mostly useless. Worse, when we rely on that information, we do so at great risk to ourselves, our businesses, and our governments, both financially and psychologically. So why do we persist in seeking that information?

The answer, according to leading psychologists who specialize in the area of human beliefs, is that we humans are a gullible lot. There is a lot of evidence to support this theory. A 1990 Gallup study found that nearly half of all Americans believe that psychic capabilities are possible and concluded that "Americans express a belief in the existence of paranormal, psychic, ghostly, and other worldly experiences and dimensions to a surprising degree."[10] Superstition and the ancient art of divining the future, using anything from animal entrails to smoke, are thriving in many parts of the developing world today. Even in more advanced countries, astrology remains as popular as ever, and new strains of superstition like New Age philosophy attract large followings.

Daniel Gilbert, of the University of Texas, is a specialist in the psychology of belief and has concluded that we tend first to believe what we see and hear, and question it second—if at all.

Bertrand Russell similarly observed, "Believing seems the most mental thing we do."[11] We find it very easy to believe—and difficult to doubt—everything we see and hear. We have a hard time discerning probabilities of events and cannot easily distinguish a long-shot prediction from something that is likely to occur by pure chance. And we are heavily influenced by authority figures. In short, we are vulnerable to being duped by experts' predictions, regardless of their poor track records.

This is as true today as it was in ancient times. Commenting on how readily his fellow Romans were duped by fortune-tellers, Cato the Censor observed, "I wonder how one augur can keep from laughing when he passes another."

However, just because we cannot predict it does not mean we can ignore the future. We must continue to plan for the future by considering scenarios of what might happen and adapting our plans accordingly. To do otherwise would be foolhardy. We cannot blind ourselves to all predictions, because some contain vital information about our environment—not necessarily what *will* happen but what *could* happen.

Our success in our work and personal lives depends to a large degree on which futuristic information we choose to believe and act on. We need to learn how to pluck the gold nuggets of advice, whether it comes as a warning sign or a clue to an opportunity, from the flood of erroneous and often sensational predictions. For example, it is important for us as citizens with some voice in our country's priorities to understand predictions of global warming, a subject that generates a continual flood of doomsday predictions. The nugget to pluck here is that scientists are concerned that the buildup of carbon dioxide and other greenhouse gases could seriously affect our future climate, but they currently do not know how, when, or even whether these effects will occur. There is a big difference between this forthright scientific perspective and, for example, Dr. Ehrlich's prediction that by the year 2000, global warming will melt Antarctica and put us under twenty feet of water.

This book is about how to select the nuggets of valuable future advice from among the $200 billion worth of mostly erroneous future predictions put forth each year, starting with weather forecasting, a familiar and at times frustrating subject.

2

When Chaos Rains

L ate one afternoon on August 18, 1991, a perfect summer day at the beach near the Massachusetts–Rhode Island border, cloudless and mild, a friend and I struck up a casual conversation about what would happen to our modest beach club if someday a hurricane were to strike the area. Twenty-four hours later, the building was ripped off its foundation and demolished by Hurricane Bob, which passed directly overhead. I was amazed that we could be so surprised by a hurricane in our modern era of advanced meteorological science, satellites, and supercomputers. Although we had known that there was a tropical depression hovering off the coast of Florida a day and a half earlier, we had no idea that it would develop full strength and reach us so quickly. It turns out that while we were discussing a theoretical hurricane, Bob was off the coast of South Carolina exploding into a real Class III hurricane, with winds of nearly 100 miles an hour. But it was not until late that night that the National Hurricane Center (NHC) posted a hurricane warning for all coastal areas from Delaware to Cape Cod, a warning that we could have heard only if we had had a television or radio on in the middle of the night. And even then, we would have learned only that Bob was likely to strike at some unknown time at some unspecified location along 600 miles of coastline. Bob accelerated up the East Coast during the night, and by morning when a more detailed warning came, it was too late to take any preventive measures; the hurricane was already pushing fast on our area with dangerous winds and driving rain. Its ferocity and the timing and location of its landfall were unpredictable less than a day before it struck New England. When it was over, Hurricane Bob had destroyed or damaged $1.5 billion worth of property, making it the fourteenth most destructive storm of the century.[1]

Years later, while doing research for this book, I found that other devastating weather events have also surprised the meteorologists. On October 15, 1987, the worst storm to strike England since 1703 hit with no advance notice. The day before the storm, the U.K.'s Meteorological Office—the equivalent of the U.S. National Weather Service (NWS)—was unaware of the approaching hurricane-force winds and thus failed to alert the British populace, instead issuing the following forecast: "Light showers, bright intervals, and moderate winds."[2] In the United States a decade earlier, the disastrous blizzard that struck southern New England on February 6, 1978, came with little warning. The storm blanketed the area with so much snow that it took a full week to clear the roads enough to open them to traffic. Far worse, the storm packed hurricane-force winds that destroyed many coastal homes, displacing ten thousand people, and President Carter declared eight coastal cities in Massachusetts to be federal disaster areas. The weather forecast for February 6 in the preceding day's *Boston Globe* predicted that the winds would be "easterly, 10 to 15 mph."[3]

The flood on the upper Mississippi River during the summer of 1993 was the worst flood to strike that part of the Mississippi River valley since records have been kept. Vast areas surrounding miles of the river and its tributaries were inundated, causing forty-three deaths and an estimated $3 billion in damage. During the first nine months of 1993, the area experienced above-normal precipitation, and rain during June and July was almost nonstop. However, the NWS, in its *Monthly and Seasonal Weather Outlooks,* predicted below-normal precipitation for every month from January to April 1993, normal precipitation for May, and above-normal precipitation only for June—a full five months after the abnormally wet weather began.

In contrast, one of the finest examples of weather prediction was the NWS's accurate forecast of the terrible winter storm that struck the eastern United States from March 12 to 14, 1993, which deposited the most extensive snowfall across that region in many decades, covering an area from Alabama to northern New England. The storm was so destructive that the Commerce Department blamed it for that year's downturn in the U.S. economy. Coastal flooding caused severe property damage from Cuba to New York, and tornadoes and squalls caused much wind damage and sank several large container ships. The NWS, however, provided reliable warnings to local communities twenty-four to forty hours in advance as the storm progressed northward along the eastern United States, giving them time to prepare for the storm. This enabled them to save lives and property by increasing staffing at power plants, emergency services, shelters, and health care facilities; by forewarning the public with announcements; and declaring states of emergency and calling up the National Guard.[4]

The weather has always been a force of death and destruction. Extended droughts meant starvation. Harsh winters meant death through exposure and sickness, and starvation set in when rivers froze and mills ceased grinding the flour so critical for making bread, the main food staple in Western countries. Flash floods came unannounced, drowning those living in floodplains; severe ocean storms killed innumerable seafarers and coastal inhabitants.

Weather has also changed the course of history many times, especially in influencing the outcomes of major battles that determined the fate of nations and even the world. In 480 B.C., King Xerxes of Persia sent his navy to invade Greece and fought the Greeks in the Battle of Salamis off the coast of Athens. Choppy seas during the battle helped the Greeks, who were equipped with vessels that were more seaworthy, to rout the Persians and retain their own freedom, thus preserving their dominance of the region and enabling the spread of Greek civilization during the next several centuries. In A.D. 394, fierce winds blowing down from the Alps blew dust into the eyes of the opponents of Theodosius the Great, Roman emperor of the Eastern Roman Empire, tipping the scales in his favor in the closely fought battle between the Eastern and Western Roman Empires. In the thirteenth century, Japan was twice saved from Kublai Khan's invasion by typhoons that wrecked the Mongol ships and drowned many of the invaders. In 1588, after the Spanish Armada failed in its attack on the superior English navy in the English Channel, a great storm drove the retreating Spanish ships to their final destruction on the dangerous coasts of the northern isles, leaving England to rule the seas for centuries thereafter.[5]

More recently, the weather shaped events during World War II. The harsh winter of 1939–1940 depleted Germany's coal supply and diminished its ability to run trains and make military maneuvers, thus forcing

Germany to postpone its attack on the weak and ill-prepared British and French forces until spring 1940, when it was able to rout the Allies and occupy most of Western Europe. Although the Soviets had signed a pact with Nazi Germany in 1939, the Germans turned their attention east when the Soviets began expanding into Eastern Europe, posing a threat to Hitler's ambitions there. Hitler's meteorologist, Franz Baur, predicted that the winter of 1941–1942 in the Soviet Union would be normal or mild, and the German army was mobilized on its eastern front in June 1941 for a full-scale invasion of the Soviet Union. But that winter turned out to be one of the severest on record. As the German forces were poised for victory twenty-five miles from Moscow, the weather worsened, immobilizing tanks and trains and freezing the poorly equipped German soldiers. When told of the extreme weather conditions in the Soviet Union, Baur replied with incredible arrogance, "The observations must be wrong." But the Germans could not win under those conditions, and when the Soviets launched a counteroffensive, Hitler shifted the main attack to the south.[6]

Catastrophic large-scale storms—tropical storms and hurricanes (called typhoons or cyclones in the Eastern Hemisphere)—are a matter of life and death in many parts of the world. The United States is exposed, on average, to twelve storms per year with winds of at least fifty-five miles per hour, which develop in the North Atlantic; thirty such storms develop each year in the western North Pacific and wreak havoc on the Philippines, Southeast Asia, and South Asia. The countries surrounding the Bay of Bengal are the most vulnerable to violent large-scale storms, 15 percent of which occur in that area even though the bay represents just 0.3 percent of the world's ocean. Over the years, millions of people have been killed in Bangladesh (formerly East Pakistan) as a result of cyclones' smashing into its low-lying coastline. A single cyclone in 1970 caused 200,000 Bangladeshis to drown. Although catastrophic weather kills few people in the United States today, each year, according to the NWS, Americans must cope with the world's most severe local weather, including 5,000 floods, 10,000 violent thunderstorms, and 1,000 tornadoes, as well as five or six hurricanes and a similar number of other large-scale storms, which wreak an enormous amount of destruction. As U.S. coastal areas and floodplains have become thickly settled with homes and businesses, these areas have been increasingly exposed to weather-related property damage, which has been especially costly during the past ten years. In 1992, Hurricane Andrew became the most expensive natural disaster in U.S. history, causing $25 billion worth of damage. Had it struck Miami, just twenty miles farther north, a million homes might have been destroyed and the costs could have soared to $100 billion.

In addition to these periodic catastrophes, the U.S. Department of Commerce estimates that U.S. businesses routinely lose about $34.5 billion each year due to incidents of bad weather, such as frost, drought, hail, and violent wind. As shown in Figure 2.1, bad weather is especially hard on agriculture and construction businesses, which each year lose $22.4 billion and $2.7 billion, respectively, because of it. The Commerce Department estimates that $14.4 billion of the $34.5 billion of weather-related business losses would be avoidable if businesses were forewarned by weather forecasts, both long and short term.[7] With a few months' warning, farmers could switch the types of crops they plant to take advantage of unusually dry or wet conditions or temperature extremes; construction firms could better protect equipment and partially completed building sites; and transporation companies could avoid dangerous storms and chart more fuel-efficient routes. Is accurate weather

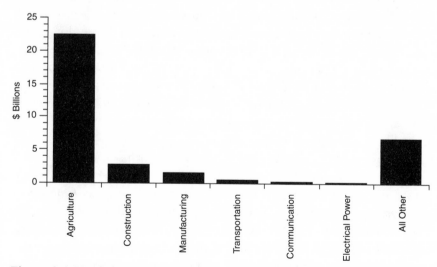

Figure 2.1 Yearly business losses due to adverse weather. (*Source of data:* U.S. Department of Commerce National Technical Information Service, *Benefit Cost Analysis for the Modernization and Associated Restructuring of the National Weather Service,* July 1992.)

forecasting so long in advance possible? Is accurate weather forecasting possible even a day or two in advance?

A BRIEF HISTORY OF WEATHER FORECASTING

Until the mid-eighteenth century, it was thought that the atmosphere was empty space. For much of human existence, the weather was believed to be the province of the gods, whose fickle desires brought about the vagaries of the weather and whose wrath was expressed in the form of storms, droughts, and floods. The Egyptians credited their Sun God, Ra, with control over the life-giving flooding of the Nile; the Greeks considered their sea god, Poseidon, responsible for setting devastating gales in motion; and North American Indians paid homage to the powers of their gods of nature with rain dances and other rituals.

Weather forecasting has existed for thousands of years in the form of weather lore, astrology, and almanacs. Folk sayings derived from eons of weather observation were passed down through the generations, such as, "Red at night, sailors' delight." (In the northern half of the Northern Hemisphere, a reddish sunset might be caused by dust in the air resulting from clear, dry weather to the west, which might reach the observer to the east the next day.) Astrologers were among the first weather-forecasting professionals, predicting the weather—along with war, plague, pestilence, and other major events—by divining the influence of the heavens from the movements of stars and planets. Almanacs contained the first published weather forecasts, dating back as far as 3000 B.C. in ancient Egypt, and have remained popular ever since. Then, as now, almanacs contained astrological interpretations, weather forecasts, and advice to farmers on what and when to plant; they were also one of the few reliable calendars and sources of information on tides and planetary movements. Columbus is reported to have used a German almanac during his voyage across the Atlantic. In colonial America, a Pennsylvania farmer who was frightened by a meteor shower is reported to have called to his wife to bring the Bible, and when she said she could not find it, he replied, "Well, hurry, then, and bring the Almanac."[8] Farmers relied heavily on their almanacs in making all kinds of farming decisions, as Albert Lee has noted in a folk history of weather prediction: "All planting, reaping, building, and butchering were dictated by the information the almanacs provided. Though they were often wrong, belief in them was great."[9]

When credible sources, as almanacs surely were, published dooms-day predictions for specific times and places, panic often erupted. The worst of all documented weather forecasts in history was published around 1500 in *Johannes Stoffler's Almanac,* which predicted that a great flood would occur on February 2, 1524. As the specified day of doom approached, some terrified people built huge arks reminiscent of Noah's, others boarded available ships, and the rest headed for the hills.[10]

Italian astronomer Galileo could well be considered the father of weather science. In 1643, he invented the thermometer, and one of his students invented the barometer, which ultimately enabled scientists to discover that air has mass and is not empty after all. After Galileo's conflict with the church, weather science languished for more than one hundred years, until the latter half of the eighteenth century, when three French scientists from diverse fields took an interest in the weather. Antoine Lavoisier, a chemist, set up the first chain of weather observing stations (which he personally financed until he was sent to the guillotine during the French Revolution); Jean-Baptiste de Lamarck, a naturalist, developed a system for classifying clouds; and Pierre Simon de Laplace, a mathematician and astronomer, perceived that the laws governing the nature of gases could be used to predict the weather, which is the basis for modern, computer-generated forecasts.

Lavoisier's network of weather stations was the forerunner of modern weather observation; however, its success was inhibited by the slow transmission of information. The fastest mode of communication of the day was the solo horse rider, who could not hope to keep pace with fast-changing weather conditions such as storms moving at thirty miles per hour. The telegraph, invented in 1794—the year of Lavoisier's death—solved the response-time problem, thus enabling large networks of weather observation stations to distribute weather data quickly. In 1849 Joseph Henry, secretary of the Smithsonian Institution in Washington, D.C., arranged for telegraph companies to have their operators collect local weather data, using meteorological instruments supplied by the Smithsonian, and telegraph the information to Washington, where it was used to create weather maps for the parts of the country covered by the stations. Although the process was disrupted during the Civil War, by 1869 Henry had built a network of 600 weather reporting stations. In 1870, after severe storms on the Great Lakes the year before caused the loss of 1,914 ships and 209 lives, the U.S. Congress appropriated $50,000 for the creation of a nationwide weather service under the jurisdiction of the Army's Signal Corps. (That same year, the term "weather forecasting" entered the meteorological vocabulary.) In 1890 the service was reorganized, under the newly created Department of Agriculture, as the National Weather Bureau; it was renamed the National Weather Service in 1970.

The use of ground-based weather stations was woefully inadequate, because they could not measure upper atmospheric conditions. The first measurement of these conditions was made in 1894 using kites, which the National Weather Bureau employed from 1900 to 1920 as its primary source for such data. Although kites could reach heights of 1,000 feet, they were useless in winds of less than 10 to 15 miles per hour, or whenever it rained. (Incredibly, kites were periodically used as recently as 1933.) The next innovation came in 1909: the weather balloon, which when tethered could reach a height of 6,000 feet, and when set free could go as high as 10 miles up. The problem with untethered balloons was the difficulty of retrieving the weather data from their on-board instruments. The first solution was to design the balloons to explode at a specified air pressure (or at an approximate height) and float the instruments safely to earth via parachute. Weather forecasters traipsed over hill and dale looking for their popped balloons and sometimes took two weeks to retrieve their data, which by then belonged to ancient history. Radio balloons and airplanes armed with detectors helped solve this problem.

Despite these advances, traditional weather forecasting was more art than science until the use of radar for weather detection in 1954 and the development of computer-forecasting models in 1955, when the Weather Bureau and the Census Bureau became the first civilian users of computers; and it improved in the 1960s with the use of satellites and faster computers (the latter still quite slow and cumbersome, though, compared to today's supercomputers). But a scientific method of forecasting based on computers had been envisioned years earlier, when English meteorologist Lewis Richardson—the da Vinci of modern weather forecasting—developed a blueprint in 1922 for an elaborate weather prediction factory. Richardson's plan included a grid of 2,000 weather observation stations located 120 miles apart throughout Europe, taking weather readings for five levels in the atmosphere every 6 hours, and an army of 64,000 workers equipped with primitive calculators who would solve the complex gas law equations and generate the daily weather forecast. Unfortunately, like da Vinci and his on-paper invention of flying machines, Richardson lacked the technology to implement his brilliant plan. Three decades later, Richardson's dream began to become a practical reality when the electronic computer (invented in the 1940s) was first applied to weather forecasting. Initially, the vast amount of weather data overloaded the early computers, which took twenty-four hours to crank out a by-then-outdated twenty-four-hour forecast. Later, more advanced computers could do the same work in five minutes, and in the 1960s, computer-generated forecasts started to outperform those generated manually by humans.

Today, the NWS operates an extensive network of weather-sensing devices—weather stations, satellites, balloons, radar, ships, and buoys—which sample current weather conditions and record the data, which are then input into the NWS's supercomputers to generate its forecasts. And since weather forecasting has become an extensive global business—not surprising, considering its economic impact—the United Nations has a global organization, the World Meteorological Organization (WMO), which coordinates the sharing of weather data from around the world. (For decades the United States has freely shared with the former Soviet Union weather data collected from U.S. satellites, even during the cold war.) In 1995, the WMO "estimated that the global budget for weather services was about $4 billion."[11] About half of that is spent in the United States by the National Oceanic and Atmospheric Administration, usually referred to by its acronym, NOAA (pronounced like the name of the biblical prophet, and thus appropriate for the world's largest predictor of precipitation). NOAA is the parent organization for the NWS and its three other weather-predicting divisions: the Climate Analysis Center, the Severe Storms Forecasting Center, and the National Hurricane Center. The NWS is responsible for issuing the daily weather forecast and three-to-five- and six-to-ten-day predictions. The Climate Analysis Center issues monthly and seasonal "Weather Outlooks," which predict deviations from normal weather patterns for the next thirty and ninety days (published on paper until 1995, and now published electronically on the Internet); and at the end of 1994 it introduced forecasts for eighteen months into the future. The NHC in Coral

Gables, Florida, keeps a watchful eye on the Atlantic Ocean during hurricane season, via satellite, and sends intrepid meteorologists into the eyes of hurricanes to gauge their strength and probable landfall.

The federal government maintained a near monopoly on weather observation, reporting, and forecasting in the United States for eighty-three years, from the formation of its weather service in 1870 until 1953. Private forecasting firms have existed since around 1930, but the National Weather Bureau constrained their activity by controlling access to and the price of the weather data it collected. In 1953 Sinclair Weeks, President Eisenhower's secretary of commerce, commissioned an investigation into public- and private-sector forecasting and established several key steps toward fostering a thriving private-sector weather forecasting industry. The most important of these was requiring the National Weather Bureau to provide free access to its weather observation data to any party requesting it. Although the NWS has retained its monopoly on the gathering of weather data affecting the United States (which makes sense, given its massive investment in infrastructure), it peacefully coexists and competes with numerous private-sector forecasting firms that comprise a $300 million subindustry.

These private-sector firms, such as the Weather Services Corporation and Accuweather Inc., obtain weather data from the NWS and generate their own forecasts, which they sell to major newspapers and television news departments. The newspaper USA Today uses the Weather Services Corporation's forecasts for its elaborate multicolor, full-page weather analysis. Weather forecasting has always played a prominent role throughout the news media and is still an important feature of daily newspapers, drive-time radio, and television news programs and the primary focus of the Weather Channel's twenty-four-hour weather coverage. Weather events are often the top stories of the day, especially floods, rainstorms, severe winter precipitation, deadly tornadoes, and hurricanes.

Many other organizations employ their own meteorologists and weather forecasters. Because the weather has always been a crucial factor in surveillance and warfare, the U.S. armed services have staff meteorologists. Major transportation firms employ weather forecasters to find safer and more cost-effective routes; agricultural firms use them to make important decisions such as when to spray and harvest crops.

Then there are the institutions that train future practitioners in the science of weather: meteorology. Meteorology is a natural science like physics and is taught at MIT, Cal Tech, and many other universities with leading science and engineering programs. Anyone who has taken college courses in thermodynamics or fluid dynamics can appreciate the sophistication and complexity of meteorological science. Whereas traditional weather forecasters may have only a high school education and minimal understanding of the science of weather, meteorology is a distinct profession with specific educational requirements. Its professional association, the American Meteorological Society, defines a meteorologist as one "who has had a minimum of a B.A. or higher degree in meteorology or atmospheric sciences and who uses scientific principles to explain, understand, observe, or forecast the Earth's atmospheric phenomenon."[12] Note that the emphasis is not so much on forecasting as on understanding the science underlying weather events.

Even after all the scientific and technological advances in weather forecasting, though, certain superstitions continue to exert a fascination on the public, especially Groundhog Day, which every year on February 2 attracts intense media coverage and 2,000 onlookers to Punxsutawney, Pennsylvania, home of Punxsutawney Phil, a groundhog. Tradition has it that if he comes up out of his burrow on that day and sees his own shadow, there will be six more weeks of winter. The tradition started in 1887, and now the Punxsutawney Groundhog Club has thousands of members from all over the world, including the top-hatted members of its inner circle, who conduct the annual ritual.

THE BUTTERFLY EFFECT

The complex phenomenon that we call the weather is merely the exchange of heat among the land, water, and air, flowing from warm to cold according to a set of established natural laws called the gas laws, thermodynamics, and fluid dynamics. These laws specify the interrelationship among temperature, pressure, humidity, density, and the velocity of air in the heat-exchange process. Essentially, hot air from the equatorial areas rises and flows toward the cooler air at the two poles, where the cooler, denser air sinks and is pulled toward the equator, filling the void left by the rising warm air and thus completing the circular flow of air. This process is called convection, and it can be observed by watching the currents in a hot glass of water circulate as the hot water rises, cools at the top, and then sinks, creating circulating currents. Convection currents can also be observed at the beach on a warm summer day, when hot air rising off the land brings in cooler air over the water, creating the typical afternoon onshore breezes. The rotation of the earth complicates this northerly-southerly air flow by twisting the currents of air into either westerly or easterly flows, depending on the latitude. In the United States and other parts of the midlatitudes of the Northern Hemisphere, air typically flows west to east. Most forms of precipitation occur along fronts, the boundaries between masses of air with different pressures, temperatures, and humidity levels.

So if the weather follows proved laws of nature, why, you might reasonably ask, are weather forecasters so often wrong? The answer lies in what I will call scientific predictions. The ability to predict the course of the future from some point A in the present to a future point B depends on two conditions: (1) you need proved laws of nature that take you from A to B, and (2) you need to know where your starting point A lies. (Scientists call starting point A an "initial condition.") Scientific predictions work extremely well in predicting the path of planets, for example. Newton's proved laws of gravity and motion enable us to project accurately where a planet will be at some time in the future (point B) given a reasonably accurate estimate of its initial conditions at starting point A (the planet's mass, speed, and location).

The two biggest underlying problems in predicting the weather are that (1) the laws that govern our weather are so volatile that they greatly amplify mistakes in the estimates of where any starting point A lies, and (2) it is very difficult to specify accurately all the A starting points, since the scale of our weather system is massive and our weather-sampling grid—the network of observation stations, satellites, and so forth—is not extensive enough to capture that level of detail. Scientists describe such complex relationships as "nonlinear." Linear relationships cause variables to increase or decrease at a uniform rate; nonlinear relationships cause variables to increase or decrease at more or less exponential rates.

To illustrate the nature of nonlinear relationships, consider two hypothetical banks. Bank A pays you interest each year on your original investment, so that interest earnings are constant over time (a linear relationship). Bank B pays you interest on a compound basis, which essentially pays interest on your original investment plus interest on your accumulated interest earnings, and your interest earnings grow exponentially over time (a nonlinear relationship). Now let us assume that you deposited $100 in each bank for thirty years at a fixed interest rate of 12 percent and that both banks made a mistake and paid you only 10 percent. As illustrated in Figure 2.2, the same mistake made by both banks is greatly amplified at Bank B. The two percent error made at Bank A cost you only $60 over thirty years; the same mistake at Bank B cost you $1,250. Scientists call this amplification of mistakes by nonlinear relationships "sensitivity to initial conditions."

However, the formula for compound interest is rather tame compared to the nonlinear natural laws that drive the behavior of the weather.[13] To demonstrate some of the complexity of this behavior, consider the following hypothetical nonlinear equation (indicated by the squared term), which behaves very much like the complex forces of weather. For the purposes of this discussion, let's have A stand for the current temperature and B stand for the temperature one hour into the future:

$$B = 0.4A - 4A^2$$

By plugging in an initial condition for A (current temperature), I was able to simulate the fluctuations in temperature for several hypothetical days. As shown in Figure 2.3, these future temperatures bounced

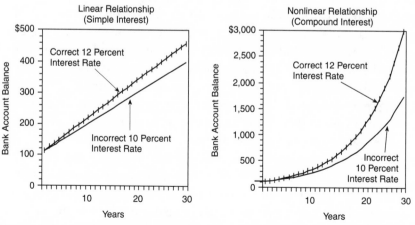

Figure 2.2 Nonlinear relationships greatly amplify mistakes, as shown by the dollars accumulated in two hypothetical bank accounts.

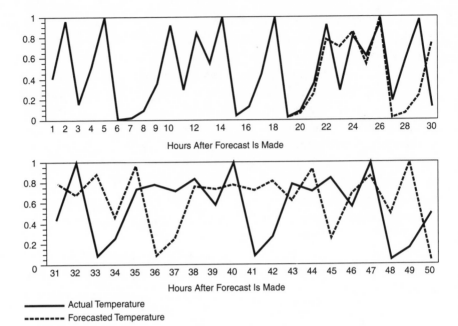

Figure 2.3   Simulated chaos illustrates deterioration of weather forecasts.

around in a noisy fashion, which was caused only by the complex nature of this simple, nonlinear equation.

Despite appearances, the noisy temperature fluctuations in Figure 2.3 are neither random nor cyclical. Although the temperature swings and dips sharply from hour to hour, it does not explode off the page but, rather, stays within a narrow band of temperatures, just as actual temperatures hover around seasonal norms (the earth would be uninhabitable otherwise). Also, although some of the peaks and valleys may look alike, that is merely an illusion; the simulated temperature patterns in the figure never repeat themselves. Similarly, even though weather patterns occurring at different times might occasionally seem similar, the weather has an infinite number of potential patterns, none of which ever repeat themselves exactly.

This nonlinear equation is also much more sensitive to initial conditions than the compound interest relationship. Recall that I plugged in an initial condition to start up the temperature simulation, which is depicted by the dark line in Figure 2.3. As a second part of my experiment, I attempted to "forecast" the simulated temperatures in this figure by plugging an estimate of the initial condition—current temperature—into the same equation. In this case, my estimated initial temperature is off by only one-millionth of a degree Fahrenheit, a minuscule mistake relative to actual weather measurement. At the beginning of the graph in Figure 2.3, the forecasted and actual temperatures are so close that they are indistinguishable until about the nineteenth hour. From that point on, the forecast starts to take on a life of its own, and after the twenty-seventh hour, the forecast and actual temperatures diverge forever. This is precisely how and why weather forecasts quickly degrade in time.

The noisy behavior of this weather simulation and of our actual weather system can be described by the term "chaos": the erratic but bounded behavior of a system that is highly sensitive to initial conditions. The apparently chaotic behavior of heat flowing through air, the underlying basis of the weather, can easily be observed by watching smoke rise from an extinguished match. The heated air causes the smoke to rise straight up for a while, and then it starts twisting, reversing, and forming curly patterns before resuming its upward flow. The same thing happens when you pour cream into hot coffee: the clouds in your coffee form as heat exchanges between the hot coffee and the cooler cream, causing the fluids to flow in apparently chaotic patterns.

Scientific purists credit French mathematician Henri Poincaré as being the Father of the Mathematics of Chaos Theory. His 1892 theoretical insights challenged the premises of Newtonian physics that suggested a forever stable solar system. Poincaré found that the physics of planetary motion involves more than isolated planets revolving around the sun; rather, they are not independent of one another but are each attracted to one another, however minutely, as part of an interconnected system. The multiple-body motions and attractions cause complex and chaotic behaviors on a very small scale that are mathematically unsolvable and totally unpredictable. Poincaré's insights, though, were overlooked for many decades.[14]

MIT professor Edward Lorenz, a mathematician and meteorologist, discovered the concept of chaos in 1961 while conducting an experiment very similar to the one shown in Figure 2.3. In resuming a long-running weather simulation after an interruption, he decided to save time by restarting the simulation using some rounded-off figures from the middle of his prior run rather than start from the beginning. After a brief time, Lorenz noticed that the new simulation diverged from the original run. In noting the sensitivity of the nonlinear weather relationships to initial conditions, Lorenz concluded that long-range weather forecasting must be doomed.[15] He also coined the "butterfly effect" metaphor, according to which a butterfly flapping its wings deep in a Brazilian jungle could ignite a chain reaction of weather events, with small effects leading to ever greater consequences that could ultimately cause tornadoes to strike Texas.[16] This is an apt metaphor for the nature of the weather and for chaos in general.

The traditional method of weather forecasting, still very much alive today, uses no proved laws of nature and instead relies on manual processing of the numbers and an implicit "I've seen that one before" methodology. The traditional forecaster simply plots high- and low-pressure areas and warm and cold fronts to get the basic parameters of the now-familiar weather map and then predicts the weather, using a combination of personal experience, "analogues" (comparisons to previous analogous weather situations, using weather records that, for the Northern Hemisphere, were begun in 1873), and rules of thumb regarding how high- and low-pressure areas and frontal systems affect the weather. Underlying the traditional method is the assumption that weather patterns regularly repeat themselves, a concept that chaos theory has shown to be false.

The chaotic nature of our weather system has significant implications for what we can reasonably expect from weather forecasting. The weather is noisy and turbulent, but it is bounded by seasonal patterns with extreme variations occurring infrequently, and it never repeats itself exactly. Nevertheless, accurate forecasting is generally possible for short periods of time before the inevitable errors in estimating initial conditions cause the forecast to degrade. But even in the short term (one to six hours) "local land influences that cannot be included in the [computer] models cause errors. In the longer term (two days and more) small initial errors snowball."[17] Note that in Figure 2.3, the forecasted and actual temperatures were reasonably close for a hypothetical twenty-seven hours. After that point, however, the accuracy of the "forecast" degraded, and the forecast quickly became meaningless.

We can extend the length of accurate weather forecasts—but only slightly—by dramatically reducing the errors of the initial conditions. At some point, further improvement in the accuracy of initial conditions yields no perceptible improvement in forecast accuracy. Lorenz understood this inherent limit and was the first to proclaim that there must be some point in time beyond which weather forecasting is theoretically impossible. Recently, the American Meteorological Society has officially proclaimed that this limit is somewhere between ten and fourteen days.[18] However, it may be economically impossible to achieve this goal.

The challenge of weather forecasting, even in the short term, is to make sure that initial conditions are reported as completely and accurately as possible. This is a tall order, since the weather is a vast three-dimensional system, and much of the weather dynamics take place in the middle and upper atmospheres, where they are difficult to measure. According to Steven Zubrick, science and operations officer at the NWS forecast office in Sterling, Virginia, the NWS has to piece together upper-atmosphere weather samples from fifty upper-air site balloons, takeoff and landing data from commercial aircraft, and inferences made from satellite and radar observations.[19] Benjamin Franklin astutely deduced the multilayered nature of the weather when he observed that storms travel in a different direction from that of their winds blowing at ground level. Given the problem of "sensitivity to initial conditions," the ideal weather-forecasting model would start with an instantaneous snapshot of the weather over the entire earth at the molecular level, which is obviously impossible. Instead, the forecaster must settle for obtaining a sample of weather data from a three-dimensional grid of widely spaced observing stations as a crude approximation of any weather pattern's highly complex initial conditions—and that grid is relatively complete only over land. Weather-sampling observations over water are much scarcer, and three-fourths of the world is covered by water. Because water is much denser than air and is able to retain much more heat, the first few feet of ocean water contain as much heat as the whole atmosphere, making it a key ingredient of the heat-exchanging weather equation. An upwelling of warm water near a coast, for example, could radically change the weather over land, and anomalies in surface conditions over water far from any coast are also potential problems but are more likely to slip through the observation grid.

THE NATIONAL WEATHER SERVICE
AND THE PROBLEMS OF PREDICTION

The National Weather Bureau had the distinction of being the first fore-casting organization on the government payroll in the United States, while today the NWS is just one of numerous future-predicting orga-nizations of many types funded by taxpayers. It is now the most ex-pensive forecasting organization in the world, but sometimes it is referred to as "the world's second-best weather forecaster" behind the U.K.'s National Meteorological Office, in terms of forecasting accuracy. Typical of old monopolies, the NWS had let its service quality erode while ignoring the growing competition from a burgeoning private-sec-tor forecasting industry—much like the situation of the U.S. Postal Service's facing competition from companies such as Federal Express. The private weather forecasting firms often outperformed the NWS in forecast accuracy, for over the decades it had not improved its methods and its organized workforce resisted change. Until 1988, the NWS used 1950s radar equipped with vacuum tubes, a technology invented in 1904 that had been phased out of radios, televisions, computers, and nearly every other piece of electronic equipment after the invention of the transistor in 1948. In fact, the NWS's only remaining supplier for its vac-uum tubes is in the former Soviet Union, the world's leading maker of antiquated technology. The antiquated radar provides only vague pic-tures of precipitation in storms and indicates nothing about the storm's wind speed or direction and often fails to detect snowfall.

Like the Postal Service, the NWS was pressured to show results by a succession of presidents and Congresses, who periodically called for its privatization. In 1953 it transformed itself into a role model for public-private sector cooperation, and in 1988 it began an extensive modern-ization program, a $4 billion upgrade that it claims will substantially improve its forecasting abilities, which is expected to be completed in 1999. When the NWS's modernization is complete, many tasks pre-viously done manually will be automated, its 1950s-era equipment will be replaced with vastly superior technology, and its forecasting staff upgraded. In 1992 it switched to a new radar technology called NEXRAD (for next-generation radar), which is much better than its predecessor at detecting the reflected microwaves that bounce off par-ticles of rain, snow, and dust, and measuring the speed and direction of winds. This information enables forecasters to detect wind shear (which can down airplanes on landing or takeoff), quick-moving storm fronts, and spinning clouds that spawn tornadoes, and to probe deep inside storms to determine their intensity and probable path. By 1999, its labor-intensive, turn-of-the-century process for collecting weather data will be replaced with unmanned automated weather sampling stations called Automated Surface Observing Systems (ASOS). An ASOS records the weather every minute, twenty-four hours a day, all year long, and provides computer-generated voice reports directly to all aircraft leaving or approaching an airport, with data on cloud height, visibility, precipitation, fog, wind, and air pressure and temperature. The upgrade also includes several new satellites. Two of them have geostationary orbits—staying over the same point on earth—enabling them to provide a twenty-four-hour window on most of the Atlantic Ocean and North America and much of the Pacific Ocean basin. Two other satellites orbit over the North and South Poles with orbits that are stationary relative to the sun, thus enabling them to provide a full coverage of the entire atmosphere as the earth rotates.

But the NWS still uses the prediction-making process that it established in 1955, called "computer guidance." According to James Lee, a NWS meteorologist, it works as follows: At 7 A.M., in Washington, D.C., the central office of the NWS loads its Cray supercomputer with weather data from local weather stations, satellites, radar, balloons, ships, buoys, and other sources. After an hour and a half of grinding away, the computer spits out a national weather prediction, which the NWS ships to local weather stations to help "guide" human weather forecasters in making their predictions. The local NWS forecasters then send in their own forecasts to the central office, which finally issues the official national forecast.[20] Two things about this guidance system approach strike me as odd: If computers are better forecasters than humans, why are humans involved at all? As it turns out, there is an intense debate about this man-versus-machine competition. And second, if weather forecasts are accurate for so short a time, why are there so many delays in the process from collecting the initial weather data to issuing the official forecast (which takes about half a day)?

The NWS's modernization plan favors the use of fewer but more highly skilled meteorologists equipped with more advanced technology. Charles Doswell III, a meteorologist at the National Severe Storms

Laboratory in Norman, Oklahoma, believes that machines will eventually win out completely in the battle of man-versus-machine: "The modeling gurus in the system (generally, the NWS) have decreed that the future of weather forecasting is a non-human one. Eventually, the weather forecasts of the future can go out unsullied by contact with the human hand."[21] In fact, there is little value in human forecasters' trying to improve on the routine forecasts generated by computer models. Human forecasters can, however, do two important things: keep the models from generating acute errors during turbulent weather, and detect and project small weather events that fall through the cracks in the NWS's weather-sampling grid. To perform these functions will require greater expertise and scientific training than the traditional NWS forecaster has had. Doswell advises on this point, "Keeping human forecasters employed must eventually come down to a perception of added value beyond what one can buy with an automated system. If you think you can do that with your high school diploma, then I wish you the best."[22] Harold Brooks, a meteorologist at the National Severe Storms Laboratory, is not optimistic about the program to upgrade human forecast skills: "Left to the present course, the future of human beings in operational weather forecasting is bleak."[23]

"TONIGHT'S WEATHER IS DARK, FOLLOWED BY WIDELY SCATTERED LIGHT IN THE MORNING"

Is stand-up comic George Carlin's Hippy Dippy weatherman's forecast the best we can do? There is no independent auditing agency tracking the accuracy of the NWS forecasts that could tell taxpayers whether they are getting their money's worth. The literature is filled with contradictory claims; some diehard meteorologists claim great achievements in weather forecasting, while critics declare that forecasting skill is minimal. The vagueness of forecasts does not help. How do you assess a forecast of 50 percent chance of rain? Rain or shine, the forecaster can claim to have been at least half right. Then there are forecasts that are nearly certain to come true, like the common forecast of "partly cloudy." Few days are ever completely cloudless. Weather accuracy is meaningful only when it is measured against some benchmark. For example, before forecasters can claim to have any predictive skill, they at least have to outperform a naive forecast such as would be generated by random guessing or flipping a coin, neither of which requires any meteorological skill. The naive forecast can thus serve as that benchmark, helping to separate fact from fiction in judging forecasting skill.

As a matter of fact, meteorologists use two types of naive forecasts to gauge forecasting skill: persistence (the prediction that tomorrow's weather will be the same as today) and climatology (the prediction that tomorrow's weather will be the same as seasonal averages). According to Doswell, persistence and climatology set high hurdles for weather forecasters to beat:

> If persistence or climatology forecasts are right most of the time, which they are, then how smart does a forecaster have to be to be right most of the time: Not very! This is why meteorological statisticians . . . make such a fuss about measuring skill and not accuracy (accuracy is some measure of the difference between forecast and observed variables). On the other hand, "skill" is measured as improvement over some standard (usually stupid) forecasting method (such as random guessing, climatology, or persistence). Hence, being right most of the time says virtually nothing about skill![24]

One of the NWS's most vital and reliable functions is the detection, tracking, and short-term prediction of violent local weather events,

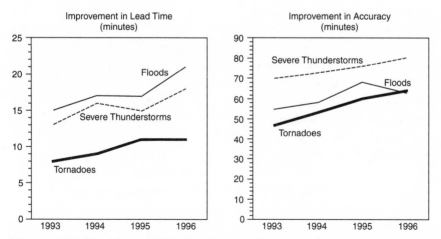

Figure 2.4   The National Weather Service's forecasting has improved with its modernization program. (*Source of data:* National Weather Service.)

such as thunderstorms, flash floods, and tornadoes, which are predictable for only a few minutes up to one hour ahead. As shown in Figure 2.4, the agency has made major gains in this task, and has thus increased air safety, due especially to its NEXRAD technology. "We see a lot more storms that we would have missed in the past," says NWS meteorologist Zubrick.[25] However, despite the improvements in forecasting, these violent weather events remain somewhat elusive. The NWS reports that in 1996 it was able to detect severe thunderstorms with eighteen minutes of lead time, 80 percent of its storm warnings resulted in actual storms and it was able to predict flash floods with twenty-one minutes of lead time, and 63 percent of these occurred as predicted, but that 58 percent of the flash floods that occurred did so with "no lead time"—that is, they were surprise events.[26]

The detection of potential tornadoes has also improved dramatically, but predicting these violent, short-lived storms is still very difficult. Less than 1 percent of thunderstorms produce tornadoes, and 80 percent of them last for less than ten minutes and cover less than a mile. As Richard A. Kerr noted in the magazine *Science* in 1993, "Twenty minutes to take shelter is no run of the mill tornado warning; it's a radical improvement over what could have been done just a few years ago. Indeed, it would have been nigh impossible if the forecasters were relying on visual sightings of funnel shaped clouds—the traditional way of triggering a warning, which may give several minutes notice but all too often none at all."[27] However, the NWS reports that the lead time for tornado warnings is not nearly as good as Kerr's "twenty minutes." In 1996, on average, it was able to predict tornadoes with eleven minutes of lead time, and 64 percent of its warnings resulted in tornadoes.

According to the American Meteorological Society (AMS), the NWS can forecast general weather conditions (excluding short-lived violent events) within a twelve-hour period with considerable skill, but its ability to predict specifically when and where various weather events will occur decreases over that period of time. Wild deviations from weather forecasts can occur when atmospheric conditions are especially chaotic or when the widely spaced weather stations fail to detect events occurring between the grid points. Large-scale weather events and conditions, such as areas of heavy precipitation or the arrival of a front, are often predictable as much as six to twelve hours ahead.

For the period twelve to forty-eight hours ahead, the NWS can produce reasonably accurate forecasts of temperature, cloudiness, and rain and of the movement of large-scale weather systems such as high- and low-pressure areas. Heavy snowfall is more difficult to predict. The NWS reports that in 1996, for each period twenty-four hours ahead, it predicted temperatures (within plus or minus 5 degrees) 86 percent of the time and the onset of freezing temperatures 74 percent of the time, as shown in Figure 2.5. Its predictions in 1996 for heavy snowfall (defined as four or more inches) were accurate only 44 percent of the time. For the period more than forty-eight hours in the future, weather forecasting enters the twilight zone, where accuracy and reliability decline to a point of very limited usefulness. In fact, the prediction of the specific time and places of precipitation beyond two days becomes indistinguishable from random guessing.

Short-term weather forecasting has improved markedly in recent decades, according to the AMS, which in 1991 found that forecasts for forty-eight hours ahead during that year were about as accurate as forecasts for twenty-four hours ahead were in 1977. Such improvement is an encouraging sign that the application of science to weather analysis and short-term prediction has paid off. The AMS's official policy statement in 1991 contained the following statement: "The notable improvement in forecast accuracy that has been achieved since the 1950s is a direct outgrowth of technological developments, basic and applied research, and the

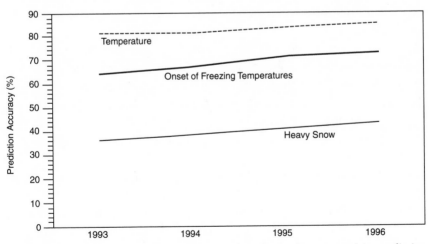

Figure 2.5 The National Weather Service's accuracy (percentage) in predicting temperature and heavy snow.

new knowledge and methods of forecasters. . . . Foremost among these has been the further development of numerical prediction models, based on the laws of physics."[28] Whenever a profession's forecasting accuracy fails to improve over several decades—despite the investment of a lot of brain power, research, and information technology—its forecasting methodologies are most likely not based on proved scientific principles.

THE STORM CHASERS

Predicting the force and landfall of hurricanes is the high-wire act of weather forecasting. We all watch and listen to television and radio broadcasts as the NHC in Miami, Florida, tracks these killer storms and predicts whether and where they are likely to strike land. Such forecasts can be deadly if the NHC fails to predict accurately where the full force of the hurricane will strike, and they can be needlessly costly if it issues warnings to areas that the storm then bypasses. The fact that hurricanes are a quickly changeable, highly chaotic force of nature increases the drama.

The vast majority of hurricanes form over warm tropical ocean waters between the tropics of Cancer and Capricorn, twenty-three degrees twenty-seven minutes north and south of the equator, and generally only during certain months, depending on the location. Those areas are (in descending order of frequency of occurrence): (1) the western tropical North Pacific east of the Philippines from October through December; (2) the tropical Indian Ocean from January through March south of the equator and October and November north of the equator; (3) the tropical North Atlantic west of Africa's western bulge from July through September; and (4) the tropical East Pacific just west of Central America from July through September. The hurricanes that form in the tropical North Atlantic cause the most damage in the United States.

The prevailing winds surrounding a hurricane, called steering winds, determine its path. In the tropical North Atlantic, the prevailing easterly winds drive the hurricanes toward the Western Hemisphere. If the hurricane stays far to the south, the same easterly winds are likely to cause it to track through the Caribbean on somewhat of a straight line. If the hurricane wanders far enough to the north, however, it will be affected by the prevailing westerly winds common to the United States, causing it to track in an unpredictable, arching north-easterly path that could strike anywhere from Florida to Maine, or it might move harmlessly off into the middle of the North Atlantic. In the absence of steering winds, hurricanes meander chaotically, circling back in a tight area and wreaking havoc on a particular location for days.

Using satellites and reports from ships and land stations, the NHC monitors hurricanes from their birth as tropical depressions or storms (depending on their wind speed) until they finally dissipate. Because hurricanes usually develop over remote areas of open ocean, it is difficult for the NHC to collect sufficient data to develop a complete three-dimensional picture of the hurricane and its surrounding weather environment. To help fill the data gap, it sends observation planes directly into hurricanes to gauge their strength and measure the speed and direction of steering winds.

Like the NWS, the NHC uses computer models to guide its hurricane forecasters in making their predictions. However, unlike the NWS models, the NHC's traditional models are essentially an automated version of the analog approach to forecasting. The model searches a database of past hurricane tracks dating back to around 1886, seeking to match the path of a current hurricane with one from the past. Once a similar hurricane track is found, the NHC uses it to predict the eventual path of the current hurricane. This methodology assumes, however, that hurricane behavior follows a consistent pattern, a shaky assumption for such chaotic weather events.

Although armed with computer guidance, hurricane forecasters are most likely to fall back on the traditional, low-tech method of projecting the hurricane's future course based on their recollections of how past hurricanes have behaved under various conditions. As one NHC forecaster explained in an interview with *Weatherwise* magazine, the most valuable tools of his trade are "a pair of dividers to measure distance, a ruler, a brush for eraser dirt, three sharp pencils colored red, black, and blue, and a large paper-plotting chart."[29] The AMS, in its official statement of hurricane forecasting, describes the current practice as being "rather subjective" with "inconsistencies in skill," and says that the quality of forecasting varies with each individual's skill and experience. It asserts, however, that "there is little skill in the prediction of hurricane-related rainfall" and that "the inability to anticipate . . . changes [in wind speed] for a storm that is less than 24 hours from landfall is of great concern."[30]

Predicting the place of landfall is the essence of hurricane forecasting. The most recent figures for the NHC's accuracy in predicting hurricane landfall—for the period from 1992 to 1996—are shown in graph form in Figure 2.6. Note that the average error at twelve hours before landfall is plus or minus 52 miles; at twenty-four hours before, it is plus or minus 102 miles; and at seventy-two hours before, the error rate increases proportionately to plus or minus 293 miles. The AMS also notes that the error rates in forecasting the tracks of hurricanes along the East Coast of the United States are 30 percent higher than the overall average error figures shown in Figure 2.6. [31] That is because whereas southern hurricanes move due west with the prevailing winds, northern hurricanes move in arching northeasterly directions that are much less predictable. Thus, a hurricane predicted to strike the Carolinas three days hence could actually strike *anywhere* along 761 miles of coastline (2 × 355 × 1.3) instead—stretching from Jacksonville, Florida, to Atlantic City, New Jersey. The AMS has noted that such large forecasting errors can be dangerous: "Unfortunately, evacuation times for some communities now exceed what can reasonably be expected from present and projected forecast abilities."[32]

In order to assess the skill of the NHC in predicting hurricane tracks, I devised a method of naive forecast that I call "rulercasting." I found the point along each hurricane's track twenty-four hours before landfall and used a ruler to extend the hurricane's path to a landfall point based on the direction in which the hurricane was heading at that time. I "rulercasted" the tracks of twenty-eight hurricanes from 1979 to 1989 twenty-four hours before each struck land and ended up with an average forecast error of 121 miles, which is only 18 percent higher than the 103-mile average error for the NHC from 1992 to 1996, and less than 1 percent higher than its average error from 1982 to 1991. This result suggests that the accuracy of my low-tech "rulercasting" is at least in the ballpark of the NHC's forecast accuracy—and it is certainly a much cheaper way of predicting where hurricanes will strike.

As shown in Figure 2.6, the NHC has improved its forecast accuracy from the 1980s to the 1990s. Mark DeMaria, chief of the Technical Support Branch of the NHC, estimates that the NHC increases its accuracy 1 percent a year, on average, and that there has been a 20 percent improvement from the 1970s to 1996.[33] The AMS reports in its

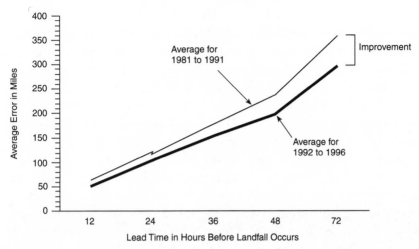

Figure 2.6 The official error rate in predicting hurricane landfalls. (*Sources of data:* American Meteorological Society and the National Hurricane Center.)

official statement: "Operational hurricane forecast errors have not decreased enough to solve the forecast problem. . . . Until such improvements can be effected, forecasting methods will continue to be subjective; disaster preparedness officials and public should be kept aware of current limitations in forecast accuracy."[34]

There is, however, one type of hurricane forecast that the NHC does especially well: predicting the impact of a hurricane for a specific landfall location. The NHC uses a model called SLOSH (sea, lake, and overland surges from hurricanes) to predict the height of the storm surge and the extent of flooding based on the strength of the storm and the geography of the coastal area it is expected to strike. Storm surge is relatively easy to predict, because the flooding depends on only the strength of the storm and the configuration of the coast it is expected to strike. There are no nonlinear relationships, feedback loops, or other chaotic behavior involved.

THE LONG VIEW

There is something inherently contradictory about long-range weather forecasts that extend a month, a season, or a whole year, given the inaccuracy of short-term weather forecasts and the fact that the theoretical limit to weather forecasting is deemed to be ten to fourteen days. Nevertheless, there are many weather forecasters providing long-range predictions, including three prominent ones: the NWS's Climate Analysis Center, which forecasts seasonal temperatures and precipitation, from a month to more than a year in advance; William Gray, a meteorologist from Colorado State University, who predicts hurricane frequency a year in advance; and *The Old Farmer's Almanac,* which forecasts daily weather conditions (including hurricanes) a year or more in advance.

Every month, the Climate Analysis Center (CAC) forecasts average temperatures and precipitation throughout the United States for the next thirty and ninety days, calculating the probability for their being above or below long-term seasonal averages. At the end of 1994, the CAC introduced its year-ahead seasonal forecast. Figure 2.7 shows a forecast it made in November 1995 for the winter of 1996–1997.

In the top diagram, the "A" and the "5%" in the southeastern United States indicate that the CAC predicted that that part of the country had odds of 5 percent better than pure chance of having above-average temperatures during the winter of 1996–1997. Given that there is a one-third random chance that any part of the country will experience above-average, below-average, or typical weather, the CAC's forecast can also be interpreted as a 38 percent probability (33 + 5 percent) that the Southeast would experience above-average temperatures. The lower chart shows that the CAC predicted that south-central areas such as Dallas, Texas, had odds of 5 percent better than pure chance— a 38 percent probability—of being wetter during that period. Interestingly, the CAC forecast for December 1996 through February 1997 shown in Figure 2.7 called for below-normal precipitation for the Pacific Northwest, when in fact the area experienced torrential rains and massive flooding for the first two months of the period.

Of what use are such low-odds predictions? Would you plan a winter vacation to Florida next year based on such a small chance of Florida's being warmer than usual? My second reaction was that the CAC was not sticking its neck out too far and that it must have some doubts about its predictions. When I asked a meteorologist at the CAC about why the forecasts are expressed in such low odds, he explained that they reflect the difficulty in getting any long-range forecasts right.

The CAC's forecasting methodology essentially involves analyzing past temperature and precipitation patterns together with persistent

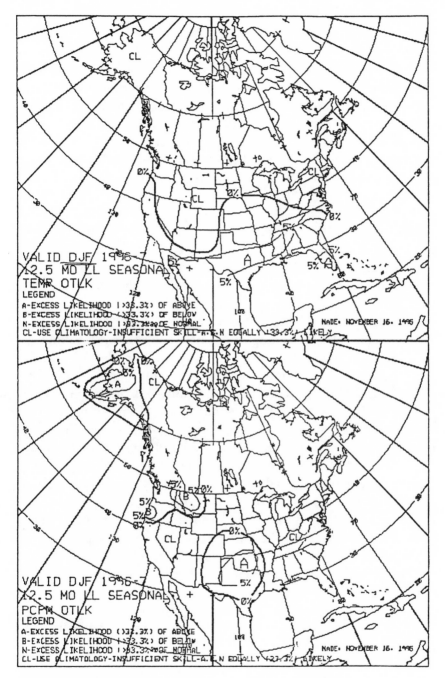

Figure 2.7 An example of the CAC's long-range climate forecast (made on November 16, 1995, for December 1995 through February 1996). (*Source:* U.S. National Weather Service.)

environmental conditions such as global sea surface temperatures, mois-
ture in the soil, and the presence or absence of snow and ice that affect
the weather. For example, if unseasonably high precipitation occurred
in the state of Washington at the same time that an unusually warm body
of water emerged off the coast of the Pacific Northwest, then one might
assume—logically, but naively—that a recurrence of the warm Pacific
water the following year would again bring unseasonably high precipitation to the state of Washington. This is another example of analog-
based methodology, which is flawed, because weather patterns never
exactly repeat themselves. There is an almost infinite number of weather
patterns that could result from any of these persistent environmental
conditions or combinations of conditions. Thus, the next occurrence of
warm ocean water off the coast of the Pacific Northwest might cause a
drought in Washington and floods in California, rather than higher levels of precipitation. It's anyone's guess.

The AMS, in its official policy statement, has raised doubts about the
CAC's methodology, asserting that "patterns of abnormal warmth and
cold and wetness and dryness are not well understood," and charging
that "slight skill exists in forecasting average temperatures and precipitation for the month or season. . . . No verifiable skill exists in forecasting day-to-day weather changes a month or a season in advance."[35] The
head of CAC's Long-Range Forecast Division, Donald Gilman, has
taken this critique a step further by admitting: "There is no usable, quan-
titative theory of long-range [weather] forecasting in a physicist's sense.
There is an empirical art and we all have to scratch our way along with
a mix of techniques. . . . Suffice it to say that the monthly and seasonal
forecasts are made by a kind of cook's mixture of empirical techniques
[and] cannot be of a very high information content or accuracy."[36] In
other words, there is little science behind the CAC's forecasts.

Furthermore, there is evidence that the CAC's predictions are no
different from random guessing—that is, it has no forecasting skill in
making long-range predictions. Imagine using a CAC weather chart
forecasting temperatures for the next three months as a dartboard, with
the three types of zones marked N for normal, A for above average, and
B for below average. Next, imagine that you are blindfolded and given
a box of darts evenly divided into the three categories marked N, A, and
B, corresponding to the zones on the weather map, which you throw
at the chart. Your accuracy in predicting the long-range weather by

blindly throwing the darts would be approximately 33 percent (one divided by the possible number of outcomes).

Next, consider that the slight skill that the AMS refers to is an improvement of only 4 percent over random guessing.[37] In other words, its overall forecast accuracy is 37 percent (the 33 percent random chance plus the 4 percent improvement). However, it turns out that the CAC's charts are drawn in such a way that certain combinations of adjacent zones cannot exist; for example, an above-average cannot exist next to a below-average, since a normal zone must separate them. This distorts the expected odds of random guessing. It's like declaring that every time your dart landed on some zones, you got another chance to throw it, which would improve your percentage hit rate. Two separate studies found that the way the CAC charts are drawn causes the figure for random guessing to approach 37 percent instead of 33 percent.[38] In other words, the 4 percent claimed improvement could just as easily be zero.

Curious about how potential users of long-range weather forecasts felt about the value of such forecasts, I interviewed two people involved in planning at natural gas companies. Natural gas companies are very dependent on seasonal weather, because it affects how much gas they store in their huge tanks, as opposed to buying gas from the open market when they need it, which might be very expensive. Kevin Cross, a meteorologist at Northern Gas Corporation in Houston, said, "We do use the information [about long-term forecasts], but with caution. We don't bet the bank on them. When we use them, we don't make any commitments we couldn't recover from, because there is too much variability [in the forecasts]." Bob Cave, executive director of the American Public Gas Association, was blunter. Involved in capacity planning in 1986, he recalls attempting to use long-range forecasts but finding them "not very reliable." He even hired a private forecaster to help him with long-range forecasts, and the forecaster eventually told him, "Bob, you're wasting your money."

GRAY SKIES

Ironically, the home of long-range hurricane forecasting is thousands of miles from any threat of being struck by one, nestled in the foothills of the Rocky Mountains at Colorado State University, where William

Gray and his associates have gained the most credible reputation for predicting the incidence of future hurricanes. Gray is currently a hot commodity and is widely quoted in the media whenever hurricanes are the topic. According to Bob Sheets, head of the NHC, "Gray's is the only credible model available today for predicting hurricane activity."[39] Peter Catalano, in *Popular Science,* gave Gray similar high praise: "No one was capable of long-term hurricane forecasting at all before Gray came along. . . . His forecasts have been uncanny. His formula accurately predicted hurricane activity in nine of the last eleven years."[40]

Gray's theory is intriguing. In studying hurricane activity and global weather conditions back to 1942, he concluded that unusually high rainfall in western Africa during the months prior to the hurricane season spawns hurricane seeds over the Atlantic Ocean just off the African coast. Prevailing easterly winds blow these storm seeds toward the Western Hemisphere, where they often blossom into full-blown hurricanes. A counterbalancing force in Gray's theory is the presence of the El Niño, a current of warm Pacific Ocean water that periodically flows up the western coast of North and Central America, temporarily creating westerly winds that push the potential hurricanes away from the Western Hemisphere.

Figure 2.8 shows a comparison of Gray's hurricane forecasts two months apart over twelve years and the number of hurricanes that actually occurred each year.[41] Commentators on Gray's accuracy often point to his direct hits, such as in 1985, 1986, and 1992. However, they overlook his misses and fail to compare his predictions to a naive forecast to assess whether they demonstrate any skill. To test Gray's skill, I used the long-term average number of hurricanes occurring per year during that period—5.9—as a naive forecast.

Gray's forecasts made in May and at the beginning of August for each hurricane season show a modest level of skill: His accuracy in predicting the number of hurricanes for each season averaged 69 percent for his May forecast and 73 percent for his August one, a slight improvement over the 60 percent accuracy of using the long-term average hurricane incidence as a naive predictor. However, forecasts made during August should be much more accurate than forecasts made several months earlier, because by August the hurricane season is already underway. Given the complexity of our weather system, the fact that Gray's predictions demonstrate some skill is laudable. However, I

Year	Prior May Forecast	Prior July–August Forecast	Actual Number of Hurricanes
1984	7	7	5
1985	8	7	7
1986	4	4	4
1987	5	4	3
1988	7	7	5
1989	4	4	7
1990	7	6	8
1991	4	3	4
1992	4	4	4
1993	7	6	4
1994	5	4	3
1995	8	9	11
1996	7	6	9

Figure 2.8 William Gray's long-term track record for hurricane forecasting.

would hesitate to call an overall 9 percent improvement over naive guessing in his May forecasts "uncanny."

That some people see them as being uncanny is a prime example of what some psychologists call the Rorschach factor, named after the famous test where patients describe the meaning of random inkblots. The human brain, trained over eons of evolution to decipher the environment quickly, often attributes meaning to meaningless patterns and truth to coincidental events that can be explained by laws of probability. As you will see throughout this book, the Rorschach factor has caused many forecasters to see relationships and trends that do not exist and to claim forecasting accuracy that is no better than could be explained by chance.

THE ART OF ALMANACMANSHIP

Despite the improbability of long-range forecasting's achieving any kind of consistent accuracy, almanacs seem to have retained their influence among a large segment of the American public. For example, in autumn 1994, both *The Old Farmer's Almanac* and the *Farmers' Almanac* predicted a stormy 1995 winter with a record snowfall. Over the weeks and months that followed, snowblower sales soared 120 percent, the sale of rock salt for use on highways increased 42 percent, snowmobile sales increased 46 percent, the sale of four-wheel-drive vehicles increased an average of 60 percent (and more than twice that for one model), and snow shovels sold out early in the season.[42] Moreover, administrators from the city of Buffalo and the city of Chicago contacted *The Old Farmer's Almanac* for further information regarding its snowy forecast, to help them justify an increased budget for salt and sand for the coming winter. And what kind of winter actually occurred? "In the United States, December 1994–February 1995 was especially warm, ranking as the 5th warmest since 1985," according to the NWS's Climate Prediction Center.[43]

Among the hundreds of almanacs that once existed in America, *The Old Farmer's Almanac* has survived as one of America's oldest pieces of literature continuously in publication through the present day. Sherrin Wight, its publisher, estimated that the *Almanac* had a circulation of 4.4 million copies in 1996 and noted that it has been on the *New York Times* best-seller list for at least the last twenty-five years.[44] In its home page on the Internet, the *Almanac* claims that it is "the only institution in America making day-to-day, nationwide forecasts 18 months ahead of time." In each of its annual publications (and now on its Internet home page as well), the *Almanac* describes its long-range weather forecasting methodology as follows: "Our weather forecasts are determined both by the use of a secret formula (devised in 1792 by the founder of this Almanac, Robert B. Thomas), enhanced by the most modern scientific calculations based on solar activity, particularly sunspot cycles. We also analyze weather records for particular locales. We believe nothing in the universe occurs haphazardly; there is a cause-and-effect pattern to all phenomena, including weather. It follows, therefore, that we believe weather is predictable."[45] The *Almanac's* success is due less to the brilliance of its secret weather forecasting formula than to two hundred years of self-promotion and claims of accuracy, such as the comments that founding editor Robert B. Thomas put in his second edition in 1793: "As to my judgment of the weather, I need say but little: for you will, in one year's time, without any assistance of mine, very easily discover how near I have come to the truth."[46]

The editors of *The Old Farmer's Almanac* have generally stated that its forecasts are 80 to 85 percent accurate, although in the 1950s they claimed that it was "almost one-hundred percent right."[47] To test the validity of the *Almanac*'s accuracy claim, I analyzed its track record in predicting monthly average temperatures for the past thirty years from the vantage point of a farmer in Omaha, Nebraska. I found that the *Almanac* had a 48.99 percent success rate in predicting whether average monthly temperatures were above or below seasonal norms, which is essentially the same fifty-fifty odds of flipping a coin. Its accuracy in predicting temperatures was 73 percent—not too far from its claimed 80 percent accuracy. Surprisingly, however, using seasonal average temperatures as a naive forecast yields 90 percent accuracy. In other words, even if the *Almanac* were 80 percent accurate as it claims, that would be 10 percent *less* than just using seasonal averages, which requires no skill. My analysis shows that the *Almanac*'s lower accuracy relative to using seasonal averages is due to its occasional bold predictions (e.g., exceptionally hot or cold seasons) that generate huge forecasting errors, because these bold predictions mostly prove to be erroneous.

The *Old Farmer's Almanac* has also claimed to have made several remarkable direct hits in forecasting unusual weather conditions with uncanny precision, such as Hurricane Andrew in Florida in 1992 and bizarre winter weather in New England on July 13, 1816. I looked up the *Almanac*'s prediction for August 1992 and, sure enough, there it was: the prediction for Florida for August 30 to 31 said, "Possible hurricane South." Not bad, given that Andrew struck on August 24. Did the *Almanac* pull off a virtuoso prediction, or was this just dumb luck? Actually, it was neither. The prediction was nearly a sure thing, since the southern half of Florida gets hit with an average of 1.15 hurricanes per year, and most of them occur during August and September.

The *Almanac*'s accurate prediction of winter weather for July 13, 1816, was due to an extraordinary coincidence. Founding editor Thomas became ill just as the 1816 *Almanac* was going to print. A copy boy informed him that the prediction for July 13 was missing. "Put in anything you want," Thomas told him, so the boy inserted, "Rain, hail, and snow." Upon discovering the joke, Thomas destroyed most of the copies and spent considerable time denying the extreme forecast, which inevitably got into general circulation. But in New England on July 13, 1816, it did in fact "rain, hail, and snow"—unusual weather caused by the 1815 eruption of Mount Tambora in the East Indies. The volcano generated a cooling dust cloud that caused what is called the "Little Ice Age" in New England that summer, during which ponds and lakes never thawed. When the original "forecast" came true, Thomas changed his tune and declared, "I told you so." Judson Hale, the current editor of the *Almanac*, has called this scenario "one of the earliest and best examples of a subtle skill my uncle always referred to as 'Almanacmanship.' "[48]

In spite of the claim of uniqueness made by *The Old Farmer's Almanac* for its forecasts, similar long-term weather forecasts are provided by several other almanacs, which the publisher of *The Old Farmer's Almanac* dismisses as "imitators."[49] The *Farmers' Almanac,* founded in 1818, is the second-oldest almanac in continuous publication; it had a circulation of 500,000 books (retail edition) in 1996. Like the *The Old Farmers' Almanac*, it is published on August 15 of each year, which provides forecasts for the balance of that year and for all of the following year and appears to use a similar forecasting method. According to Sandi Duncan, its managing editor, the *Farmers' Almanac* predictions are based on a "secret formula which originated in 1818 using sunspot activity and the tidal action of the moon and the planets."[50] A newer almanac is the *Almanac for Farmers and City Folk,* founded in 1983, which had a circulation of 1 million books in 1996. Like the others, this almanac, which comes out in September rather than August, contains forecasts for the balance of the year and for all of the following year. According to its editor, Lucas McFadden, it too relies on sunspot activity for its long-range weather forecasts, along with such factors as the declination of the moon (degrees above or below the equator). It also includes predictions for the best time to catch fish and an astrological guide to gardening.[51]

So what do these almanacs claim about their accuracy today? Judson Hale, of *The Old Farmer's Almanac,* provides a tongue-in-cheek answer: "Weather forecasting in 1792 was what you might call an imperfect science. Today, two hundred years later, it still is." And, "Our accuracy? Still 80 percent. Of course."[52] Duncan asserts that the accuracy of the *Farmers' Almanac* is 80 to 85 percent, which is, she says, "better accuracy than other almanacs."[53] McFadden claims that the accuracy of his *Almanac for Farmers and City Folk* is 85 percent and "one of the best in the market."[54] It is not at all surprising that all three major long-range weather forecasting almanacs claim accuracy in the 80 to 85 percent range, given that just using historical seasonal norms as a naive forecast requiring no skill yields a 90 percent accuracy rate. Any forecaster of long-range weather would be crazy not to rely mostly on historical seasonal norms.

A more brazen claim of accuracy was made by the weather forecaster for the *Almanac for Farmers and City Folk,* Boyd Quate, who in a *Forbes* article declared, "I always get the number of storms right, but sometimes

I'm off by a day."[55] On the surface, it seems that Quate is claiming that he alone can do what the billion-dollar NWS has never been able to achieve: forecast violent storms more than a few hours or (occasionally) days in advance—indeed, that he can do so more than a year in advance. However, to put Quate's "achievement" in perspective, consider that, according to the NWS, 10,000 storms strike the United States each year, which means that twenty-seven storms occur each day in the United States and approximately 1.4 storms per day in each of the nineteen zones for which Quate makes predictions. Further still, his "off-by-a-day" disclaimer would be hard to validate, because Quate's forecasts are not for individual days but for blocks of days ranging from as few as two to as many as twelve days.

Let us evaluate the three almanacs' forecasting skills by comparing the forecasts that they published in the summer of 1996 for a single day—January 18, 1997—to the actual weather for that day across the mainland United States. On January 18, there was clear weather over most of the country, and a massive cold front was gripping the eastern two-thirds of the United States from Canada to Miami, with clear skies and bitter cold persisting there for several days. Figure 2.9 gives the local weather for that day for ten major U.S. cities, as reported by the Weather Services Corporation, and the forecasts made by the three almanacs for that day in those cities.

Assessing the predictions versus the actual weather with some generosity, I found that both *The Old Farmer's Almanac* and the *Farmers' Almanac* were right for five of the ten areas of the country and that *The Almanac for Farmers and City Folk* was right for three of the ten. This is an inconclusive analysis, however, because the sample is so small and because the forecasts are too vague to assess accurately. None of the three almanacs predicted the weather just for January 18, but rather for a multiday interval including January 18, and the interval was different for each almanac. If I had adjusted the forecasts for sure bets—for example, all three almanacs correctly predicted that Seattle would be rainy or cloudy and that Minneapolis and Chicago would be cold and snowy—their scores would be lower.

At least *The Old Farmer's Almanac* adds a refreshing dose of realism on its Internet home page: "Modesty requires, however, that we add this caveat: It is obvious that neither we nor anyone else has as yet gained sufficient insight into the mysteries of the universe to predict weather long-range with anything resembling total accuracy."[56]

City	Actual Weather, January 18, 1997	The Old Farmers' Almanac	The Farmers' Almanac	The Almanac for Farmers and City Folk
Seattle	Seasonable, rain	+Heavy rain	+Showers	+Cloudy
San Francisco	Seasonable, cloudy	−Sunny	−Fair weather	−Rain, mild
Los Angeles	Warm, sunny	+Sunny	+Fair weather	−Light rain, mild
Denver	Seasonable, partly cloudy	−Cold, flurries	−Light snow	−Light snow
Dallas	Sunny, cold	−Ice to rain	−Showers	−Light rain
Minneapolis	Very cold, flurries	+Flurries, very cold	+Light snow	+Cloudy, cold
Chicago	Very cold, flurries	+Very cold, few flurries	+Cold, blustery winds	+Cold winds, light flurries
Miami	Sunny, cold	−Mild, showers	+Fair skies, windy	−Cold winds, rain
Washington, D.C.	Sunny, very cold	−Heavy snow, then rain	−Especially wet	−Snow
New York	Partly cloudy, very cold	+Windy, cold	−Wet	−Moderate to heavy snow

Figure 2.9   Comparison of actual weather with the forecasts from three almanacs for January 18, 1997. +, mostly correct; −, mostly incorrect. (*Sources of data: Weather Services Corporation; The Old Farmer's Almanac, 1997; Farmers' Almanac, 1997; The Almanac for Farmers and City Folk, 1997.*)

HOLD THOSE SNOWBLOWERS—
AND FLIP A COIN

In the past few years, meteorologists have harnessed the laws of nature and advanced technology to make great strides in weather observation, storm detection, and short-range forecasting in the one- to two-day range. Long-range prediction, however, remains the voodoo aspect of weather forecasting. Whether using the NWS's billion-dollar technology or a 200-year-old almanac formula locked in a tin box, long-term weather predictions should be discounted heavily, and long-term predictions for specific days should be ignored altogether. There is little or no evidence of forecasting skill in making such predictions, and whatever skill that may exist is too minimal to be of value to anyone. The best we can do is to prepare ourselves for the worst weather extremes that have occurred over the past several decades.

Ignore those who use long-range forecasts to sell their products; it is simply exploitation. For example, car dealerships in the Northeast used the dire almanac predictions in autumn 1994 to sell their four-wheel-drive vehicles. A typical ad contained the following pitch: "*Farmers' Almanac* predicts a fierce winter! Be prepared! Buy Jeep 4 × 4s now!" Sales of $53,000 Range Rovers increased 131 percent in the following months.[57]

Ignore false prophets of long-term doom-and-gloom weather predictions. Their spiel typically goes like this: "We Americans have sinned in the past by building cottages on hurricane-prone coasts, and have gotten away with it most of the time in recent years because the weather has been especially tame. But we will soon pay for our sins because we are entering a disastrous weather phase of the cycle." William Gray's long-term outlook for hurricane activity fits this mold; after discussing our sins of coastal development, he advises, "We've gone 25 years with relatively little activity—a long cycle by historical standards. Inevitably, long stretches of destruction will return. . . . Florida and the East Coast will see hurricane devastation such as they never experienced before."[58] *Popular Science,* which interviewed Gray, embellished his dismal predictions: "Imagine hurricanes the size of Andrew slamming into metropolitan regions along the East Coast with almost yearly frequency, for a decade or more. Impossible, you say: Try probable."[59] It is one thing to warn the populace that we have become vulnerable to disastrous weather because of the heavy development of our coastal areas and floodplains—which is true. It is quite another to predict the onslaught of a cycle of devastating weather; the weather does not *follow* any periodic cycle.

Do not take the daily weather predictions as gospel either. Despite the modern weather forecasters' considerable skill in short-range forecasting, weather conditions can change rapidly, and the forecasters observe only a sample of the weather conditions. Severe storms and precipitation can emerge quickly, undetected by grids of weather stations.

The big storm predicted to be coming your way in a day or two might veer off or dissipate—or it might strike as predicted. If you are in need of a reliable weather forecast, get it as current as possible from either radio or television; newspapers print weather predictions that are about a day old, and by the time you read them, they are largely incorrect. If you have a two-day-old forecast, you might as well flip a coin.

This raises the question of the value of weather forecasting. Is the $4 billion spent each year worldwide on weather forecasting worth the investment? Charles Doswell provides a succinct answer: "Forecasts have value . . . from the resources that are saved."[60] The savings in human lives alone probably more than justifies the $4 billion spent. Furthermore, the World Meteorological Organization estimates that this $4 billion expenditure yields $20 to $40 billion in saved property and business expenses, a nice return on investment. This does not mean, however, that all of the money is spent wisely. As you can see, there is no reason to spend any money on providing the public with long-range forecasting, although research on long-range forecasts should continue. It would also be a mistake for the NWS to continue much longer to invest money in creating ever denser grids of weather sampling stations, since at some point—probably soon—the increased detail in sampling current weather conditions will not proportionately improve its forecasting ability much beyond the current range.

When I started writing this book, I was skeptical about the validity of weather forecasting, a sentiment that I am sure is widely shared. I was surprised to learn, though, that modern weather forecasting is the most successful of all the future-predicting professions examined in this book. In fact, meteorology is the only forecasting profession that employs proved laws of nature to make predictions—if only for the very near future. Meteorology is also the only forecasting profession among the fortune sellers that has shown clear signs of improvement. From a scientific perspective, it's all downhill from here throughout the rest of this book. Here's a hint. *Question:* Why did God create economists? *Answer:* In order to make weather forecasters look good.

3

The Dismal Scientists

E conomists have been unable to shake their mistaken moniker, "the dismal scientists," for more than 120 years. The phrase derives from historian Thomas Carlyle's reaction to the dire future envisioned by Thomas Malthus in his 1798 treatise, *An Essay on the Principle of Population,* which predicted that population growth would inevitably surpass the growth in food and cause mass starvation. In a pamphlet written in 1850, Carlyle referred to economists as those "respectable Professors of the Dismal Science."[1] Although Malthus was considered to be an economist in his day, his "dismal treatise" is clearly a study in demographics and has little to do with what we call economics today.

Today it is the generally perceived poor track record of economists that has caused the nickname to stick. Consider a 1995 *Business Week* article, entitled "A D+ for Dismal Scientists? Even the Fed's Gurus Often Goof," and a 1996 *Forbes* article, "Dismal Days for the Dismal Science."[2] Economic forecasters have routinely failed to foresee turning points in the economy: the coming of severe recessions, the start of recoveries, and periods of rapid increases or decreases in inflation. It is jokingly said that economists have forecast nine of the last five recessions. In fact, they have failed to predict the past four most severe recessions, and most of them predicted growth instead for these periods. After the October 1987 stock market crash, most economists predicted a severe downturn in the economy similar to what happened after the 1929 stock market crash, yet during the last quarter of 1987, the economy continued expanding vigorously. Like all other types of fore-casters, economists' vision of the future is clearly clouded with situational bias.

ECONOMISTS: WHO ARE THEY AND WHAT DO THEY DO?

The leading intellectuals of social science during the eighteenth and nineteenth centuries were called economists, including such broad-gauged thinkers as Adam Smith, John Stewart Mill, and Karl Marx. Just as Isaac Newton discovered the fundamental laws of physics and artic-ulated the principles of modern scientific inquiry, so these economists sought to ascertain the principles and natural laws of commerce, gov-ernment, and society, by which they hoped to explain economic be-havior and thus predict the future of peoples and nations. In contrast, economics today is focused almost entirely on matters of commerce and money, and, according to economist and historian Robert Heilbroner, "has become a technical, often arcane calling."[3] It is a highly theoreti-cal and mathematical discipline that has almost no ties to other social sci-ences yet is essentially about human interaction—a social science with dollar signs. Treated more like a pure science—a "soft physics"—eco-nomics even has its own Nobel Prize, which was first awarded in 1969.

Economics, like meteorology, is heavily involved in forecasting. Among all the sciences, hard and soft, these two fields are by far the most heavily involved in making predictions for broad public consumption. Nearly every day the media shower us with an economist's predictions. How often do physicists and chemists make predictions about the future? Hardly ever. Even seismologists are cautious about predicting earthquakes, despite the public's appetite for such speculation.

The 1996 *Statistical Abstract of the United States* estimates that there are about 148,000 economists in the United States, and in one way or another, most are involved in making or interpreting predictions. At the very top of the economic prediction pyramid are the high-level gov-ernment officials who are intimately involved, directly or indirectly, in setting economic policy for the nation. The most influential economists in the United States are the governors and chairman of the Federal Re-serve, members of the president's Council of Economic Advisors

(CEA), and the Congressional Budget Office (CBO). All three organizations are involved in running the U.S. economy from the very top of government, and each publishes its own economic forecasts.

Twice each year, the chairman of the Federal Reserve presents his economic forecasts to the U.S. Congress. He is surely the most powerful economist in the United States; only he can make a prediction about where the economy is headed and then, without anyone else's approval, change the nation's supply of money and raise or lower short-term interest rates. Every other government official, the president included, must receive the approval of another official or government body before taking any significant action.

Paul Volcker, who headed the Federal Reserve from 1979 to 1987, demonstrated the power of the Federal Reserve chairman when he declared war on inflation in 1979. By tightening up the money supply and jacking up short-term interest rates from 10 to 19 percent, Volcker successfully rid the U.S. economy of dangerously high inflation rates, while triggering the severe 1980 worldwide recession that caused the highest unemployment rates since the Great Depression, the bankruptcy of tens of thousands of U.S. businesses, and the default of many developing countries such as Mexico, Argentina, and Brazil on $300 billion worth of bank loans. Volcker's actions also helped scuttle President Carter's bid for reelection. That's power. Some, including William Greider, think it is too much power, especially for a nonelected official. In his book *Secrets of the Temple,* Greider, a political writer and a former assistant managing editor of the *Washington Post,* argued that "the governors of the Federal Reserve decided the large questions of the political economy, including who shall prosper and who shall fail, yet their role remained opaque and mysterious. . . . The Federal Reserve System was the crucial anomaly at the very core of representative democracy."[4] Alan Greenspan, the current chairman of the Federal Reserve, has continued Volcker's war on inflation, and Wall Street cautiously anticipates Greenspan's manipulation of short-term interest rates and the money supply.

The CEA was established in 1946, with the passage of the Employment Act, to "provide the President with objective economic analysis and advice on the development and implementation of a wide range of domestic and international economic policy issues."[5] Every week, the chairman of the CEA advises the president, vice president, and other high-level officials on the state of the economy. Members of the CEA help the president in formulating specific policies on a wide range of issues, such as determining the implications of welfare reform, or helping the president prepare for trade negotiations with China on protecting intellectual property rights and market access for U.S. corporations. The CEA also prepares economic forecasts that serve as a basis for the president's budget proposals and publishes its forecasts in the *Economic Report of the President* at the beginning of each year.

The CBO was founded in 1974 with the Congressional Budget and Impoundment Control Act, to provide Congress with "detailed budget information and studies of the budget impact of alternative policies."[6] Providing Congress with its own economic analysis and forecasting group independent of the executive branch, the CBO publishes its forecasts several times each year in its *Economic and Budget Outlook*. Although critics have voiced suspicions that the CEA and CBO tilt their forecasts to support the political policies of the president and the Congress, a study by Michael Belongia, a research officer at the Federal Reserve Bank of St. Louis, found that "neither the CEA nor CBO forecasts exhibit any discernible bias."[7]

Economic forecasters are working at every level of government— national, state, and local—and internationally as well. Among the most influential internationally are those at the International Monetary Fund and the World Bank, and, nationally, at the Federal Reserve banks and federal agencies such as the Commerce Department and the Bureau of Labor. All publish volumes of economic forecasts. In fact, there are so many government economists that they have their own professional association, the Society of Government Economists.

There are also hundreds of private-sector organizations that sell economic forecasts. The economic forecasting business started with Wharton Econometric Forecasting Associates (WEFA) in 1963 and grew to about a $100 million industry at its peak in the early 1980s, when it was dominated by the "big three": WEFA, Data Resources, Inc. (DRI), and Chase Econometrics. The big three were founded by influential economists: Otto Eckstein, a professor at Harvard and a former member of the CEA, founded DRI; Michael Evans, a professor at Wharton Business School and well connected with congressional Republicans, founded Chase Econometrics (and more recently founded Evans Economics); and Lawrence Klein, a professor at the University of Pennsylvania and a former chairman of the CEA founded WEFA (our current Federal Reserve chairman was once a key principal in the economic forecasting firm Townsend-Greenspan & Co.; and Larry Meyer, appointed a governor of the Federal Reserve in 1996, headed up his own forecasting firm, Laurence H. Meyer & Associates). A number of universities, such as UCLA, Georgia State, Kent State, and the University of Michigan, are also in the business of selling economic forecasts. Typically these commercial forecasting organizations provide time-shared access to their forecasts and models, extensive databases, and software tools, as well as a modicum of consulting advice, paid for by subscriptions and time-sharing usage fees. In their heyday, these forecasting firms—the big three in particular—were instrumental in helping major corporations with their planning and budgeting.

The next tier consists of private-sector forecasters who provide forecasts for free as a service to clients. This is a diverse lot, including most major financial institutions: banks, such as Bankers Trust and Chase Manhattan; major insurers, such as Prudential and Metropolitan; and Wall Street firms, such as Merrill Lynch and Prudential Securities.

Hundreds of corporations have their own chief economists and economics departments, who advise senior management on where the economy is headed and how it will affect their industries. Typically, chief economists make short-term forecasts every quarter that extend a few years into the future; some also prepare long-range forecasts each year for as many as ten years ahead. The chief economist's forecasts often become the firm's official forecast, which is then required to be used for business planning by divisional management. The mandating of the chief economists' forecasts gives them considerable power in the company, as Ken Militzer, chief economist for AT&T, observed: "The chief economist can influence the fortunes of his company far beyond what the typical size of his staff might suggest."[8]

There are thousands of economic forecasters who make a living selling economic newsletters, primarily to individual and institutional investors. While most provide their own forecasts, a few sell what is mistakenly called "consensus forecasts." The publishers of consensus forecasts obtain forecasts from individual economists and simply average the figures; "consensus" implies an interactive pooling of economic outlooks, which does not actually take place. The most popular consensus forecast is the *Blue Chip Consensus Forecast,* a monthly newsletter published by Robert Eggert; others are provided by the Conference Board, a business trade association dedicated to economic and managerial research; the Bureau of Economic Analysis, the division in the Commerce Department that maintains economic statistics; and the *Economist* magazine.

Finally, there are the media, which inundate us monthly, weekly, or daily with economic predictions, sometimes as front-page news, which may also make it onto television news programs. All major business magazines routinely publish their own economic forecasts.

There is considerable debate about the effectiveness of man versus machine in making economic predictions. Some economists rely on their own subjective judgment, while others employ a form of computer model. The larger economic forecasting firms, like the big three, have created—and rely on—intricate computer models with thousands of equations. The economic model builder starts with theories concerning the relationships among economic variables—for example, how interest rates affect corporate investment. The economist then attempts to validate his or her theories statistically and derive parameters for the equations that are programmed into the computer model. Once the model is completed, the economist tests its forecasting ability by running it with historical data from the preceding decade or two and comparing the forecasts it produces for that period against the actual trends and events the model was supposed to predict. After tweaking and tempering the model equations to produce a more accurate forecast, the economist reruns the program with the same historical data and repeats the process until the model's forecasts more closely replicate the events of the historical period. The economist is now ready to use the model to predict the future. However, unlike meteorology, where computer models are on the verge of winning the man-versus-machine contest, economic models are prone to produce obviously erroneous predictions requiring considerable human intervention to fix.

Whether using computer models or subjective judgment, economic forecasters are heavily influenced by their particular economic "religion": their set of assumptions and beliefs about how the economy works. And the differences in beliefs held by economists are enormous—so much so that their various camps have names. The Keynesians believe that the economy is driven by the amount of government spending, whereas the monetarists see the supply of money as the key driver of the economy. Neoclassicists believe in laissez-faire commerce and a minimal role for government, while Marxist economists believe in controlled economies and are concerned about class struggles. These beliefs are so varied and conflicting that economics is jokingly said to be the only field in which two people can get a Nobel Prize for saying exactly the opposite thing. And there is truth to the joke: James Tobin, who won a Nobel Prize in 1981, believes that international capital flows are too volatile and should be restricted, while Robert Lucas, who won the Nobel Prize in 1995, believes that markets should be free from government intervention. Derived from these differences is the First Law of Economics: For every economist, there is an equal and opposite economist.

But despite the ideas they hold sacred, most U.S. economists share a belief in a common god called the Theory of General Equilibrium, which asserts that the national economy is inherently stable, that all economic fluctuations are caused by external shocks (such as oil embargoes), and that the economy has natural forces that dampen these shocks and restore it to its natural resting point, or equilibrium. A corollary to the Theory of General Equilibrium is that the economy is predictable: If the economy is stable and seeks a point of equilibrium, economists must surely be able to predict its future course. Is this sound logic or just wishful thinking? Economists' forecasting track record provides the answer.

MISLEADING INDICATORS

So how good are these economic forecasters? To find a detailed answer to this question, I reviewed the leading research on forecasting accuracy contained in twelve studies published during the sixteen-year period from 1979 to 1995 and covering forecasts made during the 1970 to 1995 period.[9] Looking beyond the cognitive dissonance and wishful thinking and adjusting for all the variables in the research, the following picture emerged regarding economists' ability to predict the future:

Economists cannot predict the turning points in the economy. That economists cannot predict the precipitous changes in the economy is obvious from their forecasting track record during the 1970–1980 period when economic growth and inflation were highly volatile. Victor

Zarnowitz, a professor at the University of Chicago and one of the leading trackers of economic forecasting accuracy, analyzed the error rates
for six prominent economic forecasters—the big three plus GE, the Bureau of Economic Analysis, and the National Bureau of Economic Research—in predicting real gross national product (GNP) growth and
inflation for eight quarters into the future during four periods of significant economic change that occurred between 1970 and 1974: the mild
recession in 1970 and the recovery in 1972, the sharp increase in inflation and the oil embargo in 1973, the deep recession in 1974, and the
rapid upturn in the economy in 1975. He found that of the forty-eight
predictions made by the economists, forty-six missed the turning points
in the economy.[10] The single worst set of predictions during that period
were those for 1974, when, as Zarnowitz noted, "forecasters across the
field missed the onset of a serious recession."[11] Six years later the big
three economic forecasting firms failed to predict the severity of the
1980 recession, the worst since the Great Depression, and missed the
drop in real GNP for the second quarter of 1980 by 270 percent.

How well do the economists who directly or indirectly run the U.S.
economy predict its turning points? Worse than chance. Based on the
forecasting track record of the Federal Reserve banks between 1980 and
1995 published by another leading observer of economic forecasts,
Stephen McNees, vice president and economist at the Federal Reserve
Bank in Boston, the Federal Reserve was three for six in calling the
turning points in real GNP growth (the same as chance) and zero for
two in calling turning points in inflation, for a combined score of 38 percent.[12] According to my own analysis, between 1976 and 1995, the CEA
was five for eleven and the CBO seven for eleven in calling real GNP
growth (see Figure 3.1); and both the CEA and CBO were zero for
three in calling inflation. The CEA's combined turning point score was
36 percent; the CBO's was 50 percent.

Economists' inability to foresee turning points in the economy is
most damning and raises serious questions about the value of economic
forecasting. Who cares if inflation forecasts for next year are off by a percentage point? What decision makers in business and government need
most from forecasters is advanced warning of major economic change,
which they cannot provide. The *Economist* observed in 1991 that "the
failure of virtually every forecaster to predict the recent recessions in

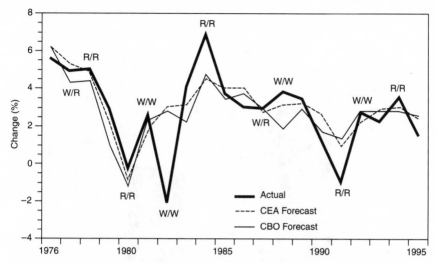

Figure 3.1 CEA and CBO forecasts are hardly better than chance in calling the turning points in the economy, as shown by the comparisons of percentage growth in real domestic product. W = wrong and R = right, with the CEA score given first, followed by the CBO score.

America has generated yet more skepticism about the value of economic forecasts."[13]

Economic forecast accuracy drops with lead time. The accuracy of economic forecasts diminishes in months into the future. Victor Zarnowitz has noted that "the predictive value of detailed forecasts reaching out further than a few quarters ahead must be rather heavily discounted."[14] As shown in Figure 3.2, the average forecast errors percentages for real GNP growth are 45 percent at the beginning of the year being forecasted and 60 percent six months in advance of the year being forecasted; the average percent forecast errors percentages for inflation are 30 percent at the beginning of the year being forecasted and 40 percent six months in advance of the year being forecasted. These averages were derived from the most statistically significant database on forecasting errors, compiled in 1989 by Steve Swidler, a professor at the University of Texas, and David Ketcher, then a graduate student at the University of Missouri. Their large sample included 5,000 forecasts made between 1976 and 1988 by fifty leading economic forecasters.[15]

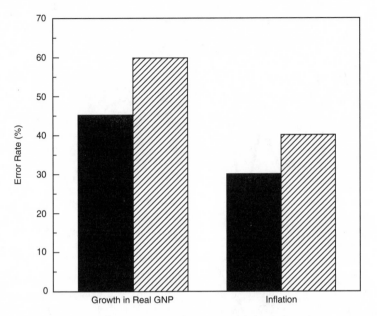

Figure 3.2   Economic forecast errors increase with lead time (percentage error rates). The solid bars represent forecasts made at the beginning of the year, and the open bars represent those made six months ahead.

Economists' forecasting skill on average is about as good as guessing. It turns out that most economic forecasts are about as accurate as guessing that next year will be the same as this year—an example of a naive forecast, which economists use to gauge the skill of their own forecasts. In fact, the naive forecast of assuming no change is theoretically the most accurate means of forecasting the statistical change of events that vary randomly period to period. In other words, if you have no clue as to whether the statistic for a series of events will increase or decrease in the next period, your best prediction is to assume no change; if you forecast either an increase or a decrease in the statistic, you stand a good chance of getting even just the *direction* of the change wrong and thereby creating huge errors.[16] I found that one could reasonably make the following conclusions about economists' ability to beat the naive forecast:

• The naive forecast is a better predictor than economists for highly volatile economic statistics, such as interest rates.

- Economists can predict with greater accuracy than the naive forecast for some highly stable economic statistics, such as government spending.
- Economists are about as accurate as the naive forecast for a middle ground of important statistics, such as real GNP growth and inflation.

There are no economic forecasters who consistently lead the pack in forecasting accuracy. The leaders in one quarter are as likely to be the losers in the next. In his research, Zarnowitz found that none of the "forecasters were consistently and generally superior to others . . . [and] the rankings of forecasters vary depending on the variables, periods, and spans covered as well as on the criteria and measurements applied."[17] Stephen McNees similarly noted, "For most variables, the most accurate forecaster varies depending on the horizon of the forecast."[18]

There are no economic ideologies whose adherents produce consistently superior economic forecasts. Such are the conclusions of Roy A. Batchelor and Pami Dua, professors at City University in London and the University of Connecticut, respectively. They analyzed whether any of the six most popular economic ideologies proved to be more accurate in forecasting economic growth, inflation, and interest rates than any others. In analyzing the track records of thirty-two forecasters, they found almost no differences in forecast accuracy among the different economic schools of thought and declared that "in no case have we found significant differences in the accuracy rankings from Keynesian (the predominant belief) and non-Keynesian ideologies."[19]

No economic forecaster has demonstrated a consistently higher forecasting skill in predicting any particular economic statistic. There are no "inflation specialists," for example. The most accurate forecasters for a particular statistic during one quarter fail to match that achievement during subsequent quarters. This random pattern of accomplishment was clearly evident in comparing the track records for the same group of forecasters included in Stephen McNees's 1983 and 1992 studies.[20]

Increased sophistication provides no improvement in economic forecast accuracy. Forecasters using computer models do no better than those

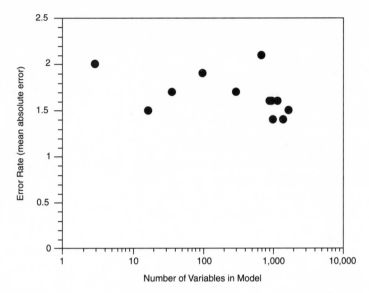

Figure 3.3   Increased sophistication does not improve forecasting accuracy (as measured by size of forecasting models). (*Source of data:* Stephen K. McNees and John Ries, "How Large Are Economic Forecast Errors?" *New England Economic Review* [July–August 1992].)

relying on only their subjective judgment, and those using large models with over a thousand equations do no better than those using simpler models with only a few, as shown in Figure 3.3.[21] In fact, the Benchmark, a forecasting service created more than twenty years ago, uses a model with only three equations and is every bit as accurate as more sophisticated forecasters with thousand-equation models. The Benchmark forecast is, in fact, a fancy version of the naive forecast. Whereas the naive model presumes that next year will be just like this year, the Benchmark model presumes that next year will be some combination of this year and several prior years.[22]

Apparently educational and professional sophistication have little to do with economic forecasting prowess. In 1995, the *Economist* published the results of a contest it held in 1985 to see who among a variety of professionals could most accurately predict the condition of the British economy ten years into the future. The sanitation workers in the study tied for first place with a panel of four chairmen of multinational firms. In presenting the study results, the *Economist* commented, "The contents of dustbins [British term for "garbage cans"] could well be a useful leading economic indicator."[23]

Forecasts may be affected by psychological bias. Some economic forecasters are extremists who consistently produce overly optimistic or pessimistic predictions, despite ample evidence that their extreme views have often been wrong. Roy Batchelor and Pami Dua found that "the same forecasters are at the top and bottom of the forecast ranking at all forecast horizons. . . . The persistence of optimistic or pessimistic forecasts cannot have been accidental."[24] Batchelor and Dua see extremist behavior as a marketing ploy—a way to target a group of forecast consumers who fit a certain psychographic mind-set: "Economic forecasters have therefore differentiated their products by adopting what we labeled an 'extremist' strategy." They found, however, that extremists do no better or worse than their more moderate counterparts.

From my involvement in the forecasting industry, I believe forecasters consistently put forth extremist forecasts because *they themselves* are extremists; their forecasts merely reflect their own psychological outlook on life. No amount of reality checking will moderate their mind-sets. In a perverse way, extremists fill a market need by reinforcing certain customers' own extreme views of the future.

Consensus forecasts offer little improvement. Averaging faulty forecasts does not yield a highly accurate prediction. Consensus forecasts are theoretically slightly more accurate than the predictions of individual forecasters by only a few percentage points, due to the averaging effect that evens out the egregious errors that individual forecasters periodically make.[25] But consensus forecasts are no more likely to predict key turning points in the economy than the individual forecasts on which they are based, and the few extra points of accuracy gained by averaging do not necessarily make them superior to the naive forecast.

There is no evidence that economic forecasting skill has improved over the past three decades. In fact, one could as easily conclude from the record that forecasting skill has decreased over time. Although some economists have proclaimed significant improvement in forecast skill, their data do not support their conclusions. Assertions of improvement are often based on faulty analysis, such as the use of small samples. Some studies based their findings on the results of a single forecaster. The biggest flaw was the comparison of forecasting errors over a period of time when the economy was becoming less volatile and thus more predictable, giving a false sense of improvement. A comparison of economists' forecasting errors with errors resulting from naive forecasts shows no gain in forecasting skill by the economists.

Two prominent international organizations that have made insupportable claims of improving their forecasting skill are the Organization for European Cooperation and Development (OECD) and the International Monetary Fund (IMF). In 1992 the OECD declared that "the accuracy of the *Economic Outlook* projections has improved over time."[26] And in 1993 the IMF stated that "the accuracy of the *World Economic Outlook* projections for output growth and inflation improved after 1985."[27] Indeed, the two organizations' forecasts have become more accurate, but they demonstrate no gains in forecasting skill. I found that although the two organizations' error rates declined over the past decade, so did the error rates of the naive model. In fact, the error rates of the naive model over this same period declined at a greater rate than the two economic forecasters, suggesting that the organizations' forecasting skill has declined, not improved.

Commenting on the lack of progress in forecast accuracy, Paul Samuelson (a Nobel laureate, MIT professor, and father of Economics 101) observed, "I don't believe we're converging on ever-improving forecast accuracy. It's almost as if there's a Heisenberg . . . [Uncertainty] Principle."[28] That economists are unable to predict the turning points in the economy suggests that the practice of economic forecasting is a game of chance, not skill, with no one consistently beating the odds and excelling at making economic predictions. After many years as a prominent economic forecaster, Michael Evans, founder of Chase Economics, confessed, "The problem with macro [economic] forecasting is that no one can do it."[29]

FROM CHAOS TO COMPLEXITY

Is the economy unforecastable because it is a chaotic system, like the weather? No, but after James Gleick popularized the concept of chaos in his 1987 book, *Chaos: Making a New Science,* there were in fact many attempts to apply chaos theory to economics and other social sciences. As it turns out, chaos theory applies to only a very limited class of physical systems, such as the weather and fluid turbulence. The economy, like other social systems, is unpredictable, because it is a "complex system," a term popularized by the Sante Fe Institute, a think tank established in 1984 to explore the science of complexity. Steven Durlauf, a professor at the University of Wisconsin and current director of the institute's economics program, found that "chaos proved to be a flop in economics. It provided no deep insights, while complexity has been much more compelling."[30]

Chaos and complexity are distinctly different concepts. Chaos refers to turbulent behavior in a system where the behavior is totally *determined* by nonlinear laws, which amplify the smallest of errors in the initial conditions of the system, making the system unpredictable beyond the shortest of periods. Complexity refers to the phenomenon of order emerging from the complex interactions among the components of a system *influenced* by one or more simple guiding principles. Structures such as the economy emerge out of what would otherwise be anarchy by a process called "self-organization." Complex systems organize themselves without some form of internal control. For example, Charles Darwin discovered that the earth's ecosystem developed out of the complex interaction of life forms over several billion years guided by the principle of "natural selection" (survival of the fittest).

The discovery of self-organization could well be attributed to eighteenth-century British economist Adam Smith. Smith was puzzled about what held economies together, given that individuals and businesses pursued their own agendas. Why did anarchy not prevail instead? In his seminal 1776 book, *The Wealth of Nations,* Smith concluded that the simple principle of "self-interest" was sufficient to create a "self-regulating" economy that would operate as if guided by an "invisible hand." Smith observed, "It is not from the benevolence of the butcher, the brewer, or the baker that we expect our dinner, but from their regard to their self-interest."[31] Smith's model is intuitively logical. Self-interest brings the supply of goods and services in balance with demand, because when the shortage of a good arises, prices and profits increase, and suppliers pursuing their self-interest in higher profits would produce more of the good to fill the shortage. If some suppliers tried to earn higher profits by overpricing their goods, other suppliers pursuing their own self-interest would seek to steal away the price gouger's customers by charging a fair price, which would eventually curtail the price gouging. If there was a shortage of products in a particular craft, wages in that craft would rise, and self-interest would encourage new trainees to become skilled in the higher-wage craft, thereby fulfilling the market need. Smith reasoned that this "complex stew" of interactions among individuals and businesses pursuing their self-interest would create a functioning economy all by itself, with no one in charge.

There are a number of characteristics of complex systems like the economy that make them unpredictable:

1. Complex systems have no natural laws governing their behavior at either their microlevel (individual humans) or their macrolevel (the economy); thus, complex systems cannot be scientifically predicted. Alfred Marshal, an English economist and John Maynard Keynes's teacher, noted in his 1890 book, *Principles of Economics,* that economic phenomena "do not lend themselves easily to mathematical expression," advice that has largely been ignored since World War II.[32]

2. Complex systems cannot be dissected into their component parts, because the systems themselves arise from the numerous interactions among the parts. Charles Morris in the *Atlantic Monthly* aptly noted that the U.S. economy is "just a metaphor for the enormously complex stew of daily personal and commercial transactions among some 250 million Americans."[33]

3. Complex systems are so highly interconnected with numerous positive and negative feedback loops that they often have counterintuitive cause-and-effect results, as when the addition of a new highway to alleviate a traffic jam causes the traffic jam to become worse or in the situation described by the following headline that appeared on the front page of the the *Boston Globe* in 1996: "Jobless Rate Up; Stocks Skyrocket."[34]

4. Complex systems exhibit periods of order and predictability, punctuated by unexpected moments of self-generated turmoil, which is why economists cannot predict the turning points in the economy.

5. Complex systems adapt to their environments and evolve, exhibiting new behaviors that can invalidate previously established theories.
6. Complex systems have no fixed cycles; their histories do not repeat themselves.

A classic example of the invalidation of a previously established theory is the Phillips Curve, which was introduced by New Zealand economist William Phillips in 1958 and is still contained in most basic economics texts. The theory behind the Phillips Curve is that there is a fundamental trade-off between unemployment and inflation; you could reduce unemployment only at the expense of increased inflation, and vice versa. As shown in Figure 3.4, the economy during the 1960s seemed to function according to the Phillips Curve, but thereafter any evidence of the Phillips Curve vanished.

The notion that the economy has regular business cycles is a myth; there is no statistical evidence to support their existence. Although the

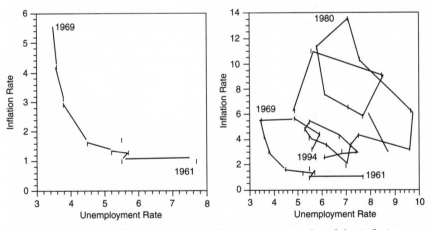

Figure 3.4   The Phillips Curve as an illusion, using graphs of the inflation rate (vertical axis, as indicated by the consumer price index) versus the rate of unemployment (the horizontal axis). The graph on the left shows that the economy seemed to follow the Phillips Curve during the 1960s. After 1969, the graph on the right shows that the Phillips Curve seems to have vanished. (*Source of data: Economic Report of the President, February 1995.*)

Date of Turning Point	Direction of Turning Point	Number of Months Between Turning Points
December 1969	Peak	—
November 1970	Trough	11
November 1973	Peak	36
March 1975	Trough	16
January 1980	Peak	58
July 1980	Trough	6
July 1981	Peak	12
November 1982	Trough	16
July 1990	Peak	91
March 1991	Trough	8

Figure 3.5   The time between officially declared turning points in the U.S. economy demonstrates the absence of business cycles that occur with any regular frequency. (*Source of data:* National Bureau of Economic Research's official designated turning points in the U.S. economy.)

economy surely fluctuates between good times and bad, it does so irregularly with no prescribed frequency of repetition, as shown in Figure 3.5. Indeed, why should the economy, a complex system that exhibits somewhat erratic behavior, have fixed periodic cycles imbedded in it? The fluctuations in the economy create the illusion of periodic cycles, helped along by the Rorschach factor.

One of the most curious examples of business cycle folklore is the Kondratieff Wave, named after Soviet economist Nikolai Kondratieff, who published a series of reports in the 1920s propounding his theory that capitalist economies experience long-term cycles of boom and bust every fifty-four years. To declare that capitalist economies go bust was wholly consistent with Marx's theory; to declare that they would also recover from downturns was sufficiently heretical to earn him a one-way ticket to a gulag in Siberia, where he eventually died. There is no statistical evidence that the Kondratieff Wave—or any other economic wave—exists. Joseph Martino, a senior research scientist at the University of Dayton, has surveyed existing statistical studies on the Kondratieff Wave and concluded that "the search for repeatable cycles in the data has been disappointing." [35]

THE ECONOMY AS A COMPLEX NONLINEAR ADAPTIVE SYSTEM

Making the economy even more unstable and unpredictable is the Sante Fe Institute's more precise classification of the economy as a "complex nonlinear adaptive system." Although this may seem like overly technical jargon, the underlying ideas are simple and logical. The nonlinear forces in the economy result from positive feedback loops that tend to amplify economic events. For example, the notion that success breeds success involves a positive feedback loop: a modicum of initial success breeds confidence and credibility, enabling one to achieve ever greater things. Another notion with implied positive feedback is that the rich get richer.

The existence of these nonlinear relationships does not conform to the general principles of the Theory of General Equilibrium, central to which are negative feedback loops that dampen shocks and restore economic stability. A simple example of this dampening effect is foreign trade. If country A sells more goods to country B than it imports from country B, then the currency rate for country A will rise against country B's currency, causing country A's goods to become more expensive and less attractive to country B, thereby pushing the trading situation toward a more stable outcome. (This is what took place between the United States and Japan in the mid-1990s.)

Yet examples of positive feedback loops are clearly evident in the U.S. economy, such as:

- *Economies of scale.* Higher-production volume reduces production costs, which lead to lower product costs, which lead to lower prices and increased sales, which lead to higher production.
- *Learning curves.* The greater the cumulative experience in performing a particular task, the lower the cost to perform the task becomes, thereby creating opportunity to lower prices and thereby increasing sales, profits, and cumulative experience (e.g., semiconductor manufacturing).
- *Brand equity.* A product with the highest cumulative amount of adertising becomes so well known to consumers that the product

continues to sell itself until it becomes a dominant brand (e.g., Coca-Cola).

- *Technological lock-in*. A technology that gains a modest advantage in market share may evolve to become the accepted standard, thereby locking out competing technologies (e.g., Microsoft).

The economy is driven by both negative and positive feedback loops in a tug of war in which the former drives the economy toward stability while the latter introduces erratic and unpredictable behavior. Contrary to traditional economic thought, external shocks are not the major cause of the economy's erratic behavior; it happens all by itself, for the economy is sufficiently unstable to create its own turmoil. The 1987 stock market crash is a good example. It was not caused by any external shock or calamitous sequence of events; it just happened due to the complex nature of the system and the interplay of events that are beyond our current comprehension. The crash came unannounced, and the market soon rebounded, reaching record heights.

Adding to the economy's unpredictability is its adaptive nature, which means simply that the players in the economy learn from experience how to play the game more effectively and to adapt to new economic climates. Brian Arthur, a research fellow at the Sante Fe Institute and a former professor at Stanford University, explained the adaptive nature of the economy as follows: "Our particles in economics are smart, whereas yours in physics are dumb. . . . Our particles have to think ahead and try to figure out how other particles might react if they were to undertake certain actions."[36] Ralph Stacey, a professor at the Hertford Business School in England and the author of two books on chaos and complexity, similarly noted, "Complex organic systems such as species or ecologies or societies [or economies] are adaptive rather than deterministic in that the rules change in the light of the consequences of the behavior they produce."[37] This means that the rules of the economic game are changing and evolving and that even if we could come up with the perfect model of the economy, our model would quickly become outmoded.

All of this makes the Theory of General Equilibrium a moving target, if it exists at all, according to John Holland, another research fellow from the Sante Fe Institute: "New opportunities are always being created by the [economic] system. And that, in turn, means that it's essentially meaningless to talk about a complex adaptive system being in equilibrium: the system can never get there. It is always unfolding, always in transition."[38]

ECON 101

Complexity theory is sufficient to explain the unpredictability of the economy and the poor track records of economic forecasters. However, what goes to the heart of economics as a scientific discipline are the data. Economic data are scant and erroneous, or "crude approximations compounded from a slag heap of samples, surveys, estimates, interpolations, seasonal adjustments, and plain guesses," according to Robert Kuttner in the *Atlantic Monthly*. [39] For example, the Federal Reserve publishes figures for industrial production based on industrial use of electricity, which ignores consideration of how and how efficiently the electricity was used. Data compiled through government surveys also are questionable. Besides the inherent messiness of survey data, respondents often provide false information, fearing—perhaps with good reason— that their answers may cause them harm. Government agencies continually revise historical statistics years into the future, trying to get them right. The inaccuracy of international economic statistics in particular is clearly evident. For example, in 1995, according to the IMF's 1996 *Direction of Trade Statistics Yearbook*, Hong Kong exported $37.8 billion worth of goods and services to the United States, while the United States imported $10.7 billion of goods and services from Hong Kong (a 253 percent discrepancy); U.S. exports to France were $14.2 billion, while France's imports from the United States were $21.3 billion (a 50 percent discrepancy); Hong Kong's exports to France were $2.7 billion, while France's imports from Hong Kong were only $600 million (a 350 percent discrepancy); and Argentina's imports from Hong Kong were $211 million, while Hong Kong's exports to Argentina were $361 million (a 71 percent discrepancy).

The unemployment rate is a classic example of a questionable economic statistic. The federal government calculates the statistic by polling a sample of households, asking how many people in the home are seeking employment. Although some respondents are evasive about answering this question, afraid that their response might end up in a permanent file on them in a government agency's database, more fundamentally, the survey does not take into account the fact that people give up looking for work after months of doing so with no success. Thus, a household full of people who quit looking for a job will be interpreted in the government's employment statistics as fully employed. For example, the true unemployment rate for 1994 was not the reported 5.9 percent but rather estimated to be about 7 percent, because 1.1 million people of working age quit looking for a job.

Forecasting real GNP growth, which the government continually updates with flash reports, monthly revisions, and restatements coming three to five years after the initial report, is certainly, and obviously, impossible to do with any degree of accuracy. Victor Zarnowitz found that one-third of the forecast error for real GNP is due to faulty historical data.[40] If the underlying data are so poor, how sound can economic theory be? How sound can forecasting models be when their underlying theory, equations, and initial conditions are all derived from erroneous data?

Apparently most academic economists have coped with the problem of erroneous information by abstaining from data altogether. Wassily Leontif, a Harvard economics professor and Nobel laureate, has harshly criticized his profession for creating theory in the absence of supporting factual data. He conducted a study of articles published in the *American Economic Review* from 1977 to 1981 and discovered that the literature was "filled with mathematical formulas leading the reader from sets of more or less plausible but entirely arbitrary assumptions to precisely stated but irrelevant theoretical conclusions." [41] He found that 76 percent of the theoretical articles had no supporting data or used irrelevant data. Less than 1 percent of all the articles drew on original, primary research to support their findings. In an update of this study, Leontif found only one article that met his research standards; it was about the decision making of pigeons.

Economics aspires to be a science but eschews the rigor of the scientific method, whereby scientific theories are created by first making hypotheses based on observing nature and then testing the hypotheses with controlled experiments. In contrast, economists derive their theories in the privacy of their academic offices, deducing consistently logical but potentially irrelevant concepts. No doubt this ivory tower approach to theorizing is why economists mistakenly assume that consumers and business managements are uniformly rational in their motivations and behaviors. This runs counter to common intuition, as Robert Heilbroner has noted: "At the root of the [economic] matter lies man, but it is not man the 'economic' being, but man the psychological and social being, whom we understand only imperfectly."[42] Steven Durlauf believes that "the notion that economic agents (humans) are rational is an assumption we may want to get rid of."[43] Economists' remoteness from the real world has given rise to numerous jokes, such as the following: There were two economists walking down the street. One sees a dollar lying on the sidewalk and says so. "Obviously not," replies the other. "If there were, someone would have picked it up!"

Irrationality abounds. Consumers do not behave according to rational equations built on the assumption that money is the only driver of human behavior. Indeed, many other powerful human motives—including power, prestige, fame, influence, revenge, conformity, hope, love, and affiliation—play major roles in people's behavior as consumers. There is little that is rational about corporate behavior either, starting with the economic theory that the goal of senior management is to maximize shareholder wealth. Typically the only maximization happening in the ranks of senior management is that of personal wealth and preserving positions of power. In fact, there is so little rationality to corporate life and decision making that many readers of the comic strip "Dilbert" swear that its author, Scott Adams, must be one of their coworkers, working under cover.

Surprisingly, economists also eschew insights from other social sciences, such as psychology, sociology, and anthropology, which they regard as being either too soft or completely irrelevant, despite the fact that information from these fields could provide deeper insights into people's collective and individual behavior.

IT'S THE DATA, STUPID!

Economic prophecy plays a prominent, and sometimes injurious, role in our society. Perhaps the most harmful aspect of economic prediction is its undue influence in the election of those who run governments at all levels. Presidents, governors, and other elected officials often gain office predicting (or promising) that their new theory for managing the economy will bring greater prosperity to the electorate. This was surely the case when Bill Clinton deposed President George Bush in 1992 with the central campaign theme, "It's the economy, stupid."

The truth is that elected officials—the president included—cannot do much to change the course of the economy radically in the brief span of their term in office. They lack the authority to put effective measures into place quickly enough to address current economic problems, and it remains unclear how the complex system of the economy can be influenced; there are no quick-fix buttons to push to remedy our various economic ills. For these reasons, the *Atlantic Monthly* concluded that "the main criterion on which our presidential elections have come to be decided—managing the economy—is a sham."[44]

The poor quality of economic data exacerbates the problem. For example, two years after the 1992 U.S. presidential campaign, the government revised its figures for the GNP for the period from 1990 to 1993, increasing real GNP growth for that period by 25 percent and real disposable income by 70 percent—the largest revision to the GNP in the past several decades.[45] So, as Paul Magnusson in *Business Week* noted, "Just as Bill Clinton was hammering away at Bush's economic performance, growth was running at a blistering 5.7 percent."[46] There is no doubt that numerous political decisions are decided on false predictions and faulty data.

What is a voter to do? Ignore all economic promises and predictions; they are likely to prove false, if for no other reason than that elected officials do not have the power to influence the economy as quickly as they promise. I would also question any claims made using historical data, because politicians can manipulate the data—which are mostly erroneous anyway—to tell almost any story they want. Instead, I would carefully consider whether the candidates' proposed policies and positions would influence the economy in a positive direction over the long haul.

A second negative impact of economic forecasts is that they result in faulty decision making by policymakers, business executives, and we as individuals, based on erroneous information. The *Economist* was right to declare that economic forecasters "are worse than useless: they can do actual long-term damage to the economy."[47] Everyone in the government, from the president, members of Congress, and governors down to midlevel managers in the numerous federal, state, and local agencies, make thousands of misguided long-range policy decisions based on faulty forecasts all the time. It is small wonder that our nation seems to make little progress in achieving the economic goals that are continually set.

Business executives who make long-term commitments predicated on economic forecasts are in the same boat. If they could really know what the economic climate will be for the next several years, they could plan accordingly; for example, if a manufacturer was thinking of building a new plant and then got *accurate* information that a prolonged recession was imminent, he would postpone it. But such an accurate economic forecast is impossible, and making long-term commitments based on long-range forecasts is foolhardy. Because economic forecasts are reliable for only a few months into the future, they have almost no value in aiding managements in making decisions involving such commitments. The best we can do in making such important decisions is to assume that the future economy will be just like it is today (this naive forecast is at least as accurate as economic forecasts) and to be ready to adapt to any radical departure from today's economic conditions, if it occurs.

In fact, economic forecasts can interject more uncertainty and risk into a company's operations than the fickle competitive environment. For example, the automobile industry works on long production cycles where plant capacity takes a long time to adjust. If auto executives relied on economic forecasts to set their production plans, they would do so at great cost: building new capacity, paying for overtime, and increasing inventories in response to a rosy outlook, and shutting plants and cutting supplier relationships in response to a dismal one. Japanese auto manufacturers' strategy for dealing with the vagaries of the economy is to ignore economic forecasts. Stephen Sharf, a columnist specializing in the auto industry, noted that orders to parts suppliers from Japanese auto manufacturers tended to vary by only 2 percent from original forecasts, which he believes has contributed to their success in producing high-quality cars and high profit margins. In contrast, orders from U.S. auto manufacturers are "all over the map," because they listen to vacillating economic forecasts, and the "result of listening to these seers . . . is a chaotic condition that continues throughout the year."[48]

Nearly forty-five years ago, in 1954, Peter Drucker made a similar evaluation of economic forecasts in *The Practice of Management:* "The business cycle is too short a period for a good many business decisions—and for the most important ones. A plant expansion program in heavy industry, for instance, cannot be founded on a forecast for the next four or five or six years. It is a fifteen- or twenty-year program. And the same is true . . . of a decision to build a new store or to develop a new type of insurance policy."[49] Instead of relying on forecasts, Drucker suggests that management should stress-test their business plans to see if they remain viable under varying economic conditions.

What should the average consumer do, who mostly uses economic forecasts in making investment decisions? We are flooded daily with predictions published in business magazines, newsletters, and the general press and delivered by business commentators on radio and television. Watch out! Remember the First Law of Economics: For every economist, there is an equal and opposite economist—so for every bullish economist, there is a bearish one. The Second Law of Economics: They are both likely to be wrong.

The third negative impact of faulty forecasts is the needless anxiety caused by doomsday predictions. A large segment of the public is hooked on predictions of disaster, from earthquakes to economic collapse, and the publication of books that forecast economic doomsday is a microindustry unto itself. Go into any modest-size library and you will find shelf after shelf devoted to books with such sensational titles as *The Bankruptcy of America, The Coming Economic Earthquake, The Downfall of Capitalism, Econo-Quake, The Great Reckoning, Financial Armageddon,* and *The Economic Time Bomb.* Perhaps our attraction to predictions of economic doom is rooted in guilt. As William Rukeyser observed in *Fortune* magazine, "The perennial popularity of doomsday forecasters reflects a quasi-biblical view of economics: Can there be no sin without retribution?"[50]

Economic doom books are formulaic. The authors start by claiming that we are finally about to pay the high price for our many years of excess and living beyond our means. Then they present evidence of a long-term cycle of boom and bust by massaging the data—averaging, filling in holes, explaining exceptions, adjusting time periods—and show that we are right on schedule for our inevitable economic downfall. Finally, they cite numerous present-day parallels with the period leading up to the Great Depression of the 1930s. This is precisely Ravi Batra's formula for his book *The Great Depression of 1994*. His prophecy, like the others, did not come true, but the book was a best-seller.

Belief in periodic economic cycles is close to superstition, akin to astrology and numerology. In 1990, the research director at the National Taxpayers Union predicted that economic collapse would occur in the United States in the year 1992 because "92" is "29" backward and 1929 was the year of the stock market crash that led to the Great Depression in the United States.[51] The Kondratieff Wave, in particular, has been the source for a number of false prophecies such as those contained in Edward Cornish's 1980 book, *The Great Depression of the 1980s,* and Jay Forrester's 1979 book, *A Great Depression Ahead.* Forrester, a retired professor in systems dynamics at MIT, predicted in 1985 that the world was due for another 1929-style severe depression, based on his belief in the Kondratieff Wave: "Present worldwide economic crosscurrents suggest that we are entering another such downturn of the long wave."[52]

Although it must be admitted that excess debt and government spending at extreme levels impede the health of our economy, no one knows how, when, or even whether such excesses will come to haunt us in the future. Nevertheless, we should support political leaders brave enough to tackle these problems. Commentators who draw parallels between the 1990s and the period just before the Great Depression are greatly mistaken, given the current controls over interest rates and the money supply that were absent back then. Today, as MIT professor and Nobel laureate Robert Solow has noted, "We're not helpless, thanks to the arsenal of fiscal and monetary responses honed since the 1930s."[53]

SELF-INFLICTED WOUNDS

How to succeed as an economic forecaster: forecast often and don't keep records. Such was the jocular advice a colleague of mine gave to a group of executives in the mid-1970s when economic forecasting was hot. The audience laughed nervously. While they saw the perils in sticking their necks out with economic forecasts, they placed high value in the predictions made by the largest economic forecasting firms and paid huge fees for their subscriptions and consulting advice.

Ten years later, this joke would no longer have been funny. The heyday of economic forecasting peaked around the early 1980s and has declined ever since. Having tired of being fed erroneous forecasts, corporations cut their subscriptions to forecasting firms, and companies such as GE, Kodak, and IBM disbanded their in-house economics departments; few of the superstar companies of the 1990s, such as Intel and Microsoft, have ever seen the need for chief economists. Many of the smaller forecasting firms went out of business, and the once-elite forecasting firms shrank in size and prestige and, to survive, repositioned their services from selling predictions to providing economic advice.

Prediction is an albatross for the economic profession that continually undermines its credibility. As management sage Peter Drucker wisely declared, "The future is unpredictable. We can only discredit what we are doing by attempting [to predict] it."[54] At least one leading economist has agreed that there is a backlash from faulty forecasting. "One of the great mistakes of the past 30 years of economic policy has been an excessive belief in the ability to forecast," admitted Harvard economist Martin Feldstein, former chairman of the CEA.[55]

Yet economists are still hung up on linking their scientific prowess to the notion of economic determinism and their ability to forecast at a time when other sciences have long abandoned this notion and instead have embraced principles of uncertainty, chaos, and complexity. According to Brian Arthur of the Sante Fe Institute, "Economics in the twentieth century has lagged about a generation behind a certain loss of innocence in all the sciences."[56]

Therein lies a huge opportunity: to remake economics into a much more scientific field by casting off deterministic economic theories and perspectives and starting to study the economy as a complex system that is far more dynamic than the ideas about the economy contained in today's textbooks. In fact, Steven Durlauf believes that "complexity has given us new ways to think about the economy, providing explanations and insights into many phenomena."[57] Economists should look more to biological science than to physics for explanations of how the economy works, since the economy is made up of biological units. Economists should give up on the false assumptions that humans are homogeneous and rational and that economies are mechanical with repeating behavior, however inconvenient that might be to developing economic theories. Finally, for economics to become a true science, it must use the scientific method, which requires developing theories based on real-world observation and then testing them through ever more observation, as opposed to academic economists' current arcane practice of making up theories out of thin air.

This transformation will not be easy, nor is it sure to happen anytime soon, since establishment economists are not amused by the new perspectives of complexity. It is equally uncertain whether we will free ourselves from erroneous economic forecasts anytime soon. So long as we do not question the validity of forecasts and think for ourselves, we will be destined to be deluged by a constant rain of error from those dismal scientists ever eager to fulfill our need for prediction.

4

The Market Gurus

In no other area of prediction is the payoff in getting it right so high as the stock market. Not surprisingly, the quest to predict the stock market has persisted since its birth some four hundred years ago, and market prediction has grown into an ever more financially powerful and lucrative business. In the United States alone, it employs hundreds of thousands of people in the business of investing more than $7 trillion annually. For most people, however, the odds of getting it right are little better than chance.

The stock market is part of the economy and thus a complex system. It behaves as if it were some form of synthetic life with a brain composed of millions of minds. Brian Arthur, a research fellow at the Sante Fe Institute, has called the market "a form of artificial life all by itself."[1] Controlled by forces comparable to Adam Smith's invisible hand, it functions in a self-organizing fashion based on the simple concept of self-interest (some might use a stronger word, such as *avarice*). Speed, however, makes the stock market much more dynamic and complex than the economy. Millions of investors can respond almost immediately to perceived moneymaking opportunities by calling their brokers or using their computers to conduct online transactions. In fact, the stock market is so adaptive and nonlinear that its prices fluctuate randomly.

The idea that stock prices are random, first determined by French mathematician Louis Bachelier in 1900, was later dubbed the Random Walk Theory based on a 1905 article in *Nature* magazine on how to predict the location of a drunkard walking randomly through a field. In the

1960s, financial economists Arnold Moore and Eugene Fama statistically analyzed daily stock prices over the periods 1951–1958 and 1958–1962, respectively, and found that they had only a 3 percent correlation one day to the next, which means that only 3 percent of the total variation in daily stock prices is explained by historical patterns, and the rest is pure noise.[2] Essentially this means that past stock prices are useless in predicting the stock market.

Despite recent innovations in information technology and decades of academic research, successful stock market prediction has remained an elusive goal. In fact, the market is getting more complex and unpredictable as global trading brings in many new investors from numerous countries, computerized exchanges speed up transactions, and investors think up clever schemes to try to beat the market. Overall, we have not made progress in predicting the stock market, but this has not stopped the investment business from continuing the quest, and making $100 billion annually doing so.

THE PAGANS OF WALL STREET

To a sociologist from the distant future, the efforts of Wall Street brokers and analysts to predict the stock market at the end of the twentieth century might seem comparable to the behavior of an ancient tribe. Such an observer might describe their behavior as follows:

Wall Street was a tribe that inhabited the southern tip of a small island and wielded enormous influence throughout the globe. The tribe worshipped a superior life form called "The Market," and their lives were completely consumed by contemplation about The Market's moods, what it thought, and how it reacted to global events. They fretted over whether The Market was depressed, overexcited, acting irrational, or correcting its past mistakes. The tribe derived its power from its professed ability to answer a single question—"What's The Market going to do?"—posed constantly by people from all over the world, who paid the Wall Street tribe billions and billions of dollars to answer this question. One way or another, every member of the tribe was involved in predicting The Market.

Judging from paintings, sculpture, and names of Wall Street eating places, it seemed that the tribe also worshipped two important idols: the Bull and the Bear, symbolizing The Market's good and bad moods. The tribe formed two rival cults consisting of Bull and Bear worshipers. The Bulls believed that The Market would shower them with untold material wealth; the Bears believed The Market would steal back their material riches. From an ancient text by someone named Joseph de la Vega, it was clear that Bull and Bear worship was a centuries-old practice:

> The bulls are like the giraffe, which is scared by nothing or like the magician . . . who in his mirror made the ladies appear much more beautiful than they are in reality. They love everything; they praise everything; they exaggerate everything. The bears, on the contrary, are completely ruled by fear, trepidation and nervousness. Rabbits become elephants; brawls in a tavern become rebellions; faint shadows appear to them as signs of chaos.[3]

The Wall Street tribe had two more rival cults: the Fundamentalists and the Technicians. The Fundamentalists believed that The Market was rational and they could predict its behavior simply by using logic to deduce how The Market would respond to the various events on the planet. In contrast, the Technicians believed that The Market was neurotic and irrational and that they could predict what it would do by analyzing its recurring irrational behavior in the past. The Technicians' beliefs seemed to derive from the ancient practice of divination, through which primitive people used to predict the future by interpreting smoke patterns, bumps on heads, animal entrails, and the movement of the planets. In fact, the Technicians had their own zodiac consisting of The Market's patterns, which they believed provided clues to what it would do in the future.

Back to the present, the question, "What's the market going to do?" certainly seems to rank high in importance with questions regarding our daily lives—and the wealth and influence of Wall Street suggest that much of the world believes it can answer it. De la Vega, a seventeenth-century Dutchman who wrote the above-quoted description of the bulls and bears in his book *Confusión de Confusiones* (1688), further observed in the same book that "the [stock] exchange resembles the Egyptian temples where every species of animal was worshipped."[4] The stock exchange in downtown Manhattan, where twentieth-century stock traders have worshiped the bull, was built in 1903 in the style of a Roman temple.

Ever since Dow, Jones & Co. developed its first of several market indexes in July 1884, investors have eagerly analyzed them, searching for recurring patterns they could use to predict stock prices. In the search for such patterns, actual stock analyst technicians primarily use historical stock prices to predict the market, a practice called "technical analysis," without taking into consideration the state of the economy, new products, management changes, mergers, or acquisitions. William Eng, in his book *The Technical Analysis of Stocks, Options and Futures*, describes technical analysis as follows:

> All "price-sensitive" techniques use only one kind of data: the recent past history of prices. Users of these techniques manipulate this data in various ways to identify the current price trend and also to pinpoint when the trend might be about to end or when the trend may have been broken. . . . The market usually behaves in more or less the same way when it is going to do something.[5]

Technicians look for signs of "major tops" marking the end of a bull market and "market bottoms" marking the end of a bear market. They search for "confirming" signals to support their predictions. According to Eng, the trick to technical analysis is to "buy bear market reversals on confirmation, sell bull market reversals and hold or initiate positions on trend continuation signals."[6] In plain English, this means "buy low and sell high."

Technicians believe that stock price patterns reflect the irrational behavior and mass psychology of the market. They believe that the market is driven primarily by psychological momentum—that it gets on a roll, uphill or down, and is as hard to stop as a Mack truck. They speak of the market being overbought or oversold, running into congestion, and having breakouts.

Technicians employ different techniques to predict the market. Some prepare stock price charts and look for graphic patterns, such as those shown in Figure 4.1. They are similar to inkblots in a Rorschach test, only with prescribed interpretations. According to technicians, the head-and-shoulders pattern signals the advent of bull and bear markets, the diamond reveals that the market is about to lose its optimism and

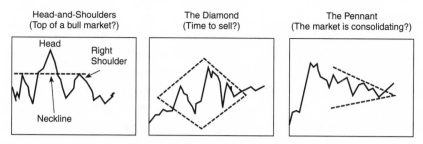

Figure 4.1 Examples of price patterns chartists use to predict the stock market.

become bearish, and the pennant indicates the market's ambivalence and unpredictability.

Burton Malkiel, a professor of economics at Princeton University and author of the popular book *A Random Walk Down Wall Street,* is a skeptic. "Under scientific scrutiny," he wrote, "chart-reading must share a pedestal with alchemy."[7] Malkiel conducted an experiment to support his point. He had his students construct stock price charts by flipping coins and showed one of the more interesting charts to a Wall Street technician he knew. The technician immediately responded, "What is this company? . . . We've got to buy immediately. This pattern's a classic. There's no question the stock will be up 15 points next week." The technician was not amused when told how the chart was made.[8]

Other technicians use more elaborate methods, such as the Dow Theory and the Elliot Wave Theory. Robert Rhea, cofounder of the *Wall Street Journal,* created the Dow Theory based on his belief that the market fluctuates between major bull and bear markets that last several years, which contain shorter cycles lasting weeks or months. Elliot, a little known depression-era accountant, devised the Elliot Wave Theory based on his belief that the market has predictable cycles containing exactly eight turning points. Of course, a random-number generator could just as easily generate the Dow Theory's bull and bear trends and the Elliot Wave Theory's cycles of turning points, especially if your interpretation of which blips on the chart are or are not turning points is sufficiently vague.

I was surprised to learn from Eng's book that technicians also use astrology to predict the market. He introduces his chapter on astrology by warning, "Readers may be surprised to read a book written in the 1980's which is going to seriously discuss the use of astronomical cycles for trading the markets." Indeed! He goes on to explain, "There are a number of individuals who make their living primarily by giving the market community astrological advice and that many successful traders who are the founders or main exponents of more 'scientifically' based methods have used astronomical cycles and astrology as well in their work."[9] In fact, the use of astrology may be quite prevalent on Wall Street. For an article in the *New York Times,* Douglas Martin interviewed a Wall Street astrologer who claimed to have 15,000 clients seeking astrological books, software, and consulting advice on how to play the stock market and who asserted that even the largest money management firms use astrology to predict the market. He added, "There are billions of dollars both influenced and managed by astrologers. If you knew some of the firms, you'd be shocked."[10]

Eng says that astrology is useful in predicting the market because heavenly events affect people's moods and psychology, which is what technicians believe the market is all about. Astrologers believe that planetary alignments and lunar cycles influence investor psychology. For example, full moons indicate high prices, and new moons suggest lower ones. Simple enough: buy stocks during new moons and sell them when the moon is full. Apparently astrologers construct birth charts for the stock market and individual corporations just as they do for people. Eng suggests, however, that birth charting is a bit complicated and advises the use of an "astrological market consultant."[11]

To get a feel for astrological market prediction, here is Eng's after-the-fact astrological explanation for the October 1987 stock market crash: "The planet of constriction and want, Saturn, is in the tenth house, the house of fame and reputation. For the whole month of October 1987, the planet of good fortune, Jupiter, is transiting the tenth house, first forward, then backward, finally continuing forward again in November." Eng decodes this astrological babble as follows: "There would be continual bouts of fame and fortunes being made for the New York Stock Exchange. . . . The groundwork was being laid for constriction and contraction. All that was needed was a trigger to set off the chain reaction of ultimate contraction."[12] So *that's* what happened.

Technical analysis is doomed to fail by the statistical fact that stock prices are nearly random; the market's patterns from the past provide no clue about its future. Not surprisingly, studies conducted by academicians at universities like MIT, Chicago, and Stanford dating as far back as the 1960s have found that the technical theories do not beat the market, especially after deducting transaction fees.

It is amazing that technical analysis still exists on Wall Street. One cynical view is that technicians generate higher commissions for brokers because they recommend frequent movement in and out of the market. On this point, Malkiel commented, "The technicians do not help produce yachts for the customers, but they do help generate the trading that provides yachts for the brokers."[13]

RANDOM HARVEST

The only form of stock market prediction that contains an element of science is fundamental analysis. The fundamentalist approach to predicting stock prices has three simple steps: (1) estimate the intrinsic value of the stock, (2) determine whether the market has over- or undervalued the stock, and (3) assume that the stock's price will eventually rise or fall as the market properly values it.

One cornerstone of fundamental analysis is the theory that the intrinsic value of a stock is simply the present value of the firm's future earnings discounted at an interest rate reflecting the riskiness of the stock. For example, Company X is expected to generate $2 in earnings per share for the foreseeable future and has an appropriate discount rate of 10 percent; its share price is theoretically worth $20 ($2 divided by 0.10)—no more, no less. This simple theory has only two variables: future earnings and a discount rate.

The most scientific aspect of fundamental analysis and stock market prediction is the theory that higher-risk investments generate higher returns. Economists say that this happens because investors are "risk averse" and thus demand higher rewards for bearing greater risks. This is quite evident from Figure 4.2, which shows that more volatile investments generate higher returns. For example, the stock market is a far superior investment vehicle than Treasury bills if you can hold your stock investments long enough to weather the ups and downs in the market.

In theory, then, the market applies a higher discount rate to corporate earnings for higher-risk stocks. If Company X's stock in our simple example were riskier, the market might demand a 15 percent

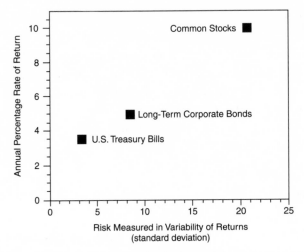

Figure 4.2   Long-term studies show that higher-risk investments generate higher returns.

discount rate rather than 10 percent. Thus far, financial prediction is on solid ground.

The barriers to predicting the stock market begin with the "future earnings" part of the equation, which, it turns out, is nearly as random as the stock market itself. In 1962, an interesting study of British corporations found that their growth in earnings per share was essentially random from period to period; further studies in the United States confirmed this surprising finding.[14] Corporate earnings growth in one period was only 6 percent correlated with growth in the prior period; 94 percent of the fluctuation in earnings growth was pure noise. This means that projecting future earnings' growth from historical earnings growth is a useless exercise.

Having advised many firms on how to improve their earnings, I found this notion of random earnings unsettling at first. After all, management works hard to improve and control reported earnings. On reflection, however, it seems logical that if share prices are random, then their key determinant—future earnings—should be random as well.

The findings that stock prices and corporate earnings growth are random are two strikes against predicting the stock market. Strike three is the Efficient Market Hypothesis (EMH), first proposed in the 1960s by financial economists such as Eugene Fama, who presented the idea in his seminal *Journal of Finance* article, "Efficient Capital Markets: A Review of the Theory and Empirical Work." The EMH states that the stock market knows everything that is knowable about future corporate earnings and thus prices all stocks at their true values. If true, this means that you cannot find over- or undervalued stocks, and you cannot beat the market or predict it in any way.[15] Suppose, for example, you believe that biotech stocks are the wave of the future. According to the EMH, the market already knows whether that is true and has priced current biotech shares accordingly. Suppose you like Coca-Cola because it has always increased its dividends. Well, that is already reflected in Coke's share price. Suppose you get a hot stock tip from your broker. Most likely, by the time you get the tip, the market has already responded to any relevant information—unless the tip is too hot, in which case you might end up in jail for insider trading.

It appears that the vast majority of economists believe in the Random Walk Theory, the EMH, and the notion that the stock market is unpredictable, and yet they believe that the economy is essentially stable and predictable (remember the General Equilibrium Theory), despite the obvious inherent contradiction.

The EMH seems logical when you consider the enormous amount of competition to make money in the stock market and the speed with which investors can respond to new information. In the United States alone, there are tens of millions of people trying to beat the market either by playing the market for themselves or managing other people's money. With global investing, the numbers multiply further. Equip all these tens of millions of professionals and amateurs with computer databases and models, investment research and advice, and immediate access to market trading and you get a massive scavenger hunt that should drive share prices toward their true value.

There are three versions of the EMH. The strong version says that the market is omniscient with respect to all known information, which means that there is no way to outsmart the market, since the market knows even the best-kept secrets. The semi-strong version says that the market knows all published information, such as annual reports, news stories, and analysts' reports. The weak version says that you cannot predict the market using historical share price data. At the very least, the weak version of EMH is true, since stock prices are at least random enough to make it impossible to predict stock price movement based on their historical patterns, thus dooming technical analysis as a forecasting tool. As would be expected, the stronger versions of the EMH have stirred much controversy since they were proposed because they imply that fundamental analysis is also doomed, that what the hundreds of thousands of investment professionals do for a living is useless, and that the $100 billion industry that manages several trillion dollars provides no value. The validity of these stronger versions of the EMH hinges on what the market is *really* capable of knowing.

WHAT DOES THE MARKET REALLY KNOW?

What the market can be reasonably expected to know is illustrated in Figure 4.3. With the thousands of analysts investing trillions of dollars, mostly in shares of large corporations, the market must surely know all publicly available information for major publicly held firms, including annual reports, 10ks, analyst reports, news coverage, and so on—all that is, but the best-kept secrets, if such things exist.

Every major corporation has scores of executives, thousands of em-

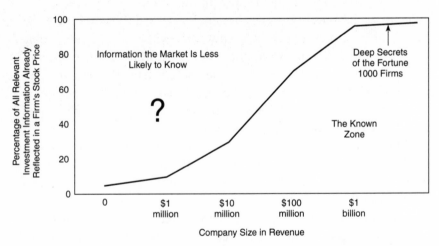

Figure 4.3   An illustrative model of what the market probably knows.

ployees, and hundreds of investment bankers, lawyers, accountants, consultants, and other advisers, all with access to proprietary information about the firm's financial condition. It would be naive to believe that these insiders resist the opportunity to make money on their privileged information, if by no other means than passing the information along. Gene Marcial, who writes *Business Week*'s "Inside Wall Street" column, believes that if you do not have access to insider information you are a "turkey, an outsider trying to play an insider's game."[16] In fact, courts often permit insiders to trade on some kinds of general knowledge about a firm, such as the existence of successful new products under development.

The market also learns much illegal insider information. What is clearly illegal is trading on "material information"—information so specific that it has a short-term effect on stock prices—for example, knowledge of mergers, tender offers, undisclosed earnings reports, and the like. Many of these deep secrets obviously get leaked. A 1994 *Business Week* study found that one-third of the merger and acquisition deals it examined were "preceded by stock-price runups or abnormal volume that couldn't be satisfactorily explained by publicly available information."[17]

In contrast, the market must know considerably less about the 10,000 publicly traded firms in the United States that fall below the Fortune 1000 rankings. There are just too many small, publicly traded firms for stock analysts and investment advisers to track, even using public information. Furthermore, most of the money going into the stock market is from pension funds, which invest strictly in the large blue chip firms listed in the Fortune 500, thus concentrating attention on those companies. In many respects, the market remains ignorant about small firms and for most lacks the all-important inside view of them.

The strong form of the EMH seems mostly valid for large, publicly traded companies, and therefore it would be very difficult for investors to outsmart the market in buying shares of these large organizations, unless illegal insider trading were involved. As firm size diminishes, however, the strong and semi-strong versions of the EMH become shaky, and opportunities should exist for the diligent investor to uncover market imperfections and capitalize on them. And so the true test of the validity of the EMH is the ability of the investment professionals to beat the market.

FIFTEEN MINUTES OF FAME

Mark Twain once warned that "October is one of the peculiarly dangerous months to speculate in stocks. The others are July, January, September, April, November, May, March, June, December, August, and February." Those failing to heed Twain's advice are variously called market timers, strategists, traders, asset allocators—and their clients.

Predicting the overall direction of the stock market is considered the gutsy part of the investment business. Those who do it believe that they are doing the important work and that picking individual stocks is for wimps. Some of these market seers acquire devout followings. A few become market gurus whose predictions convince enough people to invest in or pull out of various sectors and thus "move the market," creating a self-fulfilling prophecy.

One of the earliest market gurus was Roger Babson, who is credited with predicting the stock market crash of 1929. Throughout the 1920s, Babson was like Chicken Little, continually predicting a major downturn in the stock market. On September 3, 1929, the booming stock market of the 1920s reached a peak that would not be attained again for another twenty-five years. Months earlier, the economy had slowed (as measured by indexes of industrial and of factory production, etc.), and the market, after increasing steadily over the summer, began stagnating at the beginning of September. On September 5, Babson gave his usual doom-and-gloom speech at a luncheon of the Annual National Business Conference, declaring, "Sooner or later a crash is coming, and it may be terrific. . . . The vicious circle [of factory closings and layoffs] will get in full swing and the result will be a serious business depression."[18] Babson's comments were broadcast that day across the Dow Jones financial news tape used throughout Wall Street. That afternoon, the market dropped sharply, and it remained ragged in the days that followed. Although Wall Street denounced Babson's latest prediction, in October large numbers of investors began losing confidence, and the stock market went into a series of further declines that culminated in its collapse at the end of October. On September 3, the Dow Jones Industrial Average had reached a peak of 381; after several declines over the next few weeks, the collapse began on October 24, with panic selling and the Dow Jones falling to 299, followed four days later by the largest one-day drop in the Dow until that time, down 39 points to 260, and a further 30-point drop the next day. By the time the market reached its all-time lows in 1932, most blue chip stocks had lost 95 percent of their value.

Babson had predicted so many times that the stock market would fall that, sooner or later, the prediction was bound to come true, since every now and then the stock market does drop precipitously. Perhaps it would be more accurate to say that he fomented the crash rather than predicted it. His pessimistic speech was broadcast at a delicate time, when Wall Street had the jitters about the economy and the stock market had been driven up artificially with speculative shares bought with borrowed money—a house of cards that had to collapse eventually.

Given that there are thousands of stock market predictors, pure chance guarantees that at least one of them will make what seem to be remarkably accurate calls and attain guru status. Being a market guru, however, is a short-lived honor, because the likelihood of a repeat performance is remote. The odds of making a truly spectacular prediction in any year is one in a thousand, the odds of a repeat performance is one in a million, and the odds of getting it right three times in a row is one in a billion. The eventual fall of the market guru is inevitable.

Most Wall Street firms employ market predictors called "strategists," who either keep a low profile or lose their jobs, because their Wall Street employers have too much at stake to be embarrassed by a loose cannon. This is what happened to strategist Elaine Garzarelli, who became famous as the guru of Black Monday, October 16, 1987. On September 9 of that year, Garzarelli, then a research analyst and money manager at Shearson Lehman Bros., noted that her market-predicting model consisting of fourteen monthly indicators turned 75 percent bearish. When the Dow Jones Industrial Average reached 2641 on October 12, her model turned 92 percent bearish—the worst bearish signs she had seen since she created the model in 1980. That day on Cable News Network's *Money Line* program, she announced her prediction of "an imminent collapse in the stock market."[19] Amazingly, four days later the stock market did crash, with the Dow falling more than 500 points to 1739—a total drop of 902 points from where it was at the time of her prediction. *Business Week* declared it the "call of the century."[20] Unfortunately for Garzarelli and her clients, she remained bearish *after* the crash, and when the Dow closed at 1939 in December 1987, she declared that "the odds favored a drop in the Dow to as low as 1,000 to

1,500." After the market steadily increased over the next couple of months, she reversed her prediction on February 28, 1988, saying, "I'm a little late, but my indicators didn't confirm until recently."[21]

With her reputation guaranteed by her October 1987 prediction, Garzarelli's fame and fortune has grown ever since (at least until this writing). The mutual fund she managed, the Sector Analysis Fund, quickly acquired $700 million in assets after it was launched in the summer of 1987. She became one of the highest-paid strategists on Wall Street, with an annual salary estimated to be between $1.5 and $2 million. The *Institutional Investor* rated her, in many of its annual surveys, as the top quantitative research analyst. Her media presence continued to grow, including appearing in print and TV ads for No-Nonsense pantyhose in 1993. Garzarelli was especially popular with *USA Today*'s financial columnists Daniel Dorfman and Daniel Kadlec.

In February 1994, Kadlec wrote, "The 1990's belongs to Lehman Bros. strategist Elaine Garzarelli."[22] (Garzarelli stayed with Lehman Bros. when it split with Shearson in July 1993.) In July 1994, Dorfman called her "the USA's most famous stock market guru."[23] Her calls often moved the stock market, the true sign of a market guru. For example, in February 1994, she announced on CNBC that the market would drop 4 to 7 percent, and "within minutes" the Dow Jones Industrial Average lost 37 points.[24] Several months later, the Dow started its steady rise, reaching record heights in 1995.

In a surprise move in October 1994, however, Lehman Brothers terminated Garzarelli's position with the company. Her problems with Lehman Brothers, which had been building, culminated when her highly publicized predictions ran counter to those of Lehman's chief strategist, Katherine Hensel, generating widespread embarrassing publicity for the firm. For example, during the first week of September 1994, Garzareli declared that "the market is on an upward track again," while Hensel issued a bearish report noting, "We do not believe that investors have fully digested the impact of higher [interest] rates on [earnings] growth in 1995."[25] Although Lehman Bros. officially declared that Garzarelli was a victim of the firm's cost cutting as part of its downsizing effort, there was considerable speculation that she was just too hot to handle. (Hensel also lost her job later when she remained bearish during the 1995 bull market.)

In retrospect, Lehman Bros. did Garzarelli a huge favor by firing her, because her fame and fortune continued to grow as an independent market guru. Four months after leaving Lehman Bros., she founded Garzarelli Capital Management in Boca Raton, Florida, with the objectives of selling her investment research and managing money for pension funds. She started a financial newsletter, *Garzarelli Outlook,* with a subscription rate of $149 a year. By 1996, the newsletter had attracted 55,000 subscribers, generating an annual income of $8.2 million for her. The evidence is strong that she could still move the market as recently as July 23, 1996, when Bloomberg Business News announced her prediction that the market might drop 15 to 25 percent, and by the end of the afternoon, the Dow Jones Industrial Average closed down 44 points, a 0.7 percent drop.

When you look carefully at Garzarelli's track record, however, a very different picture emerges. I analyzed all of Garzarelli's verifiable stock market predictions that *Business Week,* the *New York Times,* and the *Wall Street Journal* published from 1987 to 1996. In total, these three sources mentioned thirteen calls where she clearly predicted that the stock market would go either up or down (I excluded her call on December 31, 1989, because she essentially said that the market would go either up or down). As shown in Figure 4.4, Garzarelli was right only five out of thirteen times, or 38 percent—a record that is worse than the 50 percent chance of flipping a coin. Figure 4.5 shows that except for October 1987, Garzarelli has failed to predict the major turning points in the market, which is what strategists are supposed to do. She also made two especially embarrassing consecutive calls during July 1996. On July 21, the *New York Times* published her prediction that the Dow "could go up from 5,529 to 6400," and just two days later she announced to her institutional clients that "the market could fall 15 to 25 percent," a crash-magnitude drop of nearly 1400 points.[26]

A further test of Garzarelli's investment acumen is her track record in running her mutual fund. As shown in Figure 4.6, she outperformed the stock market for only one year out of the six years the fund was in existence: in 1991 she beat the market by the slim margin of 31.5 to 30.5 percent. In particular, Garzarelli got off to a horrendous start in 1988, causing her fund to lose 13.1 percent when the market gained 16.6 percent. She had kept her fund out of the stock market in early 1988 because she believed that the market crash that occurred in October 1987 would continue into 1988, just as the 1930 after-shocks of the 1929

Date of Prediction	Dow at Time of Prediction	Prediction for Dow	Actual Dow for Time Predicted	Evaluation	Source of Prediction
January 9, 1987	2005	"Could go up another 15% to 20%"	1939 (December 31, 1987)	Wrong	WSJ, January 9, 1987, p. 23
October 12, 1987	2471	"An imminent collapse in the stock market"	1739 (October 19, 1987)	Right	WSJ, October 28,1987, p. 35
December, 1987	1939	"A drop in the Dow to as low as 1300 to 1500"	2169 (December 30,1988)	Wrong	NYT, February 28,1988, p. III, 10:02
July 13, 1989	2538	"Could hit 2900 before year end"	2753 (December 29,1989)	Wrong	WSJ, July 13,1989, p. C1
August 25, 1989	2732	"2850 to 3000 by year end"	2753 (December 29, 1989)	Wrong	WSJ, August 25,1989, p. C16
December 31, 1989	2753	"2400 to 3100 for the next six to twelve months"	2905 (July 31, 1990)	Doesn't count; could be right either way	WSJ, December 13, 1989, p. C1
March 12, 1992	3205	"20% gain over next six to twelve months"	3457 (March 31, 1993)	Wrong	WSJ, March 12, 1992, p. C1
July 23, 1992	3290	"Could go to 3800"	3765 (July 29, 1994)	Right	WSJ, July 23, 1992, p. C1
May 4, 1993	3446	"Could shoot up over next twelve to eighteen months"	3758 (May 30, 1994)	Right	WSJ, May 4, 1993, p. C1
July 12, 1993	3524	"4500 in 1994"	3978 (January 30, 1994; high for year)	Wrong	WSJ, July 12, 1993, p. C1
May 16, 1994	3671	"Could easily fall . . . seven to twelve percent"	4465 (May 31, 1995)	Wrong	WSJ, May 16, 1994, p. C1
February 24, 1995	4011	"4400 before there are any problems"	5486 (February 28, 1996)	Right	WSJ, February 24, 1995, p. B10
July 21, 1996	5426	"Could go to 6400"	6448 (December 31, 1996)	Right	NYT, July 21, 1996, p. III-3
July 23, 1996	5346	"Market could fall 15 to 25%"	6448 (December 31, 1996)	Wrong	BW, August 12, 1996, p. 75

Figure 4.4 Elaine Garzarelli's track record as reported in the media. "Dow" is the Dow Jones Industrial Index (figures are monthly closing prices); "WSJ" is the *Wall Street Journal*; "BW" is *Business Week*; and "NYT" is the *New York Times*.

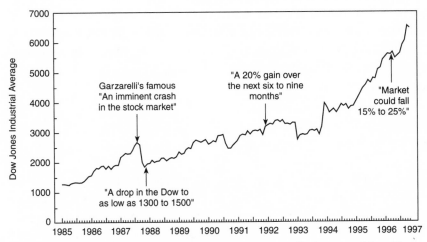

Figure 4.5 Select stock market calls by Elaine Garzarelli. (*Sources of data:* Figure 4.4 and *Business Week*, August 12, 1996, p. 75.)

crash brought the market to new lows. But 1988 proved to be no 1930; in fact, it was the start of the record bull market that has brought the stock market to all-time highs. With continued poor performance and dwindling assets, Lehman shut down Garzarelli's fund in August 1994.

It is surprising that Garzarelli has sustained her guru status with such a poor record in calling the market since the October 1987 crash. Her market-predicting model, as it turns out, is an unremarkable weighted

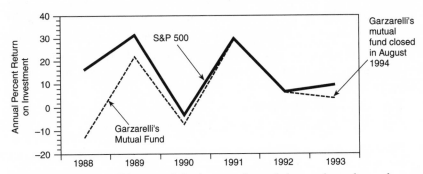

Figure 4.6 Garzarelli's mutual fund outperformed the stock market only once during its seven full years in operation. Note that Garzarelli''s mutual fund was last listed as the "Smith Barney Sector Analysis Fund." (*Source of data:* MorningStar, Inc.)

average of mundane financial statistics such as price-earnings ratios, T-bill rates, and money supply that could not even begin to capture all the dimensions of the market and its immense complexity. Without considering the facts and substance involved, the media has built up Garzarelli as a mythical guru.

FINANCIAL JUNK MAIL

Market gurus fare much better in the newsletter business. They serve a much less sophisticated audience, their track records are not as heavily scrutinized, and they can cover up their tracks with editorial comments. These free-range gurus enjoy few constraints and can—and do—say whatever they like in their newsletters, which often include social and political commentary and advice of all types. In some respects, financial newsletters are the modern-day equivalent of farmers' almanacs.

Joseph Granville, editor of the *Granville Market Letter,* a charismatic speaker with degrees from Duke and Columbia universities and author of eight books, sells his newsletter to about 3,000 subscribers annually. Granville developed a pseudoscientific market analysis tool that he calls "equity physics," which involves applying the concepts of gravity and inertia to the stock market, and he claims to have "proved" that stocks adhere to laws of "harmonic oscillation." He is noted as a user of charting and astrology to predict the market, and he has also issued earthquake predictions. Granville was the quintessential market guru in the 1970s and 1980s. He demonstrated his power in April 1980 when his recommendation to buy stocks sent the Dow Jones index up 30 points. And in January 1981, when he told his devotees to quit the market with the message "sell the market—sell everything," the Dow dropped 24 points the next day, causing a $40 billion loss in the market value of shares.

Granville is the Chuck Norris of Wall Street, as is evident from his description of his advice to clients:

> My entire theory of technical analysis forces you to follow the market and nothing else. Treat every [market] top like it is the final top. Sell everything and go short. Treat every bottom like it is the buying

opportunity of the century. I can offer little or no help for market long-termers because that is not the way the game is played. If you are going to follow me (or the market, we're interchangeable), you have got to adopt a degree of flexibility you never thought possible. Long-term investing is strictly for suckers."[27]

His track record reveals the real suckers. Although Granville had some success in the 1970s, he blew it in the early 1980s. When the Dow was in the 800s, he predicted that the market would crash and told his followers to sell everything they had and to short sell shares they did not have. Instead, the market rose to about 1200, while Granville continued to predict a market crash. According to the *Hurlbert Financial Digest*, which tracks financial newsletters, Granville's performance for the eight-year period ending January 1994 was 38 percent below the market average.

Granville has also revealed his egalitarian side. When asked the million-dollar question of why he shared his predictions with subscribers instead of making a killing himself, he replied that his mission in life was to enrich others, not himself: "Everyone I touch I make rich."[28] An alternative explanation is that his newsletter generates an annual profit of many hundreds of thousands of dollars for him with no market risk.

Robert Prechter, credited with predicting the 1980s bull market, succeeded Granville as the leading market guru. A former drummer in a rock band and a psychology major at Yale, Prechter became fascinated with the fifty-year-old Elliot Wave Theory when he was a junior analyst at Merrill Lynch and claims to have traced the theory's cycles back to 1789. In 1976, he started the *Elliot Wave Theorist* newsletter. Prechter lost his touch when, shocked by the depths of the 1987 crash, he declared that the bull market was finished and the Dow would plunge to 400 in the early 1990s. Instead, the Dow reached 3000, and in early 1994 it soared to 4000, making his prediction off by a factor of ten. Undaunted by his wrong call, Prechter predicted in 1992 that the Dow would plunge 90 to 98 percent by the year 2004. According to the *Hurlbert Financial Digest,* Prechter's performance for the ten-year period ending December 1996 was 64 percent below the market average.

AT NO TIME HAS MARKET TIMING WORKED

A mountain of evidence shows that the stock market is unpredictable. For example, it is quite clear that mutual fund managers cannot predict the stock market, as evident from the amount of cash they hold at any one time: they hold more cash when they believe that the market will decline and less cash when they feel more bullish about the future. A study of mutual fund cash holdings from 1970 to 1989 conducted by Goldman Sachs showed that mutual fund managers miscalled all nine major turning points in the stock market during the 1970s and 1980s.[29] I updated the Goldman Sachs study with an analysis of the period 1984 to 1995, as shown in Figure 4.7. From 1984 to 1986, mutual fund managers increased their cash positions, indicating that they anticipated a drop in the market; instead, the market steadily increased. The same thing happened in 1992, 1993, and 1994, with fund managers foreseeing market drops that never occurred. An examination of the three major changes in the stock market from 1984 to 1995 indicates that mu-

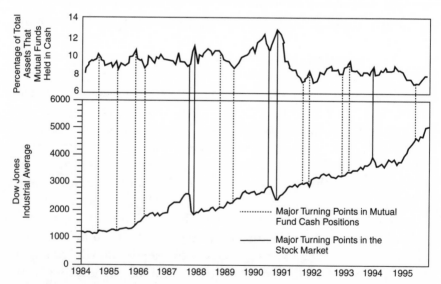

Figure 4.7   Mutual funds have been unable to predict turning points in the stock market. (*Sources of data:* Investment Company Institute and Standard & Poor's *Current Statistics.*)

tual fund cash positions are more a lagging than a leading indicator of the stock market—that fund managers reacted to market changes instead of responding to them. There are no signs that the mutual funds anticipated the October 1987 market crash, and when the market turned around in November 1987, the mutual funds were high in cash and still bearish. The market topped out again in July 1990, after mutual funds had been decreasing their cash for several months, and then declined again. The market drop bottomed in October 1990, when mutual fund cash was at record highs and stayed high well into 1991, a period during which the market steadily grew. Mutual funds made few changes in their cash positions in the months before the next market peak in December 1993. The next decline lasted six months, with the market drop bottoming out in June 1994, but mutual funds remained bearish and continued to increase their cash positions during the following months. As John Bogle, chairman of Vanguard, the second-largest mutual fund company in the United States, said to me, "There is no evidence in the record of mutual fund managers showing that they have improved their performance by anticipating market changes and changing their cash positions."[30]

A study by the *Hurlbert Financial Digest* in January 1994 showed that of the 108 market-timing newsletters it followed over the preceding five years, only one of them beat the market, which is astonishingly worse than expected by pure chance. Recent attempts to predict the market show similar ineptitude. A study by *USA Today* showed that all but a few Wall Street strategists completely missed the early 1994 market plunge, when the Dow declined from 4000 to 3600 between January and March. The newspaper commented, "Most professionals never saw what hit them." [31] By April 1994, the deep dip in the market made the vast majority of market gurus very bearish, as situational bias set in. Most market-timing newsletters predicted that the balance of 1994 would see further market declines. Both *Time* and *Newsweek* ran feature articles drawn from interviews with market gurus predicting a bear market. The market gurus failed to foresee the record 1995 bull market, which took the Dow above 5000.

Many leading financial economists and investment professionals have expressed their belief that the stock market is unpredictable. British economist John Maynard Keynes concluded fifty years ago that "we have not proved able to take much advantage of a general systematic movement out of and into ordinary shares as a whole at different phases of the trade cycle."[32] Vanguard's John Bogle told me that "the statistical evidence shows that there is about a one-in-ten chance of guessing when the market is at a high [or low] point; and that's being generous. To make money, you have to make two market calls: one to get near a low point and one to get out at near a high one, which means that your chance of success is about one hundred to one (one-tenth times one-tenth). And, doing it twice has a one-in-ten-thousand chance of succeeding."[33] Bogle summed up his position on market prediction as follows: "In the 30 years in this business, I do not know anybody who has done it successfully and consistently, nor anybody who knows anybody who has done it successfully and consistently. Indeed, my impression is that trying to do market timing is likely not only not to add value to your investment program, but to be counterproductive."[34] John McDonald, professor of finance at Stanford University, expressed a similar opinion when I asked him about market timing: "I don't believe it's worth much of your time. There's not much evidence that it can be done. If there's someone out there who can do it, I don't know about them."[35]

Peter Lynch, the leading money manager of recent times, has plainly stated, "I don't believe in predicting markets," and that market timers "can't predict markets with any useful consistency, any more than the gizzard squeezers could tell the Roman emperors when the Huns would attack." In commenting on the crash of 1987, he confessed, "I wasn't the only one who failed to issue a warning. In fact . . . I was very comfortably surrounded by a large and impressive mob of famous seers, prognosticators, and other experts who failed to see it, too." In fact, a chapter in his book, *One Up on Wall Street,* is entitled, "Is This a Good Market? Please Don't Ask."[36]

THE STOCK PICKERS

There are hundreds of thousands of investment advisers in the United States selecting stocks for their clients' portfolios. The elite stock pickers manage money for the top mutual funds and pension plans. Most of them attended top business schools, have large research staffs at their disposal, and are highly compensated. A very few, such as Peter Lynch, become legendary.

Apart from the few legends, however, the elite stock pickers do not beat the market, as clearly shown by studies dating back to the 1960s. A study by University of Rochester professor Michael Jensen showed that mutual funds over the period from 1945 to 1964 were "not able to predict security prices well enough to outperform a buy-the-market-and-hold policy."[37] A follow-up study by Richard Ippolito, covering mutual fund performance between 1965 and 1984, similarly showed that "returns in the mutual fund industry, net of fees and expenses, are comparable to returns available in index funds."[38] A recent study by Vanguard showed that from 1984 to 1994, the S&P market index outperformed mutual funds on average by 1.8 percent per year.[39]

Managers of pension fund money similarly fail to beat the market. An authoritative 1988 study by Stephen Berkowitz, Louis Finney, and Dennis Logue found that between 1968 and 1983, the market outperformed pension fund managers by about 0.5 percent per year (9.31 percent versus 8.83 percent). Deducting for management fees would widen the gap further by about 0.5 percent.[40]

The studies also show that about 70 percent of investment professionals fail to beat the market, and that they are not getting better at it. This is evident from Vanguard's findings, shown in Figure 4.8. In fact, a recent study conducted by Lipper Analytical Services showed that in 1995 the S&P index rose 37 percent, while mutual funds increased by only 30 percent and only 11 percent of them beat the market.

Although about 30 percent of mutual funds beat the market in any given year, none do so with any consistency. The winners one year are usually the losers the next. Burton Malkiel concluded from his research on mutual funds "that one cannot count on consistency of performance."[41] Jensen noted that "there is very little evidence that any individual fund was able to do significantly better than that which we expected from mere random chance."[42] I found statistical support for Jenson's assertion when I examined the track records of all mutual funds with more than $500 million in assets between 1991 and 1995. For each of the five years, I determined the number of funds that consistently performed in the top one-half for two to five years in a row. The results, shown in Figure 4.9, indicate that the percentage of funds consistently

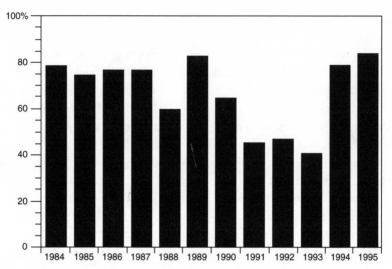

Figure 4.8   Percentage of equity mutual funds outperformed by the Standard &
Poor's 500 Index. (*Source of data:* Vanguard.)

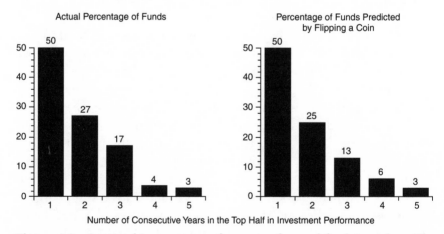

Figure 4.9   Sustained investment performance of mutual funds is random. The
graphs show the percentage of major mutual funds that remained in the top half
in investment performance for one to five consecutive years from 1991 to 1995.
(*Source of data:* Forbes annual mutual fund surveys.)

performing in the top half dropped quickly from 27 percent for two years in a row to 3 percent for five years in a row—the same odds as flipping a coin and getting heads five times in a row.

There is one instance where stock pickers have so far beaten random odds: the *Wall Street Journal*'s dartboard contest, which pits leading investment professionals against the selection of stocks by throwing darts. Every month since July 1990, the *Wall Street Journal* has been recruiting four investment professionals and asking them to pick a stock that they believe will prove to be a winner in the next six months. The *Journal*'s staff then picks a competing group of stocks by hanging the pages of the newspaper's stock listings on the wall and throwing four darts at them. Six months later, the *Journal* compares the investment of the four stocks picked by the professionals with the four stocks picked by throwing darts. As of January 1997, there have been seventy-nine such contests, of which the professionals have won forty-five and the darts thirty-four, although the *Journal* reports that there was a stretch during 1996 where the darts won six months in a row. The investment professionals have also beaten the darts in average return on investment: 10.6 percent for the professionals to 5.6 percent for the darts.

A common reaction to the notion that investment professionals fail to beat the market is, "But what about Peter Lynch?" True, Lynch has consistently outperformed the market, and everyone else, while managing Fidelity's Magellan fund. This would seem to poke a big hole in the EMH, but Lynch's investment strategy is perfectly consistent with at least the semi-strong version of the hypothesis. It is clear from his book, *One Up on Wall Street,* that his strategy is to avoid the "known zone" illustrated in Figure 4.3. Lynch looks for offbeat stocks that the investment community overlooks or avoids. He likes firms with dull-sounding corporate names, such as Bob Evans Farms, and those that he believes are falsely tainted, as Chrysler was when it was on the verge of bankruptcy. He prefers mundane industries—no high tech for him—and especially likes industries that do "something disagreeable," such as waste treatment, or "something depressing," such as funeral homes. He avoids stocks that are tracked by investment analysts and would be of interest to pension fund investment professionals, whom he calls the "Wall Street Oxymorons." He also seeks first-hand information on potential investments that is not generally known to the investment community.[43]

I asked both Stanford University's John McDonald and Vanguard's Bogle to explain Lynch's superior track record, which seems to defy the EMH. McDonald told me that "Lynch is a superior investor who beats the market by skill, not chance. This doesn't mean that he wins every time, but over time he adds value through bottom-up fundamental analysis of individual businesses. He doesn't pay attention to the overall market."[44] Bogle had a slightly different explanation: "The odds of flipping a coin and getting heads five times in a row is one in thirty-two. Peter Lynch is *the one* in thirty-two; actually he's *the one* in two hundred and fifty. The laws of probability guarantee that there will be *one* superior investor among a crowd of 250 investors." This comment puzzled me. Was Lynch the one in 250 due to skill, or was he just one in two hundred and fifty due to sheer luck, such as the winner of a coin-flipping contest? Bogle responded, "That's a hard thing to figure. A winning investment style during one period may underperform the market during another. There is statistical evidence that shows that it would take seventy years of tracking an investment manager's performance to tell if it was attributable to talent or pure luck."[45]

THE ALL AMERICANS

Wall Street firms employ hordes of analysts who give the thumbs up or down on the stocks they follow each quarter. Stock analysts at each firm are assigned a group of stocks to follow and often specialize in one or more industries. They analyze public data on their stocks' companies, examine historical earnings trends, and sometimes make a quick day trip to evaluate a company's management. Their earnings predictions and stock recommendations can influence share prices.

Most analysts' track records are poor in predicting corporate earnings. A 1993 study conducted by *Forbes* columnist David Dreman and money managers Michelle Clayman and Robin Swartz showed that analysts' earnings forecasts are off by 30 to 60 percent—a huge error: a one dollar earnings per share forecast would on average be off by plus or minus forty-five cents. Dreman concluded from his research that the analysts' earnings estimates are "utterly undependable" and of "not much value."[46] Surprisingly, Burton Malkiel found that analysts' earnings forecasts were just about as poor for staid utilities as for volatile electronics companies. And the results of a 1991 study conducted by Dreman for *Forbes,* shown in Figure 4.10, reveal that analysts have been getting worse at predicting corporate earnings.[47]

Every October, *Institutional Investor* polls 2,000 money managers about Wall Street stock analysts and taps those reputed to be the best for its All American Research Team (about seventy-five for a first team, with others assigned to lower-ranked teams). These All American analysts, however, are no better at predicting earnings growth and stock performance than their supposedly less astute colleagues. A 1992 study found that from 1981 to 1985, the All American Team had a forecast error rate of 34 percent versus a 35 percent error rate for their colleagues; however, given the wide range of error rates among the analysts, this 1 percent greater accuracy is not statistically valid.[48] Remember, too, that the All American Team is selected on the basis of reputation, not forecast accuracy.

Malkiel blames analysts' high error rates on incompetence and the drain of top talent into higher-paying sales and portfolio management positions. However true this may be, there are at least two deeper explanations. Recall that earnings growth rates are nearly random and that predicting random events is a losing proposition. Also, analysts cannot

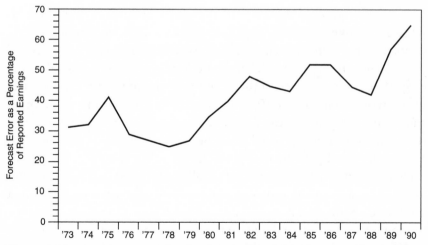

Figure 4.10 Average errors of analysts' quarterly earnings forecasts. (*Source of data: Forbes,* December 9, 1991.)

afford the time and effort to understand fully what goes on inside each of the many corporations they are assigned to follow. They are forced to rely on historical earnings trends, which provide no real clues about the future, and on public information, which is hopelessly old and usually inaccurate, and in any case is picked over by all of Wall Street. A 1968 study showed that analysts relied most heavily on historical earnings trends in making earnings predictions for the companies they analyzed, 66 percent of which correlated with those companies' past earnings trends.[49]

The corporate dynamics that give rise to quarterly earnings are much more complex and chaotic than commonly believed, and it would take an analyst many months of intense, on-site research to gain a complete understanding of the profitability of a major corporation. Even then, such an extensive effort might not lead to accurate earnings forecasts. Unexpected events, such as the loss or gain of major clients, cause erratic swings in the bottom line, and even corporate managers trading on their firsthand knowledge of the companies they analyze (within legal bounds) are often surprised by those companies' earnings growth and stock performance.

THE OLD FINANCIER'S ALMANAC

The most intriguing challenge to the Efficient Market Hypothesis is what is known as the *Value Line* enigma. The venerable weekly newsletter has a stock-picking system that seems to defy the odds and has thus become the bible of investment information. Founded in the early 1930s, it is now one of the largest investment information services in the world, with about 100,000 subscribers each paying $535 for an annual subscription, and can be found in most investment firm's libraries. Its extended readership could easily be in the millions. *Value Line* provides year-ahead performance predictions each week for 1,800 stocks, using a quaint scoring system that it calls "timeliness." It describes this as the "measure of the probable performance of a stock over the next six to twelve months. A stock ranked 1 (Highest) is expected to be one of the best performers, relative to the 1,700 others, during the next six to 12 months. Stocks ranked 2 are expected to be above-average performers; 3, average; 4, below average; and 5, lowest."[50] *Value Line* derives these rankings by analyzing fundamental characteristics such as earnings and technical factors such as past price performance. It intends for the rankings to be used as advice for actively buying and selling stocks on a short-term basis. The rankings are not meant for long-term buy-and-hold investment strategies, and, in fact, the performance of the top-ranked groups over a three- to five-year period is poor.

Value Line claims that its ranking system reliably beats the market. Figure 4.11 shows a key chart from its promotional material. Note how the graph lines for its five groups' performance over thirty years line up just as its ranking system had predicted, which seems to me to be suspiciously tidy, given the vagaries of stock prediction. Furthermore, several leading financial economists who were highly skeptical of *Value Line*'s claim have independently confirmed that it is valid. *Value Line*'s biggest break was getting the support of Fisher Black, the well-known financial economist at the University of Chicago and an ardent believer in the EMH. A joint study that Black conducted with *Value Line* seemed to support the newsletter's claim. In a 1973 letter to the editor of *Financial Analysts Journal* entitled, "Yes, Virginia, There Is Hope,"

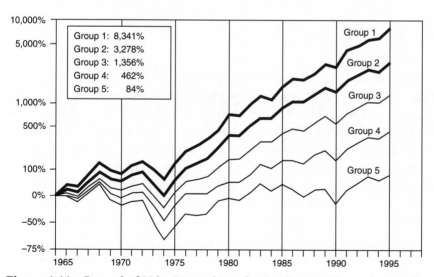

Figure 4.11   Record of *Value Line* rankings for timeliness, without allowing for changes in rank (1965–1995). (*Source: Value Line Investment Survey*, January 19, 1996, p. 7653.)

Black declared that "most investment management organizations would improve their performance if they fired all but one of their securities analysts and then provided the remaining analyst with the Value Line service."[51] In the prediction business, a recommendation does not get any better than that.

Still, there is something fishy about *Value Line*'s claim. Why should it be such a significant and rare exception to the EMH, when its self-described investment analysis is standard fare? Its timeliness formula is reminiscent of *The Old Farmer's Almanac*'s 200-year-old secret formula locked in a tin box somewhere in New Hampshire. Its ranking system can be arbitrary; stocks get bumped from Group 1 when new ones are added merely because there is a fixed quota for the top group, as *Value Line* has noted: "Since there can be only 100 stocks ranked 1, some other stock must fall to a rank 2, even though there has been no change in earnings or price."[52]

How is it possible that *Value Line* can disseminate such purportedly invaluable information to 100,000 subscribers without its mailroom staff spilling the beans in an effort to enrich themselves and their friends? If the newsletter's publishers and staff are so much smarter than the rest of the world, why don't they just keep the rankings to themselves and become infinitely wealthy instead of selling their predictions for a few hundred dollars?

Is *Value Line* some legendary exception to the EMH? I don't think so. First, to achieve its promised results (shown in Figure 4.11) would require an intense amount of buying and selling of shares at purchase and sale dates that are several days earlier than its subscribers could actually execute. The *Hurlbert Financial Digest* simulated the buying and selling of *Value Line*'s Group 1 stocks at realistic transaction dates from 1990 to 1994 and achieved an annual return of 15.5 percent, as compared to 15.2 percent for the market average, an insignificant difference.[53]

Academic studies reveal another plausible explanation of how *Value Line* seems able to beat the market: *Value Line*, wittingly or otherwise, groups its stocks according to risk, which on average would guarantee that higher-risk groups would outperform lower-risk ones. Robert Kaplan from Carnegie-Mellon University and Roman Weil from the University of Chicago, in a rejoinder to Fisher Black's 1973 letter lauding *Value Line* in the *Financial Analysts Journal* (published along with it), suggested that "Value Line ought to account for risk in its rankings."[54]

A study in 1987 stated, "Our findings show . . . that the result [of the *Value Line* enigma] may reflect an association between *Value Line* rank and beta (a measure of risk)."[55] A 1990 study concluded, "The purported abnormal returns of positions based on Value Line's rankings are compensation for systematic risk associated with these positions."[56] *Translation:* The higher returns of *Value Line*'s top groups are due to their higher risk.

The 1987 study analyzed the weekly rankings and actual returns for all of the newsletter's stocks from 1978 to 1983 and developed a model indicating that *Value Line*'s Group 1 had a 47 percent higher beta than Group 5. My own analysis of *Value Line*'s January 1996 rankings shows that its Group 1 stocks had a beta of 1.31 and that those in Group 5 had a beta of 1.04—a 31 percent difference in risk. This suggests that the success of *Value Line*'s rankings is merely an illusion; the higher returns of higher-rated groups are compensation for bearing higher risk.

I think there is also a third explanation for the *Value Line* enigma: self-fulfilling prophecy. Given the newsletter's enormous influence with millions of readers and its continual prediction of superior returns for its favored choices, it is entirely possible that its announced rankings move the market in a self-fulfilling way so as to make them come true. Recall that the pronouncements by some market gurus achieve the same self-fulfilling results.

The *Value Line* enigma is a myth. The investor service is not invincible, just enormously influential. This also suggests that the market is not nearly as rational as financial economists would have us believe.

IRRATIONAL EXPECTATIONS

The theory of rational expectations proposed by Robert Lucas, winner of the 1995 Nobel Prize in economics, and other recent developments in economic theory have pushed further and further into presuming that the world is populated with rational people making rational decisions, especially when it comes to important matters such as investments. This assumption is convenient for economic theorists, but it flies in the face of everyday practical experience.

The stock market is clearly driven by irrational herd mentality and mass psychology. Speculative binges cause stocks to surge to price levels way beyond their economic value in terms of future earnings potential. Panics cause the equally irrational effect in the opposite direction. The stock market is a psychological soup of fear, greed, hope, superstition, and a host of other emotions and motives.

Speculation and panic are inherently human behaviors. Steadily rising stock prices are just too tempting to ignore; they lure into the market more and more investors who hope to jump on the bandwagon before it is too late. It does not matter if the market is overvalued, so long as you are not the last person buying stocks—an ultimately self-defeating fallacy called the Greater Fool Theory. With mass panic, investors hope to get out while still preserving some of their money, even when prices are below their intrinsic value. Nineteenth-century historian Charles Mackay noted that investors "go mad in herds and recover their senses slowly."[57]

One of the most absurd instances of irrational investment behavior ever was tulip mania. In the mid-sixteenth century, the tulip was introduced to Europe from the Middle East and became wildly popular in Holland. Prices for tulip bulbs escalated rapidly, leading to mass speculation. People traded their whole farms for a single tulip bulb, and sometimes they sold the bulb to an even greater fool for an even higher price, enabling them to buy an even bigger farm. "The rage among the Dutch to possess them was so great," wrote Mackay, "that the ordinary industry of the country was neglected, and the nation, even to its lowest dregs, embarked in the tulip trade."[58] Inevitably, the speculative bubble broke, after which a tulip bulb sold for the price of a mere onion, creating widespread financial ruin. Mackay described the terrible results as follows: "Many who, for a brief season, had emerged from the humbler walks of life, were cast back into their original obscurity. Substantial merchants were reduced almost to beggary, and many a representative of noble line saw the fortunes of his house ruined beyond redemption."[59]

Stock prices are also irrationally volatile. According to Benjamin Graham, the father of fundamental analysis, "Most of the time common stocks are subject to irrational and excessive price fluctuations in both directions, as the consequence of the ingrained tendency of most people to speculate or gamble—i.e., to give way to hope, fear and greed."[60] The crash of the U.S. stock market in 1987 is a good example; it came and went seemingly without cause. Whatever stocks were worth on the preceding Friday, they were worth 30 percent less a few days later, with no special events or new information to account for the dramatic drop in market value. There was no reason to believe that the value of future earnings would drop by a third over the course of a few days. Similarly, there is no rational explanation for why the market rebounded over the weeks following the crash. The same questions apply to Japan's Nikkei exchange, which in 1990 lost 91 percent of its value in nine months. Clearly, Japan's commercial empire did not lose 91 percent of its earnings power.

The market also responds to news events in strange ways. For example, on March 15, 1996, when the U.S. Labor Department announced that a record number of jobs had been created during the preceding month, the Dow Jones plunged 171 points. Apparently some investors were worried that the Federal Reserve might raise interest rates in order to slow the thriving economy. Joseph de la Vega observed this counterintuitive nature of the stock market as far back as 1688: "While philosophy teaches that different effects are ascribable to different causes, at the stock exchange some buy and some sell on the basis of a given piece of news, so that here one cause has different effects."[61]

While financial economists continue to base their theories on the assumed rational behavior of human beings, their psychologist colleagues from across the campus are stepping in to fill the void by creating a new field called behavioral finance. In fact, in 1995 Harvard Medical School conducted its First Congress on the Psychology of Investing. Behavioral finance hypotheses include some of the following obviously commonsense notions: "disposition theory" (investors are reluctant to sell shares when they go below their original purchase prices), "barn-door closing" (investors will stick with a current trend even when it is changing—i.e., situational bias), and "anchoring" (investors are reluctant to change their opinions once they have made up their minds).[62] Behavioral finance theorists appear to share some common ground with market technicians, who believe that the stock market is heavily driven by mass psychology.

The irrational dimension of the market means that the EMH is at least partially flawed, especially with respect to explaining the market's volatility. According to the EMH, the variability in share prices is due to external shocks in the form of new information coming on the scene that affects investors' expectations about future corporate earnings. This is similar to economists' explanation for the fluctuations in the overall economy.

The notion that the volatility of the stock market is caused by new information is weak, and in fact, there is no scientific linkage between the EMH and the Random Walk Theory. As a student at Wharton Business School, Peter Lynch "found it difficult to integrate the efficient-market hypothesis (that everything in the stock market is 'known' and prices are always 'rational') with the random-walk hypothesis (that the ups and downs of the market are irrational and entirely unpredictable)."[63] A more complete explanation of the stock market's volatility is that the market is a complex system with rational and countervailing irrational forces at work, as illustrated in Figure 4.12.

While rational forces drive the market toward its fair value, irrational forces of speculation and panic cause the market to diverge from rational value. These irrational forces give rise to explosive nonlinearities that make the market unpredictable. Speculation and panic are nonlinear forces with positive feedback loops. The greater the surge in stock prices, the more investors are tempted to buy shares, which causes the market to surge further—until price drops set off a run of panic selling, causing a huge market decline that can result in the collapse of the market, as happened in sixteenth-century Holland with tulip mania.

The Sante Fe Institute has created a working model of a simple stock market that exhibits behavior expected from the complex market system, illustrated in Figure 4.12. The simulated market had a single stock

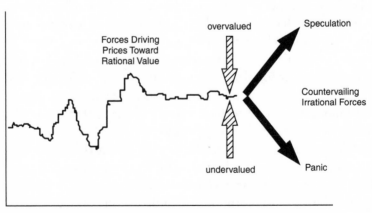

Figure 4.12   The stock market as a complex system.

that had a fair value of $30, and the hypothetical investors (economists call them agents) had to learn their own rules on how to make money in the market. Although the simulated stock price hovered around the rationally expected $30, strange things occurred when the price reached $34. As research fellow Brian Arthur noted, "The agents had discovered a primitive form of technical analysis. That is, they had come to the belief that if the price went up enough, then it would continue to go up. So buy. But, of course, that belief became a self-fulfilling prophecy: if enough agents tried to buy at price 34, that would cause the price to go up." Conversely, panic set in whenever the price dropped to $25. The model accurately captured the countervailing rational and irrational forces, even creating speculative bubbles and market crashes.[64]

MINING CHAOS

A more recent attack on the EMH involves the fact that stock prices are not precisely random, at least according to a textbook definition of random. Stock prices seem to behave as if they have some slight memory of their past (remember the 3 percent correlation) and, though erratic, seem to be bounded. These statistical observations have led to speculation that the stock market, in addition to being a complex system, might be driven by some obscure chaotic process buried deep inside it. The presence of chaos would mean that the market might be somewhat predictable in the short term. Recall from Chapter 2 that although the weather is a chaotic system, it is driven by laws of nature that permit short-term weather forecasting to be reasonably accurate. If similar principles of chaotic structure could be found for the stock market, they would be the Holy Grail of Wall Street, and those who understood them and knew how to apply them to the market would become unimaginably rich.

The potential to make money from chaos theory has attracted a number of leading scientists and mathematicians to Wall Street and has led to the creation of new companies based on the possibility. To find these patterns in the market, in 1989 Citicorp hired British mathematician Andrew Colin, who specializes in nonlinear relationships and in 1991 the Prediction Company was founded in Sante Fe by Doyne Farmer and Norman Packard, physicists who pioneered early work on chaos theory while they were at the University of California at Santa Cruz. Swiss Bank Corporation is a major financial backer and client of the Prediction Company.

The search for patterns of chaotic structure in the market involves massive data mining. Hundreds of theories expressed in the form of non-linear equations are generated and run against historical price data to find those with some statistical fit. Packard explains the Prediction Company's methodology as follows: "The idea is to throw proven pattern-finding strategies of any stripe at the data and 'keep pounding on them' . . . to find the merest hint of a pattern, and then exploit the daylights out of it. The mind-set here is that of a gambler: any positive edge is an advantage."[65] The Prediction Company admits that it has no interest in the science behind stock prices. Farmer asserts, "If the point is to make money, . . . the question doesn't need to be answered."[66]

The hype about chaos theory has also attracted authors and the media. There have been articles in *Business Week, Investing,* and other magazines hailing chaos theory as a potential savior of the money man-agement industry. Tony Vaga's book, *Profiting from Chaos,* seems to be a Trojan horse intended to restore the credibility of technical analysis by shrouding it with serious academic work on chaos and complexity theories, as he himself noted: "The vindication of technical analysis by [this] new research is heartening."[67]

We have come full circle from the pseudoscience of the market technicians to the scientific neotechnicians. Both are attempting to do the same thing: find and exploit recurring patterns in historical stock prices. So far, the results seem to be the same. Despite the optimism in the early 1990s, no one has hit a mother lode in their data mining—un-less the neotechnicians have secretly done it and have been hiding the Porsches and Mercedes they have bought with their profits. Secrecy, however, is a scarce commodity on Wall Street.

Statistical probes of stock prices nevertheless have revealed that even if rules of behavior exist for the market, they are so complex and deeply buried that no such Holy Grail equations are likely to be found. John Casti, a research fellow at the Sante Fe Institute, has concluded "that al-though stock returns do appear to exhibit chaotic structure, the depar-ture from pure randomness is probably too small to be usefully employed in any predictive scheme aimed at beating the market."[68] Even if the coveted equations were found, their effectiveness would deteriorate over time by the very process of using them to make money. For example, imagine that someone discovers that the market goes up every time there is a new moon, enabling the discoverer to buy into the market the day before the new moon and make a profit. The more that this discovery gets used—especially by the inevitable copycats—stock prices would get bid up the day before the new moon, and then the day before that, and the day before that, until the effect dissipates entirely.

A 1996 article in the *Economist,* "Chaos Under a Cloud," described the application of chaos theory to investments as "a long march up a dark alley," and concluded that "the best way to make money out of deterministic chaos is to write about it."[69]

"A TOUCHSTONE FOR THE INTELLIGENT AND A TOMBSTONE FOR THE AUDACIOUS"

Such is how de la Vega described the Dutch stock market in 1688,[70] and not much has changed since then. Betting on the random walk is perilous business. As Warren Weaver, author of the book *Lady Luck,* observed, "The best way to lose your shirt is to think that you have discovered a pattern in a game of chance."[71] So do not use the market as a gambling casino. In fact, Vanguard chairman Bogle told me that the "math of investing and gambling are a lot alike, as are their economics. Apart from long-term market growth, short-term gains are a zero-sum game: the gains of one investor are paid by the losses of another. And then there is the casino's take, which, like the investment manager's fee, reduces the zero-sum game to a losing one, on average. When you cut through it all, it's a fool's game. And never confuse skill with luck, especially during a bull market."[72]

There is more quiet wisdom to be found among the noisy investment hype. Take Benjamin Graham's advice: "The individual investor should act consistently as an investor and not as a speculator."[73] Peter Lynch further adds, "To the rash and impetuous stockpicker who chases hot tips and rushes in and out of his equities, an 'investment' in stocks is no more reliable than throwing away paychecks on the horses with the prettiest mane, or the jockey with the purple silks. . . . [But] when you lose [at the racetrack, at least] you'll be able to say you had a great time doing it."[74] Burton Malkiel advises, "The consistent losers in the market are those who are unable to resist being swept up in some kind of tulip-bulb craze. . . . It is not hard, really, to make money in the market. . . . What is hard to avoid is the alluring temptation to throw your money away on short, get-rich-quick speculative binges."[75]

Avoid market timers, for they promise something they cannot deliver. Cancel your subscription to market timing newsletters. Tell the investment advisers selling the latest market timing scheme to buzz off. Ignore news media predictions, since they haven't a clue as to what the market is going to do—although that will not stop them from publishing market predictions. Stop asking yourself and everyone you know, "What's the market going to do?" It is an irrelevant question, because it cannot be answered.

The evidence shows that if the market *can* be beaten in picking individual stocks, it is damn hard to do, and the vast majority of investment professionals fail trying. The exceptional stock pickers who consistently beat the market year after year, cycle after cycle, can be counted on one hand—that is probably an overstatement—and it is not clear whether their success is mostly due to luck. Malkiel believes that "professional investment managers are not able to outperform the broad market averages. No investor can afford to ignore this important fact of life."[76]

And so, be highly skeptical of those who claim to have superior stock picking abilities. Ask them to explain how they, unlike the vast majority of their competitors, can consistently find undervalued stocks that have eluded the tens of millions of investors, advisers, stock analysts, and inside traders. Examine their track records carefully, comparing them with market averages for the past one-, three-, and five-year periods; a good one-year track record is not good enough.

You can take advantage of the stock market's higher long-term returns—*but do so only if you do not need the cash anytime soon.* You must be able to weather the long-term ups and downs in the market. As shown earlier in this chapter, stocks generate more than twice the returns as other investments, but they come with some added risk. In the short term, the stock market is more volatile than other instruments.

Investing wisely in the market means buying and holding stocks, because their higher returns can be achieved only over long periods of time spanning bull and bear markets. Vanguard's John Bogle advises that "people around age twenty-five should be 85 to 100 percent invested in stocks and stay the course to reap the higher returns. Over the long haul, downturns will be offset by upturns in the market. Someone around seventy-five should be 20 to 40 percent invested in stocks. The extreme risk-averse should not be in the market at all, because as soon as the market drops five points, they'll abandon the market and lose their investment."[77] Investing wisely also means diversification. The risk of investing in any one stock can be alleviated by holding a diversified portfolio of stocks, such as in buying a mutual fund.

The best thing that an investment adviser can do for you is to assess your financial needs and design a tailored investment program to meet them. A good financial adviser will consider your tax situation, cash flow needs, and risk tolerance. For example, if you are investing for the very long term, do not need to tap into invested funds in the interim, and are unaffected by gyrations in the stock market, which surely will occur, then you should invest more in stocks than in bonds and short-term securities. Conversely, if you need ready cash and are intolerant of risk, then stocks should play a lesser role in your portfolio. A good financial planner can help you figure this out and determine the right mix of investments for you.

But you should also avoid the chronic pessimists, or what *Barrons* calls the "permabears." These ever-pessimistic advisers see clouds surrounding every silver lining. To them, every financial event is a signal of crash and burn, and even healthy economic growth is a sign that the economy is overheating and headed toward hyperinflation. Besides selling bad advice, these permabears create high anxiety—but perhaps that is what some customers secretly want.

Especially avoid the doom-mongers who cater to survivalist investors. The *Reaper,* for example, is a newsletter that predicts that earthquakes, floods, and tornadoes will plague the earth throughout 1997. Its editor, R. E. McMaster Jr., explains that "we are presently in the trough of the eleven-year sunspot cycle, in which the sun is retrograde." His advice: keep your money in strong foreign currencies and gold.[78] The *U.S. and World Early Warning Report* predicts that the conflict in the former Yugoslavia will lead to a third world war, and advises its readers to buy Swiss francs and invest in Fidelity's Select Defense and Aerospace fund. The *International Harry Schultz Letter* foretells war and financial collapse caused by financial derivatives and advises investing in gold and silver along with food, timber, and other basic staple industries. The *Dines Letter* envisions a sequence of disasters that started with the 1993 bombing of the World Trade Center in New York City and the Federal Building in Oklahoma City and will lead to bank failings and the collapse of the stock market; it recommends buying gold and silver stocks. The *Monetary and Economic Review* says that we are in a new Sodom and Gomorrah situation brought on by the sins of materialism and debt, and it advises its readers to buy gold, silver, and Treasury bills. The *Remnat Review* cautions that welfare recipients will soon revolt, leading to our Judgment Day, and urges city dwellers, especially those who live in New York or Los Angeles, to head for the hills.

Such dire predictions would be cause for alarm if they were believable. The real fright experts are the demographic forecasters introduced in the next chapter. These prognosticators foresee Malthusian mass starvation and ecological poisoning around the globe, and they question the very survival of the human species.

5

Checking the "Unchecked Population"

S ince prehistoric times, prophets have predicted that angry gods would punish mankind for its sins with pestilence, plague, and famine. For the past two hundred years, prophets have predicted that we would bring about our own punishment for failing to control our population growth. Today, news media and books are full of apocalyptic stories about how overpopulation will cause starvation, poisoning of natural resources, and deleterious climatic changes. More doom mongering? In many cases, yes; however, population is relatively predictable many years into the future. The challenge is to pick the good predictions from the bad. For example, consider the following three scenarios:

The Ice Age Cometh. "There is now considerable evidence that the first stages of the next ice age may really begin soon, within the next few years—and that the transitional stage of extreme and increasingly inhospitable climate may have already begun. By 1975, our rapidly deteriorating climate may well lead to massive world wide starvation by 1995 if not before, with the possibility of nuclear war over dwindling resources."[1] This prediction, from Larry Ephron's 1988 book, *The End: The Imminent Ice Age and How We Can Stop It!* has obviously not come true. In the book, Ephron follows the standard doom-monger format.

He first attempts to prove that ice ages come in predictable cycles and that we are now overdue for one, and he tells us that we are faced not only with freezing to death but with an increase in tornadoes, earthquakes, and other plagues that will accompany the advancing ice. He then attempts to show that we have brought doom upon ourselves—in this case, by environmental degradation. Finally, he offers a way out of our imminent demise, urging us to spread rock dust over the earth's surface to remineralize the soil, which, through some convoluted logic, will cause the glaciers to recede. *The End* was endorsed by two famous individuals. Visionary architect, philosopher, and inventor Buckminster Fuller, creator of the geodesic dome, called the book "completely convincing." Actor-comedian Robin Williams praised it as "one of the most relevant books since the last ice age."

Global Famine. "I call the disaster the Time of Famines and I say that the Time of Famines will be upon us by 1975. . . . The lagging productive capacity of the hungry nations shows clearly that hunger is not only here today but is steadily increasing. . . . Civil disorder, anarchy, military dictatorships, runaway inflation, transportation breakdowns and chaotic unrest will be the order of the day in many of the hungry nations—all because hunger will turn inexorably into starvation and starvation will become widespread famine."[2] Another failed prediction, this one by William and Paul Paddock in their 1967 book, *Famine—1975!* The authors, like others before them, underestimated the productivity of modern agriculture, especially that practiced in the United States. For example, they predicted that exportable grains in the United States would be 60 million tons in 1980, whereas the U.S. Department of Agriculture later estimated that the United States actually exported 102 million tons of grain that year—a 72 percent forecast error on the part of the Paddocks. Not only did the apocalyptic famine fail to appear since the time the book was published, but the United Nations estimated that the number of undernourished people in the world declined from 942 million in 1970 to 786 million in 1990—a noticeable improving trend, though admittedly still a lot of hungry people.

Ironically, the prophecy made in *Famine—1975!* is more valid for the 1990s than it was for the mid-1970s. The world's population has grown immensely since then, and we can now see elements of the predicted scenario coming true today in impoverished sub-Saharan African nations such as Somalia, Rwanda, Liberia, and Ethiopia, where over-population and famine exist and warlords foment anarchy among their desperate peoples. A 1996 *Business Week* cover story was subtitled "As global demand outpaces supply, both haves and have-nots are in for a shock."[3] As rapidly developing countries like China acquire the eating habits and lifestyles of the developed world, food and other resources may—and, indeed, have—become acutely scarce for the first time in many decades.

Societal Collapse. "The population, continuing its exponential growth, will soon reach a peak when the people have outstripped the land's resources. The forests will vanish, overharvested for agricultural purposes and wood products. Many species of trees will become extinct as the last of the larger trees are cut down and rodents eat the tree seeds and saplings. With the forests gone, streams, lakes, and aquifers will dry up and topsoil will erode to the point of infertility. Agricultural production will plummet and starvation will set in, with people eating every animal to the point where many species will become extinct, save for insects, small snails, and some domesticated animals. Society will collapse as marauding warlords and genocidal killings displace civilization. Technology will fail, and some people will resort to living in caves for protection and warmth. All forms of past culture will be destroyed in the warfare and chaos; and the hungry, barbaric people will resort to cannibalism. All told, the human population will plummet between 75 and 90 percent from its peak year."

This third prediction is not a prediction at all but rather an actual historical event that I have recast in the future tense. The societal collapse described actually began about five hundred years ago on the remote Easter Island in the South Pacific,[4] famous for its mysterious massive stone heads weighing up to eighty-two tons that stand on the shore and peer eerily out over the Pacific Ocean. How they got there has been a mystery, because it seemed impossible that the ancestors of the current native population could have made these enormous sculptures and erected them on the shore. Recently, however, scientists have solved the mystery by analyzing centuries of pollen, DNA, linguistics, human bones, and ancient trash piles.

It all began when a group of Polynesians, who were master seafarers, crossed thousands of miles of open ocean around A.D. 400 to become the first settlers on Easter Island. The sixty-four-square-mile island was a fertile paradise covered by subtropical forests with massive trees and a diversity of plant and animal species. Trees six feet in diameter were perfect for making oceangoing canoes, which the islanders used to hunt deepwater fish, since much of Easter Island is surrounded by cliffs that prevent most shallow-water fishing. There were plenty of seabirds and land birds to eat as well. With such favorable conditions, the original explorers evolved into a sophisticated society that grew to as many as 20,000 people between the years 1200 and 1500, when civilization and population on the island peaked.

A few centuries after they arrived, the Polynesians began carving the giant stone heads at inland quarries and transporting them to their shore sites using logs from the huge trees as rollers. Pollen analysis shows that the giant trees became extinct after the year 1400, due to the inhabitants' overcutting them to make these rollers and also their canoes. The trees they used as firewood to keep warm in the often cool climate also became scarce. As canoes aged and rotted, the Easter Islanders had no means of replacing them, and thus they were unable to harvest their food staples from deep-sea fishing and unable to escape their remote island, located 1,400 miles from the next inhabited island in the Pacific. When they hunted land and sea birds to near extinction, they raised and ate more chickens and, resorting to agriculture, cleared much of the island to grow food. Topsoil eroded and water sources dried up, agricultural production plummeted, and the island could feed only a fraction of its large population. Starvation drove the Easter Islanders to resort to cannibalism, evident from the piles of human bones and the curse handed down by oral tradition, "The flesh of your mother sticks between my teeth."

Eventually organized society was toppled, and the island was taken over by factions of fighting warlords by the 1600s. When Dutch explorers rediscovered Easter Island in 1722, they found a barren landscape devoid of any tree or bush over ten feet high, no land animals larger than insects, and a total population of 2,000 primitive people. Incredibly, the islanders had lost their Polynesian oceangoing heritage and by the time the Dutch arrived had only primitive canoes barely capable of plying the island's few accessible shallows.

Are we repeating the mistakes of the Easter Islanders on a global scale? Some population forecasters say that the outlook for the next fifty years is frightening. Human population on earth is expected approximately to double over the next fifty years, from 5.6 billion today to about 12 billion in 2050. Can the planet feed this many people? Will we exhaust our nonrenewable resources and cause modern society to collapse? Will we poison ourselves with industrial pollutants to the point of extinction? Population forecasters seek answers to these questions and, in so doing, may be *the* real "dismal scientists."

THE REAL DISMAL SCIENTISTS

Population forecasting seeks to predict deaths, births, immigration, and the characteristics of future generations. It is perhaps the most important form of social science prediction, if for no other reason than that it puts the "capita" in every per capita projection. Population forecasts are also a crucial component of other important predictions, such as economic growth, household formation, and income distribution. Demographers, statisticians, sociologists, and other professionals make population forecasts; for simplicity, I will call them all demographers. Unlike other forecasting professions, population forecasting is not a big moneymaking business for most of its practitioners, except for the occasional best-selling authors of doom-and-gloom predictions. Population forecasting is primarily done by public-sector entities, not-for-profit organizations, and academics.

Most developed countries have official population-predicting entities. In the United States, the Bureau of the Census creates official population projections for the nation, much as the National Weather Service creates official weather forecasts, but for decades ahead rather than days ahead. The United Nations produces the official forecasts for world population. Many universities, such as Brown and Princeton, and think tanks, such as the Rand Corporation, have population study centers that probe future demographics and explore future population issues. There are also population control advocacy groups such as Zero Population Growth, which forewarn of the dangers of excessive population growth.

The public sector makes extensive use of population forecasts to determine the future need for schools and teachers, roads, airports, hospitals, schools, power plants, waste disposal facilities, and water utilities. The federal government and state governments need these forecasts to plan for the funding of social security, Medicare, and other social programs. Corporations use population forecasts as a critical part of their strategic planning to determine future product demand—it is important for makers of blue jeans, for example, to forecast the future population of their core customers, who are fourteen- to twenty-four-year-olds—and where to locate stores, restaurants, bank branches, and warehouses.

The stakes are high in using population forecasts, especially for planning costly long-term projects. Underestimating future population causes infrastructure to become inadequate—crowded roads, for example—while overestimating population causes a costly *excess* of infrastructure, such as public utilities with too much capacity, which we pay for with needlessly higher taxes. For corporations, failure to anticipate the characteristics of future populations can lead to declining markets and missed opportunities. Population forecasting is a life-and-death matter for those living in countries dependent on food aid; if the U.N.'s Food Development Agency underestimates the future populations of developing countries, food shortages and mass famine could result.

There is a joke that demographers make fifty-year forecasts so that they will be long buried by the time their predictions are found to be faulty. In fact, demographers prefer to make shorter-term forecasts, which are more accurate, and they are the most humble forecasters I encountered in writing this book. They make long-term predictions only to satisfy their users, who are desperate for population predictions extending many decades into the future. In fact, demographers insist that they do not forecast population but, rather, "project" it, a distinction that confuses everyone who uses population predictions. According to Harvard professor of demography Nathan Keyfitz, "A demographer makes a projection, and his reader uses it as a forecast."[5]

Demographers commonly use the cohort component model to predict future populations, a technique that is a lot simpler than its name suggests. The methodology first breaks the population forecast into its key components, as shown in the following equation:

$$\text{Future population} = \text{Current population} + \text{births} - \text{deaths} + \text{net immigration.}$$

Next, demographers apply this equation to groups of people—cohorts—of the same age and sex. For example, demographers will start with an estimated count of existing females under the age of three and project the number of children they will bear in the future and when they will die. The final step is to add up the projections for each cohort group, a process that surely involves a lot of numbers but nothing more complex than arithmetic.

HUMANS AS PREDATORS AND PREY

The dynamics of populations involve the complex interplay among plants and animals in an ecosystem. When a predator thins the ranks of its prey, its population declines as a result of lack of food, subsequently causing a rebuilding of the prey population, which then stimulates a rebuilding of the predator population, and so on. The population of Soay sheep on Hirta, a remote, uninhabited island in the Outer Hebrides off the coast of Scotland, is dependent on the island's native grasses and varies according to the grasses' abundance, in an alternating cycle of population explosions and massive die-offs every three to four years. Whenever the herd grows to about 1,400 sheep, its heavy grazing makes scarce the normally bountiful summer grasses that enable the sheep to make it through the winter. Mass starvation then takes place during the winter months, killing about 70 percent of the sheep by March, which enables the island's grasses to recover. Because Soay sheep are fertile during their first year and because the grasses have once again become abundant, the herd grows back quickly, reaching the 1,400 limit in another three to four years, at which point another mass die-off begins.

Human beings, uniquely equipped with high intelligence, have easily won the predator-prey competition among large animals on earth. A stunning example is the invasion of human hunter-gatherers into North America from Asia about 11,000 years ago. For millions of years, North America was populated by woolly mammoths, giant sloths and bison, saber-tooth tigers, and other large mammals, which within a thousand years of human arrival on the continent became extinct. Even horses became extinct on the continent until they were reintroduced by European settlers in the seventeenth century. There is no proof that humans caused the mass extinction, but the timing of human arrival and the extinction of the large animals seem more than coincidence.

Historically, we have been more prone to lose out to smaller life forms. Early death and disease caused by microorganisms' feasting on human tissues has been humanity's legacy for most of the several hundred thousand years of our existence. Studies of Cro-Magnon bones show that early humans lived on average twenty-five years, long enough to procreate but too short to become civilized. Disease-causing microorganisms constrained the rate of human population growth for millennia. For example, bubonic plague killed one-third of all fourteenth-century Europeans. The population of Britain grew to 3.7 million by 1348 and plunged to 2.1 million by 1430, not reaching 3.7 million again until the year 1603. The plague-causing bacterium was a constant killer throughout the world until 1943, when antibiotics nearly eradicated it.[6]

It took 200,000 years to increase human life expectancy from twenty-five to forty-seven years, and in the last one hundred years, life expectancy dramatically increased from forty-seven to seventy-seven years (in developed countries). The gains in health and the increase in life spans can be attributed to public health programs that minimize human exposure to deadly microorganisms and to relatively recent advances in medicine that cure people already exposed.

Epidemics of infectious diseases have been by-products of civilization in every society that has existed. Large numbers of people living in close quarters have frequently hastened the spread of such diseases, often through the contamination of drinking water with human waste and its disease-causing microorganisms, such as the *Vibrio cholerae* bacterium that causes cholera. Public health improved dramatically during the Greco-Roman era, especially in Rome, where aqueducts supplying pure water from distant streams and good sewage systems minimized citizens' exposure to dangerous microorganisms. However, interest in public health declined in the West when the Roman Empire fell in A.D. 476 and was not restored until the mid- to late 1800s. In the United States, little thought was given to public health until the founding of the American Public Health Association in 1872, following two decades of continual cholera epidemics.

Until the late 1800s, with few exceptions, Western medical practice was mostly a combination of superstition and barbarous treatments such as bloodletting, which ended up hastening death rather than curing the patient. (A notable early exception, from the fourth century B.C., was the Greek physician Hippocrates, who maintained that disease has natural rather than supernatural causes.) One of the earliest printed documents was an astrological calendar published in 1462 in Mainz showing the best times for bloodletting. Sixteenth-century Swiss physician Paracelsus said of his profession, "When I saw that nothing resulted from [doctors'] practice but killing and laming . . . I determined to abandon such a miserable art and seek truth elsewhere. . . . The best of our popular physicians are the ones who do the least harm. But unfortunately, some poison their patients with mercury, and others purge or bleed them to death."[7] In fact, a mercury-based ointment was the only remedy to contain the ravages of syphilis for hundreds of years, but for many, the cure was worse than the disease, since it caused hair and teeth loss, ulcers in the mouth, and other afflictions, leading to the notion of the time that "a night with Venus meant a lifetime with Mercury."[8]

The first break in the war on microorganisms came in 1675 when Anton J. Leeuwenhoek, a Dutch naturalist, discovered the existence of bacteria using a crude microscope. Although he had no idea that such microorganisms caused disease in humans, his discovery laid the basis for the controversial "germ theory" that many years later correctly linked disease to the invasion of microorganisms. Another significant breakthrough was the creation of a vaccine for smallpox by English physician Edward Jenner in 1798, after observing that people afflicted with the relatively mild cowpox disease became immune to the more deadly smallpox disease—the founding principle of the science of immunology. French chemist Louis Pasteur proved the germ theory by demonstrating that microorganisms are living things that cause disease and that disease can be prevented by killing them. Progress continued with Robert Koch, a German physician, who linked specific microorganisms to the specific diseases they caused, and with British surgeon Joseph Lister's innovation of antiseptic surgery, which cut the death from infection among patients undergoing surgery from 12 to 2 percent. (Patients undergoing amputations previously had a death rate of up to 50 percent due to infections.) Sir James Simpson, an English physician, noted that "anyone entering a hospital for surgery in the 1860s was exposed to more chances of death than was the English soldier on the field of Waterloo."[9] Finally, English bacteriologist Sir Alexander Fleming discovered penicillin in 1928, paving the way for the discovery of hundreds of other antibiotics that would cure most of the most serious infectious diseases, such as tuberculosis, syphilis, pneumonia, and meningitis.

POPULATION MOMENTUM
AND PREDICTABILITY

Different ecosystems have different tempos. There are ecosystems of microorganisms that regenerate every few hours or minutes, whereas a forest ecosystem is extremely slow, as different species of trees compete for sunlight, water, and minerals in a battle that may persist for centuries before reaching some steady state. Like forests, the human ecosystem evolves slowly: it takes about fifteen years for the human female to reach childbearing age; the average human life span is nearly eighty years. Demographers call the slow movement of the human ecosystem "population momentum," and it makes the accurate prediction of future populations relatively easy. For example, making a prediction in 1997 about the population of thirty-year-olds in the year 2025 would be highly accurate because these future thirty-year-olds already exist.

Twenty-year population forecasts are about as accurate as one-month economic projections or one-day weather forecasts. Figure 5.1 demonstrates the accuracy of population predictions several decades into the future, as the lines representing the forecast population and the actual population are mostly indistinguishable. For example, the Bureau of the Census's 1972 prediction of the U.S. population in 1995 was off by only about 5 million people—an error of 2 percent. However, forecasts of the U.S. population become unreliable twenty-five years ahead; according to the Bureau of the Census, these long-range forecasts are "obviously subject to considerable error."[10] Nathan Keyfitz has concluded from his extensive reviews of U.S. population forecasts that "short-term forecasts, say up to ten or 20 years, do tell us something, but that beyond a quarter-century or so we simply do not know what the population will be."[11]

From the research of Keyfitz, the Bureau of the Census, and others, I have made the following conclusions about the reliability of population forecasting (note the obvious similarities to other forecasting fields):

- Forecasts of future cohort populations that *already* exist when the forecasts are made are quite accurate. As shown in Figure 5.2, the error rates for ten- to twenty-year forecasts for future cohorts that already exist are about 1 to 3 percent versus 30 to 50 percent for cohorts that have yet to be born.

• Forecasts of population counts are much more reliable than forecasts of population growth rates, as is evident from Figure 5.1a and b. (Note that the rate of change of any statistic is always harder to predict than the statistic itself.)

• Periods of steady growth allow for greater forecast accuracy than periods of great change. The Bureau of the Census estimates that its error rate in the volatile 1950s was twice as high as in the period after 1970, when the U.S. birthrate stabilized and remained steady for the next twenty-five years.[12] (See Figure 5.8.)

• Forecast accuracy is much less dependable for rapidly growing populations. The U.N. estimates that its population-forecast errors are three times higher for high-growth areas such as Africa than for slow-growing ones such as Europe.

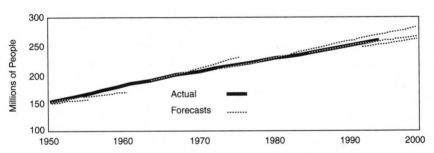

Figure 5.1a Total population predictions are reasonably accurate for several decades into the future.

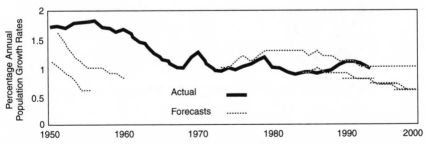

Figure 5.1b Forecast of population growth rates shows that demographers still miss the small turning points.

• The bigger the target, the better the accuracy, if for no other reason than that bigger areas even out the vagaries of migration. And so, forecast accuracy is higher for larger geographic areas.

Global population predictions are more accurate than predictions for individual countries, because the figures for individual countries are affected by migration. Whereas predictions of the world's population are reliable for four or more decades ahead, forecasts of the U.S. population are reliable only for two to three decades ahead. As shown in Figure 5.3, the forecast of the 1995 global population made in the 1960s is nearly right on target. Similarly, U.S. population predictions are four times more accurate than predictions of state populations, because state populations are affected by the migration of people from state to state. Population accuracy further degrades as you go from large counties to smaller ones, as demonstrated in Figure 5.4.[13]

The vagaries of local economies make predicting the populations of metropolitan areas and states unreliable. A client of mine from Houston once boasted in the early 1980s that the official bird of his state should be the crane, because of the heavy construction fueled by its booming oil economy. My home state of Massachusetts was struggling at the time, as many manufacturing operations either closed for good or quit the state that is sometimes called "Taxachusetts." A few years later

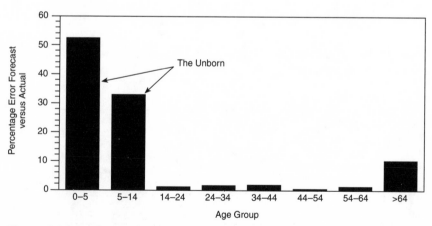

Figure 5.2   Predicting the population of age groups twenty years into the future is relatively accurate for age groups that were born at the time of the forecast.

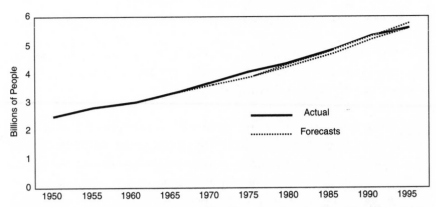

Figure 5.3 Forecasts of world population are accurate many decades into the future.

the petroleum market crashed, crippling the Houston economy and forcing many residents to find jobs elsewhere in the country. Meanwhile, high-tech industries in the Boston area started to resuscitate the Massachusetts economy. Presidential candidate Michael Dukakis called this his "Massachusetts Miracle," and he promised to apply his magic to revive the entire U.S. economy. Dukakis's miracle quickly became an embarrassment, though, when the Massachusetts economy crashed under the strains of massive layoffs by Digital, Data General, Wang, and other high-tech firms that failed to keep up with the rapidly evolving computer technology.

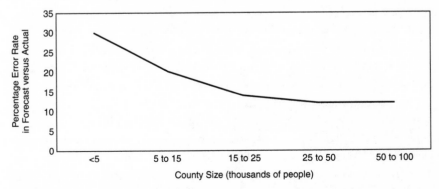

Figure 5.4 Errors in forecasting county population in the United States decrease with the size of the county.

A LOT OF ACCURACY, BUT NOT MUCH SKILL

Although population predictions are relatively accurate in the one- to two-decade range, population forecasters have the same skill limitations as their counterparts in other fields:

- They have no forecasting "skill," because their predictions are only as accurate as those made by simple, naive methods, such as using a ruler to extend past trends into the future.
- They are unable to predict turning points in any population components. (For example, they missed both the baby boom of 1947 to 1961 and the baby bust of the 1980s.)
- Their predictions are subject to situational bias, as their predictions reflect only the trends existing at the time they made their forecasts.
- They have made no progress in forecast accuracy during the six decades since track records have been maintained.

Leading academics who have studied past population forecasts have come to the same conclusion regarding the forecasters' limited skill. Dennis Ahlburg, a professor at the University of Minnesota, found that there is "no evidence that complex and/or sophisticated techniques produce more accurate or less biased forecasts than simple, naive techniques. . . . Expertise has been shown to add little to forecast accuracy."[14] Michael Stoto concluded that "simple projection techniques are more accurate than more complex techniques."[15] And Stanley Smith, a professor of economics at the University of Florida, has observed that complex models "have not led to greater accuracy in forecasting total population than can be achieved with simple, naive techniques."[16]

Forecaster error rates have nominally improved since 1970, primarily because the pre-1970 population was much more volatile than post-1970, creating the illusion of improved precision. Ahlburg came to the same conclusion from his research: "While some improvement in accuracy may be the product of changes in methodology, it is most likely that the forecasting task has become easier." Nor has demographers' understanding of population dynamics much improved over time. Keyfitz concluded: "The great volume of statistical information has contributed disappointing little to the discernment of a comprehensive causal system."[17]

The cohort component model used to predict populations is nothing more than a giant adding machine. The real challenge in population forecasting is predicting its key components: deaths, births, and migration. Leading demographers in academia and government confess that their forecasts are prone to error, and they readily admit that the forces shaping future populations—such as fertility, war, disease, and government policy—are completely unpredictable.

THE CALCULUS OF DEATH

Much about death is predictable. Actuaries can consult their mortality tables to determine when you and I are likely to die. Furthermore, the average life span of people living in developed countries has steadily increased throughout the entire twentieth century, as shown in Figure 5.5, which is the first of the very few persistent long-term trends covered in this book.

Life expectancy varies significantly around the world, with the lowest average life expectancies in the African countries of Sierra Leone and Guinea-Bissau, at thirty-nine and forty-three years, respectively; life expectancy is forty-three years in war-torn Afghanistan. The highest life expectancies are in Japan and Hong Kong, at seventy-nine and seventy-eight years, respectively. Average life expectancy can be a misleading

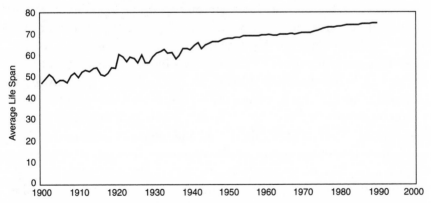

Figure 5.5 Life expectancy in the United States has predictably increased during the twentieth century.

statistic, however, masking the terrible scope of childhood death in places such as Africa. Half the newborns in Africa die by the age of twelve, mostly from disease, but most of those who escape death during childhood live relatively long lives and bring up the overall average life span. In contrast, only 2 percent of North Americans and Europeans die by the age of twelve.

Given the steadily improving human life span, demographers today can easily predict death rates many years into the future with a fair degree of accuracy, as shown in Figure 5.6. The standard error for death rate forecasts has been very low, averaging .03, which means that with an average death rate of ten people per thousand per year, the forecasts have a two-thirds chance of being within plus or minus .3 deaths per thousand people (10 × .03). Despite this high level of accuracy, however, demographers have little or no *skill* in predicting death rates; their forecasts are no better than forecasts generated by naive methods, such as using a ruler to extend past trends. Figure 5.6b, an enlarged detail of Figure 5.6a, shows that demographers have missed the various turning points in the death rates, especially the drop that occurred around 1970.

There is no guarantee, however, that human life spans and death rates will remain predictable. Scientists are only now beginning to understand the genetic mechanisms that cause cells to stop dividing after so many replications; someday they might discover a way to slow the process of aging. Conversely, there is no guarantee that death rates will not increase due to a resurgence in plaguelike diseases or diseases induced by industrial toxins.

In the 1970s, the medical community brashly predicted that it would conquer infectious diseases by the 1990s, which turned out to be another failed prediction. We now have more respect for the perennial danger of microorganisms, well expressed by plague expert and University of Chicago historian William McNeill: "Ingenuity, knowledge, and organization alter but cannot cancel humanity's vulnerability to invasion by parasitic forms of life."[18] In fact, death from infectious diseases has *increased* 58 percent since the 1980s, and infectious disease is now the third most frequent cause of death, after heart disease and cancer, up from fourth place a decade ago. New, frightening diseases such as HIV infection (the cause of AIDS), Lyme disease, ebola, and flesh-eating streptococcus A have recently emerged, and traditional ones such as tuberculosis have undergone a resurgence with the rise of new antibiotic-

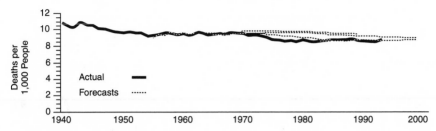

Figure 5.6a   The death rate in the United States is easy to predict because it changes little from year to year.

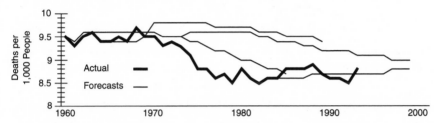

Figure 5.6b   An enlarged detail from Figure 5.6a shows that forecasters miss the turning points in predicting death rates.

resistant strains. Such new strains develop when a microorganism mutates during its replication process—a process that can occur as quickly as every twenty minutes—producing a version of itself that is no longer vulnerable to the antibiotic that had killed off its predecessor. It took only two years, for example, for the organisms that cause staph infections to become immune to penicillin. Some leading thinkers in biology and medicine, such as Nobel laureate Joshua Lederberg, now predict that people are becoming more susceptible to diseases than ever before, because microorganisms are evolving to become immune to modern medicine. Laurie Garrett, in her book *The Coming Plague,* predicts that AIDS is only the first in what will be a wave of modern epidemics.

With the emergence of AIDS in the early 1980s, everyone from medical experts to crackpots made apocalyptic predictions that it would quickly reach the dimensions of the fourteenth-century plague epidemic. One televangelist, David Jeremiah, claimed that AIDS "could kill more people than have died in all of the pestilences yet known to man."[19] Another televangelist, Jack van Impe, in his TV special "The

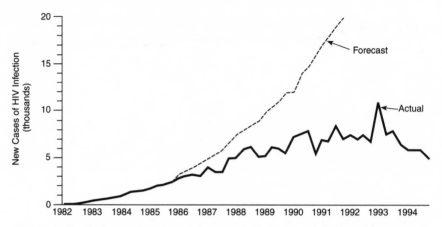

Figure 5.7 Early predictions of the HIV infection in the United States were greatly overstated.

AIDS Cover-Up," declared that AIDS will "make the Statue of Liberty the most expensive tombstone in history" and that the last human on earth could be dying from AIDS by the year 2020.[20] Some believers in the doomsday predictions of sixteenth-century physician and astrologer Nostradamus interpreted them to mean that half the world would be infected with AIDS by 1993 and that two-thirds of the world would succumb to the disease by 2000.[21] The media have sometimes fomented hysteria with their own predictions, and, as a result, public bathhouses were closed and children with AIDS were frequently prohibited from attending school.

Even U.S. health care experts got it wrong. In 1986, the Public Health Service, a division of the U.S. Health and Human Services, assembled a group of eighty-five experts to produce a five-year forecast for the spread of HIV. As shown in Figure 5.7, the number of new AIDS cases they predicted was far too high. Similarly, the Centers for Disease Control predicted that there would be 180,000 AIDS-related deaths in 1991, when in fact only 80,000 people died from AIDS-related infections that year. [22] In reviewing these predictions, David Bloom and Sherry Glied, professors at Columbia University, concluded that the experts "tended to overproject, often by sizable amounts, the number of AIDS cases in the United States."[23]

The experts overpredicted the incidence of AIDS because they extrapolated early trends in the AIDS outbreak when the incidence of the disease was small but growing exponentially. By definition, extrapolation always fails to predict turning points, such as the leveling off of HIV contagion that occurred in the late 1980s, due primarily to the testing of the nation's blood supply and to the practice of safer sex, especially among the gay community.[24] Although most of the developed world has so far avoided the worst-case scenario of the AIDS epidemic that had been forecast, the dire predictions are becoming fulfilled in parts of sub-Saharan Africa and other developing areas.

THE WILD CARD OF THE UNBORN

Forecasting future births, or what demographers call the "unborn," is the wild card in population prediction. The unpredictability of human fertility is demonstrated by the fact that demographers have routinely missed the major changes in U.S. population growth, as shown in Figure 5.8. Dennis Ahlburg has studied the accuracy of the Bureau of the Census's past birthrate forecasts and concluded, "The official forecasts failed to predict a single turning point in the series."[25] As Michael Stoto, a professor of public policy at Harvard, noted from his analysis of forecast track records, "In 1945 and 1950, the forecasters did not anticipate the baby boom, and after it began they did not realize it would not continue."[26] Afflicted with situational bias, demographers routinely extend into the future the population characteristics that prevailed at the time they made their forecasts, as most of the charts in this chapter show.

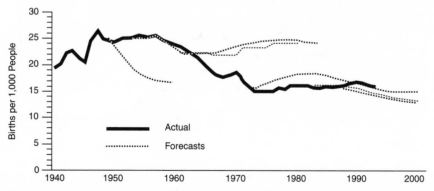

Figure 5.8 Demographers have consistently missed the turning points in predicting birthrates in the United States.

Ahlburg further observed that the Bureau of the Census's forecasts "tend to be heavily influenced by recent trends in fertility, mortality, and migration."[27]

Human fertility varies widely around the world, and the difference is especially great between developed and developing countries, which average 1.7 and 5.8 births per woman, respectively. Japan has the world's lowest fertility rate, at 1.5 births per woman, and Yemen has the highest, at 7.6 births per woman. The average for African nations as a whole is very high, at 6.3 births per woman.

The only consistent factor explaining differences in fertility is the use of contraceptives, as shown in Figure 5.9. In the absence of birth control, most human beings will produce as many children as nature will allow, just like any other animal. However, the use of birth control itself is unpredictable, as it is driven by many complex factors, such as education, women's rights, cultural norms, and religious doctrine.

Beyond the use of contraceptives, sociologists cannot scientifically explain how families decide how many children to have and when they plan to have them. In reviewing the academic literature attempting to explain fertility rates, sociologist John Hedderson found that "what is presented as theory is not that at all. Rather, they are correlations that occur often, but not consistently enough [to call them theories]."[28]

Attempts to make a science out of fertility prediction has produced

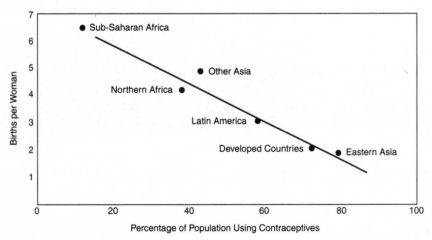

Figure 5.9   The use of contraceptives is a strong predictor of human fertility.

ludicrous results. For example, as recently as 1995, one sociologist theorized that children are the "commodity produced and consumed within the household [and that] wives with a high taste for children and a low taste for market-related activities (i.e., careers) will tend in general to seek and to receive less formal schooling than women with the opposite preference."[29] Other sociologists have theorized that families trade off having children with acquiring adult toys—trips, restaurants, and entertainment—and the more toys, the fewer the children. Others put forth the notion that the more education that women have, the fewer children they choose to bear.

Some of these fertility theories are amusing in their naiveté, and most are not statistically valid or universally applicable to all cultures. For example, the theory that the higher the woman's education, the fewer children she is likely to bear has been shown to be statistically invalid among white Americans. Fertility is deeply rooted in culture, and there may be as many partially valid theories about fertility as there are cultures and subcultures in the world.

THE BURGEONING LATE ARRIVALS

The last component of population forecasting is migration, the inflow and outflow of people from a particular geographic area. Migration is driven by complex circumstances, such as economic hardship, civil war, political oppression, discrimination, and governments' immigration policies, and it can be quite unpredictable. Who could have predicted that one-third of the Rwandan population would migrate to Zaire almost overnight. The U.S. Bureau of the Census believes that immigration cannot be predicted, as indicated by the following disclaimer accompanying one of its forecasts:

> Civilian immigration into [the] continental United States is determined largely by the relative level of economic conditions in [the] continental United States and in other areas and by the various laws controlling international migration. In view of the nature of these controlling factors, it is felt that allowances for future immigration cannot be arrived at by any extrapolation of past trends. Therefore, the immigration assumptions represent rather arbitrary choices.[30]

It is clear from Figure 5.10 that the Bureau of the Census does not much try to predict migration; it merely extends into the future the rates of migration that exist at the time it makes its forecasts. Before 1950, when migration into the United States was low, the errors made by the Bureau of the Census were small. Since then, however, migration has rapidly increased, and the Bureau of the Census has continually underestimated the migration rates, often substantially. For example, in 1982 it projected that net migration in the United States in the mid-1990s would be about 450,000 people per year, and it turned out to be closer to 1 million people per year.

And the Bureau of the Census missed one of the biggest turning points in American demography: a resurgence of legal and illegal immigrants, especially from Mexico and Central America and from Asia. In 1949 the bureau stated that immigrants were of "relatively minor importance insofar as their effect on the school age population of the future is concerned."[31] How quickly things change. The Immigration and Naturalization Service "conservatively" estimated in 1995 that "each year 300,000 to 400,000 [illegal aliens] slip into the country permanently."[32] Conservative indeed. The U.S. Border Patrol arrested 358,194 aliens along the Mexican border during the first quarter of 1995 alone. If for every arrest at least one other alien successfully enters the United States, then at least a million Mexicans and Central Americans have managed to get north of the Rio Grande every year since 1995.[33]

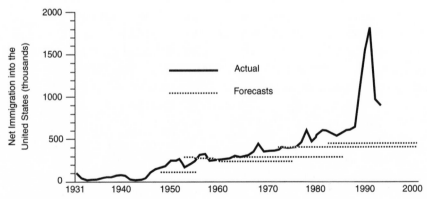

Figure 5.10   The Bureau of Census has consistently underestimated future immigration into the United States.

STANDING ROOM ONLY

Given population momentum and the relative accuracy of population forecasting, here are two seemingly safe predictions. First, the United Nations (U.N.) predicts that world population will grow from 5.6 billion people today to about 12 billion in the middle of the next century. This number is based on the simple math of population growth: today's population includes several billion females who will reach childbearing age in the next two decades, and these future mothers live in developing countries where birthrates are very high. The world's population is growing exponentially. As shown in Figure 5.11, it was not until around the year 1830 that the human population reached 1 billion; today we add 1 billion more people *every decade.*

World population growth is almost entirely a phenomenon of the developing world, as shown in Figure 5.12. Between 1990 and 1995, 88 percent of the people added to the world were in Africa or Asia. In contrast, the developed world will maintain its slow-growing populations. Some developed countries already have birthrates that are at or below replacement levels.

Surely there are events that could derail the U.N.'s prediction for world population growth, but such events seem implausible. A global nuclear war, widespread famine, or incurable plagues could curb the population explosion, but for the population to stabilize completely, hundreds of millions of people would have to die every year in an unimaginable string of catastrophes. Similarly, the success of global

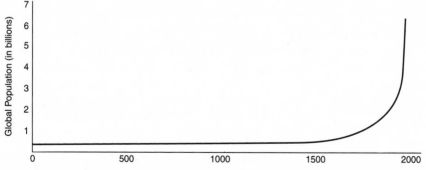

Figure 5.11 World population remained flat for eons until exponential growth took off in the past two hundred years.

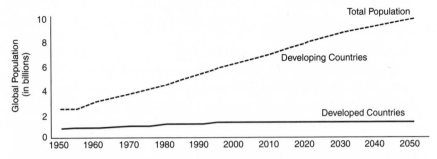

Figure 5.12   Exponential population growth is occurring only in developing countries.

efforts to influence women to have smaller families also seems doubt-
ful, if past efforts are any indication. For example, in September 1994
the U.N. held a conference on population control, which prompted vicious attacks from the Vatican and from Islamic leaders. The latter called
it the "licentiousness conference" and claimed that it was an imperial-
istic plot to destroy Islam.

The second prediction is that the population explosion in the developing world will spill over into the developed world as growing
masses attempt to flee their impoverished countries. Developed countries will no doubt try to contain the immigration explosion—but how
successful will they be when the population of the developing world
more than doubles and there are 6 billion more people pounding at the
gates? Given the thousands of miles of mostly unguarded U.S. borders,
illegal immigration into the United States seems likely to escalate beyond anything experienced thus far. And when that happens, the nation's racial complexion will change dramatically. The existing U.S.
population is predominantly non-Hispanic white and has a birthrate that
is nearly at replacement levels. In contrast, legal and illegal immigration
is escalating each year, especially Hispanic peoples from Mexico and
Central America, who have much higher birthrates than the resident
U.S. population. In 1994, for the first time, more Hispanic people were
added to the U.S. population (through immigration and domestic
births) than non-Hispanic whites.

One of the biggest questions we face today is whether the planet can
support the 12 billion people that the U.N. predicts for the year 2050.
Demographers call this limit "earth's carrying capacity," a concept

meaning how many people the planet can support before starvation, exhaustion of nonrenewable resources, and/or poisoning through pollution imposes limits to further population growth. What is the carrying capacity of the planet has been debated for more than 350 years and is much alive today. On one side of the debate is the International Food Policy Research Institute, which optimistically believes that the world will have no problem feeding 12 billion people in 2050. Conversely, doomsayer Paul Ehrlich predicts that if world population reaches even 10 billion, it's "going to resemble a cinder, if it survives at all."[34]

WILL THERE BE FEAST OR FAMINE?

The most famous doomsayer of overpopulation was Thomas Robert Malthus (1766–1834), an economics professor and ordained pastor. For the past two hundred years, the popular adjective "malthusian" has connoted a horrific scene of famine, death, pestilence, war, and/or societal collapse caused by overpopulation. Malthus came of age in an era when intellectuals believed that large populations were advantageous; after all, the strongest, wealthiest, and "happiest" nations seemed to be those with large and growing populations. It was a time of growing optimism, with widespread belief that humanity was entering an age of reason characterized by the rise of egalitarian institutions and enlightenment, and (according to the most liberal thinkers) the elimination of social classes.

Into this optimistic setting, Malthus cast his bombshell, his 1798 book, *Essay on the Principle of Populations As It Affects the Future Improvement of Society*. Malthus stated that nature firmly controls all animal populations and that it controls the human population through cycles of famine, sickness, death, and misery that especially afflicts the poor. As Robert Heilbroner writes in his book, *The Worldly Philosophers*, Malthus "perished at one blow all the fond hopes of a harmonious universe. . . . [He] pulled the carpet from under the feet of the complacent thinkers of the times, and what he offered them in place of progress was a prospect meager, dreary, and chilling."[35]

Malthus started his argument with two of the safest possible assumptions: "Food is necessary to the existence of man" and "the passion between the sexes is necessary and will remain nearly in its present state." From here, he deduced his famous hypothesis: "Population, when unchecked, increases in a geometrical ratio [while] . . . subsistence increases only in an arithmetical ratio." Malthus derived this notion from his observation that British couples before the age of twenty-five had six children, four of whom survived, thus doubling the original two that created them, *and* from his assumption that increasing food production could come from only the slow process of clearing more land for agricultural purposes. He concluded that human breeding inevitably outstrips available food production. According to Malthus's model, if you start with one unit of people and one unit of food, the people units would grow exponentially (1, 2, 4, 8, 16, 32, etc.), while the food units would grow only linearly (1, 2, 3, 4, 5, 6, etc.). He thus foresaw that "premature death must in some shape or other visit the human race . . . war of extermination, sickly seasons, epidemics, pestilence, and plague . . . sweep off their thousands [and if these fail] famine seems to be the last, the most dreadful resource of nature."[46] Malthus also proposed tough cures to control excess population: not safe sex but no sex at all, or at least greatly deferred sex through late marriages. He inveighed against birth control, calling it the "improper arts to conceal the consequences of irregular connections."[37]

Malthus's notion that nature culls the human race through famine, sickness, and death was wholly inconsistent with the Enlightenment view of humanity. He was attacked for decades for holding such views. His biographer, James Bonar, said he was "the best abused man of his age. . . . For thirty years it rained refutations."[38] Liberals vilified Malthus because he blamed the population problem on the poorer classes. Karl Marx called him "the contemptible Malthus: a shameless sycophant of the ruling classes" and condemned his work as a "sin against science."[39]

Malthus's predictions about the linear growth in food supply proved to be wrong—so far at least—for he failed to foresee the "green revolution." In his day, the only way to increase food supply was to cultivate more land, a slow, linear process. Since the beginning of the twentieth century, agricultural technology has greatly boosted food productivity through the use of fertilizers, pesticides, mechanized farm equipment, irrigation, antibiotics for animals, and, more recently, genetic engineering. Increased farm productivity over the past fifty years has caused food prices to plummet continually, especially between 1975 to 1995, when they dropped 40 percent. Although the U.N.'s Food and

Agricultural Organization (FAO) estimates that fifteen countries in Africa today require emergency food assistance to prevent massive famine, the problem so far has not been a global shortage of food but rather the fact that these impoverished countries cannot afford to import food.

The FAO's optimistic food forecasts may prove dangerously wrong, however. In 1994, for example, the FAO (and the World Bank) predicted that China would remain self-sufficient in meeting its need for grains. The next year, however, China started importing rice as its rapidly growing middle class started switching from a diet based mainly on rice to one that includes meat, and meat is an inefficient way to feed a hungry world (it takes four pounds of grain, for example, to produce just one pound of pork). According to Ed Ayres, editorial director at the Worldwatch Institute, China's importation of grains could trigger a "food crisis worldwide. China has 20 percent of the world's population, and if it were to increase its demand for grain in the years ahead, the total world demand for imported grain might exceed the entire export capacity of the world, leaving every other importer short. This raises the whole question of how are many people going to eat."[40]

The Worldwatch Institute has been critical of the FAO and World Bank food forecasts. Ayres told me that "the FAO and the World Bank forecasts are the linchpins of public policy and corporate planning for industries concerned about agricultural trade, but their forecasts were demonstrably wrong. Government and business planners were using fallacious information, because the FAO and World Bank forecasts were mere extrapolations of past trends; they didn't analyze the factors that actually drive the demand for food."[41]

Now, in the late 1990s, certain malthusian predictions are starting to sound plausible. Not only is world population growing exponentially, but so is per capita consumption of food in developing countries. Furthermore, a host of problems are hampering food production. Cropland is shrinking due to desertification, topsoil erosion, increased salinity due to decades of heavy irrigation, and the development of farm property into shopping malls, industrial parks, and housing tracts. Irrigation consumes 75 percent of the world's fresh water, which is becoming scarce. Water tables are plunging by as much as ten feet per year in some areas of the world, such as Mexico City and parts of India, and pollution is poisoning aquifers. Viruses, fungi, and insects that plague farm animals and plants are becoming resistant to the chemicals historically used to control them. Meanwhile, breeding and cultivation have created farm animals and plants that are more genetically alike, increasing the threat of an infestation that will wipe out the vast majority of crops at once.

Technology could take the green revolution to new heights, eliminating our current concerns about food production. For example, "precision farming" uses satellites to enable farmers to dispense fertilizers and pesticides only to those areas that need them, thereby reducing the chemical degradation of the environment. Genetic engineering offers enormous potential to improve food production. Geneticists are engineering varieties of barley that resist viral diseases, self-fertilizing corn with roots that fix nitrogen into the soil, and tomatoes that resist cold weather because they have acquired a special gene from a flounder. These are just a few of the possibilities. Who knows what future developments are on the horizon?

ARE WE RUNNING OUT OF GAS?

They called themselves the Club of Rome: a group of thirty noted scientists, economists, humanists, industrialists, and government officials who in 1968 gathered in Rome to discuss "the present and future predicament of man."[42] Acting independent of any political group, the Club of Rome published the most controversial malthusian prediction of the twentieth century in its best-selling book, *The Limits to Growth:* "If the present growth trends in world population, industrialization, pollution, food production, and resource depletion continue unchanged, the limits to growth on this planet will be reached sometime within the next one hundred years. The most probable result will be a rather sudden and uncontrollable decline in both population and industrial capacity."[43] The Club of Rome essentially predicted an Easter Island disaster on a global scale.

Like Malthus, the Club of Rome was concerned about exponential population growth, but it also probed the implications of escalating industrial activity, consumption of nonrenewable resources, and increasing pollution. It hired a group of MIT professors who used an elaborate computer model, World 3, to predict the ultimate limitations of human activity on the planet. To its credit, the Club of Rome tried to avoid sensationalism by omitting specific dates for their predicted societal collapse; however, these dates can be extracted from the many graphs contained in *The Limits to Growth*. According to the Club of Rome's prediction, serious problems will begin to emerge in 2010, when nonrenewable resources will become scarce and costly, causing industrial and agricultural output to decline. World population will eventually peak at 10 billion people in the year 2050 and then plummet to 5 billion by 2060, meaning that at least 5 billion people (about equivalent to today's global population) would die in the space of ten years. By the year 2100, our industrial base will collapse to a point where it would be equivalent to what it was in preindustrial times, making adequate food production impossible. Indeed, it would be difficult to feed *today's* population if we had to do it using preindustrial technology.

In 1990, the leaders of the MIT research team reexamined their earlier predictions and published their findings in *Beyond the Limits*. The book's message, which is already clear from its title, is this:

> The human world is beyond its limits. The present way of doing things is unsustainable. . . . Human use of many essential resources . . . [has] already surpassed rates that are physically sustainable. Without significant reductions in material and energy flows, there will be in the coming decades an uncontrolled decline in per capita food output, energy use, and industrial production.[44]

In updating their predictions, the authors found that doomsday has moved up two decades from 2050 to 2030, because we have done little to correct our exponential growth in population and industrialization. But they concluded that there is still time to save ourselves. Although some options have closed since the first book came out, others have emerged due to new technologies that could not have been anticipated in 1970.

The Limits to Growth opened many eyes to the future dilemma of unchecked growth in human activity. Inevitably, it also drew criticism, including a book entitled *Thinking About the Future: A Critique of The Limits to Growth*. The authors of *A Critique* stated that the Club of Rome's assumptions were too pessimistic, the underlying data were weak, and the model lacked proved laws and instead relied on "statistical guesses."[45]

A Critique makes some valid points: the Club of Rome's predictions underestimated the reserves of oil and other nonrenewable resources while overestimating the population of the world in the year 2000 by 13 percent (7 billion predicted, versus the 6.2 billion that seems more realistic today).

Although some of its specific predictions may have been wrong, the overall message of *The Limits to Growth* is simply unassailable: our planet's ecosystem has obvious limits that cannot support the exponential growth in human activity forever. This is no different from predicting that your car will eventually run out of gas if you fail to refill it. However, I question the prediction of sudden societal collapse. What seems more plausible is that human activity will be constrained earlier and more gradually, and that solutions will emerge when the problems become sufficiently acute. Some solutions may be novel, such as substituting renewable for nonrenewable resources; others may force changes in our lifestyles to curtail our escalating consumption of resources.

HAZARDOUSLY WASTED?

In 1962, an intrepid fifty-year-old marine biologist named Rachel Carson wrote *Silent Spring,* which explained how industrial and agricultural pollution was ruining the environment and endangering human health. Industrial leaders attacked her with the same vengeance that eighteenth-century liberals attacked Malthus. The chemical industry attempted to keep her book from being published and launched a massive smear campaign portraying her as "an ignorant and hysterical woman who wanted to turn the earth over to the insects."[46] However, the attack on Carson backfired; it enhanced her book's success and spawned the environmental movement in the United States. Ever since, dire pollution predictions have proliferated, contained in books like *The Dying Sea, AIR Scare, Epitaph for Planet Earth, Our Drowning World,* and *How to Survive in America the Poisoned,* among others. *How to Survive in America the Poisoned* illustrates the typical prediction of toxic terror: "In the long run, what may be at stake . . . is the very integrity of the human race. . . . Only the magnitude of the impending tragedy . . . remains to be seen."[47]

The Club of Rome explored a second scenario in its world simulation: What would happen to future societies if they did not run out of nonrenewable resources—the factor limiting population growth in the base scenario? For example, what would happen if future generations had endless access to fuels and other nonrenewable resources? Under the new scenario, the computer model indicated that world population would peak at 10 billion people in 2050 but then would plunge to 1.2 billion, or about the same human population estimated to have existed in 1850. This time, the culprit was an exponential rise in pollution and the resulting escalation in the death rate.

One of the most controversial predictions circulating today is that air pollution will cause the earth's climate to warm up, melting the polar ice caps and inundating much of the world's population that lives in coastal areas. Theoretically, global warming is caused by the "greenhouse effect," whereby the accumulation of carbon dioxide and methane in the atmosphere traps heat from sunlight, similar to the way that glass traps heat in greenhouses. Ironically, before the idea of global warming was proposed, most climatic doomsayers predicted that we were overdue for another ice age. Examples of ice age predictions include books such as Ephron's *The End* and the strangely secretive Impact Team's *The Weather Conspiracy: The Coming of the Ice Age,* as well as articles in popular magazines such as *Newsweek*'s "Return of the Glaciers" in 1992 and *Time*'s "The Ice Age Cometh?" in 1994.[48] Typically, these doomsayers have based their forecasts on the false notion that ice ages come and go in periodic cycles. Ice ages do come and go in cycles, but they are cycles of changing and *unpredictable* frequency.

The idea of global warming has some firm scientific foundations. Scientists have proved that carbon dioxide and other greenhouse gases trap solar radiation and that these greenhouse gases are growing exponentially in our atmosphere. By examining air samples from thousands of years ago trapped in glacial ice, scientists have also concluded that the warmest periods in the past have been those times with high concentrations of carbon dioxide. Despite these compelling facts, however, there is no statistical proof that the earth's atmosphere is actually getting warmer, as is reflected in the American Meteorological Society's official statement on global warming: "Observations suggest, but are insufficient to prove, that atmospheric warming caused by human activities has already occurred."[49]

One very plausible explanation for the as-yet-unfulfilled global warming prediction is that there is a counterbalancing cooling effect from pollutants that cause acid rain, such as sulfur dioxide from coal-burning power plants, because they reflect sunlight in the upper atmosphere. The climatic impact of volcanoes spewing forth vast amounts of sulfur dioxide provide strong anecdotal support for this cooling effect. In 1815, the eruption of Mount Tambora in the Pacific is believed to have caused the "little ice age" in 1816, during which ponds in New England stayed frozen all year long. More recently, the 1991 eruption of Mount Pinatubo in the Philippines is believed to have cooled the earth's climate for several years. The ironic twist is that if we get rid of acid rain by cleaning up sulfur dioxide emissions, we may see the fulfillment of the global warming predictions.

In effect, no one knows when or if global warming will take place and what the consequences will be for human activity around the world. There is even debate about whether global warming is good or bad. For example, Thomas Moore, a senior fellow at Stanford's Hoover Institution, suggests that "evidence and theory suggest that global warming would in general be beneficial for mankind. Agriculture and some services might actually benefit. An examination of the record of the last twelve millennia reveals that mankind prospered during the warm periods and suffered during the cold ones."[50] With so much uncertainty surrounding global warming predictions, it is not surprising that little has been done to curtail greenhouse gases.

THE HIGH PRICE OF SUCCESS

With modern medicine, we began to beat microorganisms, especially in the past fifty years. The high price of our success over other species, however, is our exponentially growing population and the exponential decline of other species on earth. Nature abhors exponential growth and eventually contains it. At some point, natural forces will somehow curb our exploding population. The only questions are when and how. Will it occur when world population reaches 8 billion? 12 billion? more? Perhaps the fate of the developing world will be massive famine and disease far beyond what Malthus could have envisioned, and beyond the help of the developed nations. Perhaps the fate of the rich developed world will be increased sickness, death, infertility, and other afflictions caused by the industrial pollution that accompanies our extravagant lifestyle.

Although predictions of a societal collapse on a global scale may seem unrealistic, such collapses have already happened: to the Easter Islanders, Mayans, Khmers, Anasazi, and perhaps many other vanished civilizations. Easter Island, in particular, is a powerful metaphor for planet earth. Unlike in Malthus's time, when 20 million hungry British escaped to North America, Australia, and South Africa, today we have no place to go; there are no unexploited areas that we could invade, and for the foreseeable future we cannot escape earth, if for no other reason than we have yet to find another habitable place in the universe.

However, our future could be positively shaped by global cooperation and advanced technology—two highly uncertain forces. Except for banning the ozone-depleting chlorofluorocarbons by ninety-two countries in 1990, though, global cooperation has failed miserably to address our major ecological problems, including excessive population growth, escalating greenhouse gases, and the destruction of rain forests and the millions of life forms that inhabit them.

Technology may solve many of our problems, and who knows what the limits of food production may be with advanced technologies such as genetic engineering. As you will see in the next chapter, however, technological progress is anything but certain—or predictable.

6

Science Fact and Fiction

The mind-boggling leaps in technology that have been achieved over the past fifty years have fostered our high-tech visions of the future. Older generations have witnessed the advent of the computer, the laser, television, atomic energy, manned space travel, and radar. Today, younger ones are witnessing the explosion in information technologies and genetic engineering. One example of the pace of technological change during the past fifty years is the miniaturization of electronics. It is estimated that during World War II there were about 1 billion vacuum tubes in operation around the world, powering radios, radar systems, and any other form of what was then advanced electronics. These vacuum tubes put end to end would have spanned the globe approximately four times and weighed about 200,000 tons. These days, the same electronic capability embedded in microelectric circuitry could be delivered by 182 Intel Pentium Pro chips, each carrying 5.5 million transistors, and all 182 chips would easily fit inside a single shoe box.

Widespread fascination with future technology, however, is a recent phenomenon in human history. It is hard for us to believe that the notion of steady technological progress was not envisioned by the general populace until about 1800. Before then, there had been little innovation to inspire the imagination of the public, and almost no fictional speculation on such topics. Although the steam engine had been invented in the 1770s (and a more primitive one seventy years earlier), until 1800 most mills, ships, and carriages were still powered by animals, wind, and water, much as in the days of ancient Greece and Rome. People saw the future as a mere extension of the present.

There were a few exceptional people with creative minds who envisioned future technology in earlier times. In 1260, Roger Bacon, a medieval monk who dabbled in philosophy, science, and mathematics, predicted that there would be flying machines and carlike devices that were "made so that without animals they will move with unbelievable rapidity."[1] In 1500, Leonardo da Vinci's sketches of helicopter-like flying machines and other devices anticipated future technology. These creative thinkers, however, had no broad or lasting impact on society's futuristic thinking.

Instead, we had to experience technological progress first before we could foresee it happening in the future (another example of situational bias at work). Figure 6.1 illustrates how scientific discoveries have led to innovations, which in turn inspired science fiction—the first form of technology forecasting produced for a mass public. Inventions such as the hot-air balloon signaled that air (or perhaps even space) travel was possible; the steam engine showed that sources of power were not restricted to animals, wind, and water.

The first science-fiction novel was *The Year 2400,* written by Sebastien Mercier in 1770. However, it was not until Jules Verne began writing science fiction a hundred years later that the genre became popular. Inventions of the day influenced him and other science-fiction

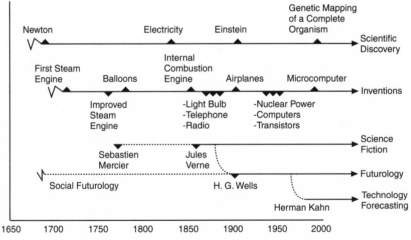

Figure 6.1   The evolution of technology forecasting.

writers. The invention of the balloon inspired Verne to write *Around the World in 80 Days* and possibly *From the Earth to the Moon*. In our own time, science fact still influences science fiction; for example, advances in genetic engineering inspired Michael Crichton to write *Jurassic Park*. But there is also some evidence that fiction has influenced science, such as nineteenth-century Russian rocket scientist Konstantin Tsiolkovsky's admission that "the first seeds of the idea [for rockets] were sown by that great, fantastic author, Jules Verne."[2]

Science fiction later spawned science prediction. In 1900, science-fiction writer H. G. Wells, author of *The Time Machine* (1895) and *The War of the Worlds* (1897), became a "futurist" when, in 1901, he wrote *Anticipations of the Reaction of Mechanical and Scientific Progress upon Human Life and Thought* in which he made the distinction that "hitherto such forecasts have been presented almost invariably in the form of fiction."[3] Although the term "futurology" was not coined until the 1940s, Wells is the true father of modern futurology, which incorporates predictions of technological progress in visions of future society. For clarity, I have defined "futurists" as those who predict the impact of future technology and other trends on the future of society and for whom technology is only one of several elements that contribute to advances in the way we live.

In the 1950s, technological innovation took a quantum leap with the introduction of the computer, laser, transistor, television, space travel, commercial nuclear energy, and many other technological achievements. Technology forecasting emerged soon after as a specialized field in the 1960s. Although interest in futurology may have peaked by the 1980s, science fiction and technology forecasting are more popular today than ever.

HIGH-TECH ANXIETY

Today the constantly increasing pace of technological innovation has become a high-stakes game with millions of jobs and national prosperity and defense at risk. As Japan got the upper hand in a number of high-tech industries such as consumer electronics, whole companies and industries in the United States have essentially vanished. Every high-tech firm in the United States has competitors all over the world trying to overtake it in the marketplace. Even the enormously successful company Intel, which makes and sells most of the microprocessors found inside personal computers (PCs), stays ahead only one product release at a time. If it misses a beat, it will be in trouble.

The scale of the technology game is enormous. In the United States alone, the amount of money spent by government and industry on technological research is approximately $160 billion each year, about the size of the entire Swedish economy. There are 2.5 million scientists working in thousands of corporate, university, and government labs. The federal government itself has 700 labs engaged in scientific research, much of it still defense related. There are 33 million patents in the world, and 1 million are added each year. Patented inventions, in fact, are only a fraction of the innovations created; an enormous number of technological concepts, ideas, inventions, and prototypes are developed or occur outside the patent process.

The risk in investing in new technologies is enormous, and failed technology ventures can cost hundreds of millions of dollars. Failure, in fact, is the norm, not the exception. Although new product failure rates probably vary by industry, surveys by the market research firm Datamonitor and the newsletter *New Product News* show that an average of about 80 percent of new products fail to become a commercial success.[4] Those that do succeed are increasingly threatened with rapid technological obsolescence as product life cycles become ever shorter. Just months or even weeks after you unpack your new PC, it will probably become outmoded by the release of even cheaper, more powerful models.

Given the massive risks associated with technological developments, it is not surprising that technological forecasting has become a sizable practice involving governments, scientists and engineers, securities analysts, trade associations, gurus, futurists, think tanks, consultants of all types, and firms selling off-the-rack technology forecasts. Their clients include businesses determining how to allocate their research and development budgets, which technology-based businesses to pursue, and which technologies they should adopt to upgrade their production processes and information technology; investors seeking to capitalize on new technology opportunities; and governments and foundations assessing how to spend their research grant funds.

Figure 6.2 illustrates the flow of technology forecasts in the form of

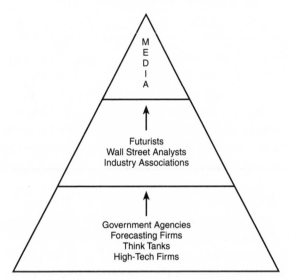

Figure 6.2 The flow of technology forecasts.

a pyramid, starting with expert predictions and leading eventually to popularization in the media, which continually floods us with technology prognostications. Forecasts originate at the bottom of the pyramid, from a large group of "experts," including scientists and others working on various projects and government-sponsored studies at think tanks such as the Rand Corporation, as well as at universities and corporate labs. The "experts" also include the many technology-predicting gurus such as Marvin Cetron, the president of Forecasting International, and Owen Davies, the former senior editor of *Omni* magazine, and numerous commercial firms that specialize in a particular industry—for example, Frost & Sullivan, International Data Corporation, Dataquest, Forester, Gartner Group, Meta, and BIS. All of these experts advise their clients on how to navigate their way through the technology industry's perils.

In the next tier are the packagers of technology forecasts, including trade associations, Wall Street analysts, and futurists. These organizations cannot afford to employ expert forecasters and so usually either borrow or buy forecasts from the experts. For example, the Information Technology Industries Association hires International Data Corporation to prepare its forecast of key trends in the computer industry, which it repackages and sells to each of its customers for a nice $250.

The news media are the capstone of the technological forecasting pyramid. Predictions of technological change help sell newspapers and television time, and over the past three decades the most respected media have flooded us with high-profile stories, such as "Where the Industries of the '70s Will Come From," "The New World of Super-conductivity," and "Dentistry's Brave New World." Except for a handful of well-known science journalists, media producers have limited technical expertise and rely on the packagers and experts for their material, giving technological predictions an air of validity that is often unwarranted.

The largest technology forecaster in the world is the Japanese government. As early as the 1960s, Japan's Ministry of International Trade and Industry (MITI), the chief strategist for that nation's program of export warfare, developed long-term technology forecasts for the use of Japanese industry. Today, no other entity or organization comes close to the Japanese government in terms of seriousness and scope of effort, which starts at the highest levels in government and extends throughout Japanese government agencies and industry, as illustrated in Figure 6.3. Technology forecasting in Japan starts with the Science and Technology Agency (STA), which reports to the prime minister's office. Under its Institute for Future Technology, the STA conducts an extensive long-range technology forecasting study every five years, as it has done since 1972. Its 1992 long-range forecast involved a panel of 3,000 Japanese scientists, engineers, and experts from multiple fields working together to address more than a thousand futuristic topics and to project the emergence of major new technologies. This is certainly the single largest forecasting event in human history, as of this writing.

MITI uses the STA predictions as part of an intricately orchestrated effort to direct Japanese R&D investments and product development into what they believe will be the most promising future markets. Industry groups and associations, such as the automobile-manufacturing and electronic industries, also undertake their own technology forecasting. One group, the Japan Industrial Robot Association, has sponsored a study of the future of personal robots, which, like PCs, support people in their daily lives. And so the forecasting cascades down to the company level in a coordinated manner, with a centrally directed research agenda and systematized information sharing.

A number of economists have credited much of Japan's commercial

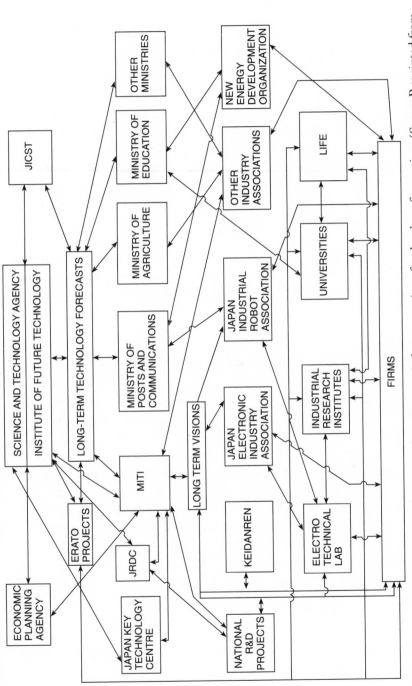

Figure 6.3 Overview of Japan's coordinated government industry practice of technology forecasting. (*Source*: Reprinted from D. Bowonder and T. Miyke, *Technology Forecasting in Japan*, *Futures*, September 1993, p. 765; copyright © 1993; with kind permission from Elsevier Science Ltd., The Boulevard, Langford Lane, Kidlington OX5 1GB, UK.)

success to this massive forecasting initiative. Two who have studied the existing research on Japan's efforts in this area, B. Bowonder, a professor at the Administrative College in India, and T. Miyake, an economist at ESCAP in Bangkok, concluded that "the strong linkages between technological forecasting, long-term planning, project selection and technology information support help Japanese organizations to plan the future with greater clarity."[5] There is no effort in the United States comparable to Japan's elaborate technology forecasting machine. In fact, industrial collaboration is illegal in the United States without special exemptions from antitrust laws, and many U.S. politicians and policy analysts see government-sponsored technology forecasting and other forms of industrial policy as misdirected, and even dangerous, efforts to control commercial events that are best left to the marketplace to resolve. Is this another case of Japan's industrial superiority over the West, or are they just fooling themselves? The soundness of technology forecasting and its track record answer this question.

THE DARK ART OF TECHNOLOGY FORECASTING

A host of analytic tools are used in the technology forecasting trade (see Figure 6.4).[6] These include brainstorming techniques such as the Delphi method and nominal group process; trend extrapolation techniques such as S-curves, trend analysis, and correlation analysis; analytic techniques such as cross-impact analysis, analytic hierarchy process, and relevance trees; simulation techniques such as systems dynamics; scenario development; and analysis of real-world situations where technology is being used in new ways via the case study method and lead-user analysis. Despite their fancy names, these techniques are useless in predicting the most significant events in the evolution of technology.

Two particular techniques warrant further explanation, given their popularity. The first is the S-curve trend analysis of technology development, illustrated in Figure 6.5. The theory behind the S-curve is that all technologies go through three predictable phases in their development: an initial slow period of growth as the new technology is not well understood, a middle period of exponential growth where the technology is a proved success and sells like hotcakes, and a final period

Delphi method: a brain-storming session with a panel of experts.

Nominal group process: a variant of the Delphi method with a group leader.

Case study method: an analysis of analogous developments in other technologies.

Trend analysis: the use of statistical analysis to extend past trends into the future.

S-curve: a form of trend analysis using an S-shaped curve to extend past trends into the future.

Correlation analysis: the projection of the development of a new technology using past developments in similar technologies.

Lead-user analysis: the analysis of leading-edge users of a new technology to predict how the technology will develop.

Analytic hierarchy process: the projection of a new technology by analyzing a hierarchy of forces influencing its development.

Systems dynamics: the use of a detailed model to assess the dynamic relationships among the major forces influencing the development of the technology.

Cross-impact analysis: the analysis of potentially interrelated future events that may affect the future development of a technology.

Relevance trees: the breakdown of goals for a technology into more detailed goals and then assigning probabilities that the technology will achieve these detail goals.

Scenario writing: the development of alternative future views on how the new technology could be used.

Figure 6.4   Major techniques for technological forecasting.

where the technology has penetrated the market and has fewer and fewer new applications. Supposedly all you need to predict the future is to draw the curve and plot your position on it, and the future course of the technology is instantly revealed.

The good news for forecasters is that most technologies do follow the S-curve in their development. However, this is somewhat of a tautology, because everything seems to go through S-shaped stages of birth, growth, and decline. The bad news is that it's hard to predict the size and shape of the S-curve with respect to how large the market will ultimately become and how quickly it will develop. Mistakes in these two estimates can create massive forecasting errors five or more years ahead. That is why the S-curve is most useful in forecasting established technologies for which the growth trajectories are better established, but even in these cases, accurate prediction is never certain. Also, there is no way that this S-curve tool will ever predict a new breakthrough

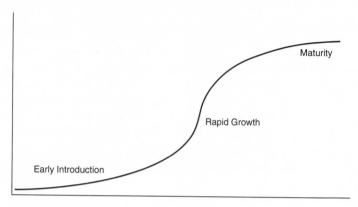

Figure 6.5   Predicting technological growth via the S-curve.

technology; that is where the Delphi method is supposed to come into play.

Named after the ancient Greek oracle, the Delphi method was invented in 1948 by several researchers at the Rand Corporation think tank to improve the accuracy of using expert predictions for policy-making. The Delphi method involves asking a panel of experts to make various predictions, either by mail or computer and with full or partial anonymity. The Delphi study team compiles the responses, determines the most common predictions, and sends them back to the experts for their reactions. During the second round, the experts can modify their answers or, if they have voiced a minority opinion, provide reasons that they deviate from the most common predictions. Multiple rounds are conducted until some degree of consensus prediction is reached.

The Rand Corporation conducted fourteen Delphi studies between 1950 and 1963, mostly of a secretive nature for the U.S. Defense Department. Use of the Delphi method spread beyond the Rand Corporation in the mid-1960s, becoming a popular tool for using experts to make predictions. TRW used the Delphi method in its 1966 study, Probe of the Future, employing a panel of twenty-seven top scientists to predict future developments in technology and other aspects of society. Japan's elaborate STA-sponsored study of future technologies conducted every five years employs the Delphi method on a large scale, involving thousands of scientists and other experts. However, in an extensive analysis of past studies using the Delphi method, Fred Woudenberg, an experimental psychologist, concluded in 1991 that "no evidence was found to support the view that [the] Delphi [method] is more accurate than other judgment methods. . . . Consensus is achieved mainly by group pressure to conformity."[7]

The experts place a lot of faith in their methods and stress the importance of picking the right ones for the right occasion. Reuven R. Levary and Dongchui Han have declared that "a good choice of a forecasting method in a particular situation could affect the accuracy of the forecast and, conceivably, the ability of a firm or government to compete in today's global economy."[8] Others believe that advances in developing forecasting tools will help avoid past errors. According to Joseph Coates, president of the J. F. Coates, Inc. consulting firm specializing in the studies of the future, "The tools for probing the future have matured so much in the last three decades that these errors are largely avoidable in any serious look at the future."[9] Let's take a look at how well the experts and their tools have foreseen future technology.

PROMISES, PROMISES

Analysis of the track record of forecasters over the past several decades shows that their long-term technology predictions have been wrong about 80 percent of the time. Such was the finding of Steven Schnaars, author of *Megamistakes: Forecasting and the Myth of Rapid Technological Change* and an associate professor of marketing at Baruch College, in a study of forecasts published between 1959 and 1989 in the *Wall Street Journal,* the *New York Times, Business Week, Fortune, Forbes, Time,* and *Newsweek.* Schnaars also evaluated technology forecasts made by the high-tech manufacturer TRW, Herman Kahn, and *Industrial Research* magazine. Evaluating the predictions in TRW's 1966 study, Probe of the Future, he found that "nearly every prediction was wrong."[10] Herman Kahn, a popular futurist in the 1960s and 1970s, and director of the Hudson Institute, another think tank, included an entire chapter of predictions in his 1967 book, *The Year 2000: One Hundred Technical Innovations Very Likely in the Last Third of the Twentieth Century.* According to Schnaars, Kahn's predictions were somewhere between 75 and 85 percent wrong, depending on the generosity of the grader.[11] In 1969, *Industrial Research* polled the research directors at most major industrial firms in the United States, asking them to identify the technologies that would emerge over the next ten years. Schnaars found that of the twenty-two predictions, nineteen (86 percent) were wrong. One of the most startling of *Industrial Research*'s predictions for 1979 was that human life spans would reach 150 to 200 years.

Can a national consortium of Japanese scientists and engineers be as wrong? You bet. An assessment by Shlomo Maital, a visiting professor at MIT, of the predictions made by Japan's STA in its 1971 study shows that 75 percent of them were wrong. The Japanese had some direct hits, such as the mass production of insulin, and some egregious errors, such as the use of laser holography to store information.[12]

The most amusing aspect of technology forecasts is the many wrong predictions regarding technologies that were supposed to change our lives. For example, the experts over the past forty years have predicted the success of the following innovations: conference television, video telephones, dehydrated foods, ultrasonic dishwashers and showers, voice recognition, moving sidewalks, and jet engine–powered cars. According to the TRW and *Industrial Research* studies, we were supposed to have the following by 1977 (about ten years after the studies were conducted): a habitable lunar base; vertical-takeoff aircraft for individuals; 3-D color teleconferencing, movies, and television; plastic dwellings; usable nuclear fusion; human exploration of Mars and Venus; and extensive use of robots. By 1980 we were supposed to be enjoying commercial passenger rockets; mass-produced houses that would be cheap and immune to fire, insects, earthquakes, and tornadoes; and our lunar base would be retrofitted with nuclear power. By 1990, we were to be driving in idiot-proof cars that would automatically take us to our dialed-in destination, and robots would replace humans in the military.

"Too cheap to measure" was the initial promise of nuclear power. In testimony before the U.S. Congress's Special Committee on Atomic Energy in 1946, Robert Hutchins, chancellor of the University of Chicago, called nuclear power "the greatest invention since the discovery of fire" and declared that "it promised to transform American society as dramatically as had electrification in the period after 1890."[13] Nuclear energy would power everything: cars, trains, planes, refrigerators, even wristwatches. Ford Motor Company created a prototype of the Nucleon, a nuclear-powered Batmobile-like car (see Figure 6.6), in 1958. Predictions that typewriter-size nuclear reactors would power every home and factory in the United States gave rise to utopian visions.

Figure 6.6 A model of Ford Motor Company's nuclear-powered car, the Nucleon, created in 1958. (*Source:* UPI/Corbis-Bettman.)

In 1955, President Eisenhower's special assistant, Harold Stassen, declared that nuclear energy would lead to a world where "hunger is unknown, . . . where food never rots and crops never spoil, . . . where 'dirt' is an old-fashioned word, and routine household tasks are just a matter of pushing a few buttons . . . a world where no one stokes a furnace or curses the smog, where the air is everywhere as fresh as on a mountain top and the breeze from a factory as sweet as from a rose."[14] In these post-Chernobyl days, as we face the multiple specters of nuclear war, nuclear accident, nuclear terrorism, and massive nuclear poisoning, we might well prefer to put the nuclear genie back in the bottle.

Robots have long been predicted to be helpers in the home and workplace. For the 1939 World's Fair, Westinghouse produced Electro and Sparko, models of a robotic man and his mechanical dog. By the 1950s, it was predicted that robots would make their own decisions on the factory floor and would fix appliances in the home. In 1964 Meredith Thring, a professor at Queen Mary College, declared that within ten to twenty years "we could have a robot that will completely eliminate all routine operations around the house and remove the drudgery from humans."[15] In 1970, futurist Kahn agreed with Thring's vision, noting that a scenario like hers "seems most reasonable by the year 2000."[16]

Some visionaries proclaimed that by 2000 people would work only ten hours a year, if at all. Thomas Bray in the *Wall Street Journal* predicted in 1966 that a typical farmer in the year 2000 "will be a sophisticated executive with a computer for a foreman." In the 1980s, the media told us that robots would soon perform much of the manual work in manufacturing and that Japan was light-years ahead of the United States in robotics, as in most other areas of technology and engineering. Though robots have transformed the manufacturing operations of some organizations, they have yet to fulfill the predictions of how they would replace human workers and create leisurely lifestyles. According to the 1996 *Statistical Abstract,* there are only 50,000 robots in the United States versus a manufacturing workforce of 20 million, which represents a 0.25 percent penetration of robots into the manufacturing workplace. As it turns out, some of the most efficient factories in the world are the least automated and employ commonsense, low-tech methods, such as designing products for ease of manufacturing. According to Herb Brody, senior editor of *Technology Review,* "The myth of a huge robot market grew in large part out of statement by Prudential Bache [now Prudential Securities] vice-president Laura Conigliaro, where . . . erroneous assumptions about manufacturers' needs [for robots] took on the weight of truth in the retelling."[17]

Although robots have failed to create a leisure-filled utopia, they are starting to make significant contributions in other ways. With recent, though humble, advances in robotic perception, cognition, manipulation, and movement across difficult terrains, robots are now being enlisted for hazardous duty, including nuclear waste removal, repairing highways, painting road markers, exploring volcanoes, space travel, and defusing explosive devices. Robots are also being used in high-precision applications like bone surgery where machine-computer capabilities exceed those of humans. Robotics is a brilliant emerging technology with considerable promise that we cannot as yet imagine; but don't count on it to free us anytime soon from workplace chores or domestic duties.

For decades, experts have predicted the development of thinking computers. In 1967, Kahn intoned that "by the year 2000, computers are likely to match, simulate and surpass some of man's most 'human-like' intellectual abilities, including perhaps some of his aesthetic and creative capacities, in addition to having some new kinds of capabilities that human beings do not have."[18] Scientists today are much less optimistic about the prospects for what they call artificial intelligence and have proclaimed that the human brain may be the most complex "machine" in the known universe. Researchers in the field of artificial intelligence have only a rudimentary understanding of how the human brain learns and interprets language with all the ambiguities of pronunciation, gesture, and emotion. Scientists and philosophers have only vague theories about what consciousness is.

Figure 6.7 lists some of Kahn's technology forecasts for the year 2000, which reveal the situational bias of 1967, a time when science seemed invincible. For example, he envisioned that we would be able

---

- Use of nuclear explosives for excavation and mining, and for generation of power.
- Some control of weather and/or climate.
- New and more reliable "educational" and propaganda techniques for affecting human behavior, public and private.
- Human hibernation for relatively extensive periods (months to years).
- Improved capability to "change" sex of children and/or adults.
- General and substantial increase in life expectancy, postponement of aging, and limited rejuvenation.
- "High-quality" medical care for undeveloped areas of the world.
- Permanent manned satellite and lunar installations—interplanetary travel.
- Application of life systems designed for outer space (or similar systems and techniques) to terrestrial installations.
- Permanent inhabited undersea installations, and perhaps even colonies.
- Automated grocery and department stores.
- Extensive use of robots and machines "slaved" to humans.
- Chemical methods for improving memory and learning.
- Greater use of underground buildings.
- Very low-cost buildings for home and business use.
- Simulated and planned and perhaps programmed dreams.
- Inexpensive worldwide transportation of humans and cargo.
- Inexpensive road-free transportation.
- Artificial moons and other methods for lighting large areas at night.

Figure 6.7 Some of Herman Kahn's miscalls for technology in the year 2000. (*Source:* Herman Kahn and Anthony J. Wiener, *The Year 2000: A Framework for Speculation on the Next Thirty Years* [New York: Macmillan, 1967], pp. 51–55.)

to control the weather; today we struggle to generate a reliable weather forecast for the next two days. Some of his predictions are frightening. Imagine using H-bombs to blow up mountains to excavate roads or "reliable propaganda techniques to control human behavior." For what end? Why on Earth would we want to hibernate, or program our dreams, or live in colonies under the sea, or use artificial moons to light large areas at night?

OUT OF THE BLUE

Worse than the blunders just visited is the nearly complete inability of experts to predict the major breakthrough technologies that have changed our lives. Innovations that were not predicted include electricity, the telephone, the light bulb, the radio, airplanes, television, radar, atomic energy, jet propulsion, space travel, cellular telephones, compact disks, and GUI (the point-and-click graphical user interface that makes PCs so easy to use today). Major innovations such as these seem to have come out of the blue; they were never anticipated in any of the literature, except for a few that were envisioned in science fiction. Experts even dismissed working models of new technologies as mere toys with no real-world application. As technology historian James Martin has noted, "All [inventions] met similar derision shortly before becoming practical realities. The derision usually came from leading scientists or engineers of the day and often from committees of them."[19]

In 1896 J. W. Rayleigh, a leading British physicist, commented, "I have not the smallest molecule of faith in aerial navigation other than ballooning."[20] Seven years later, the Wright brothers made their famed first manned airplane flight in Kitty Hawk, North Carolina. In 1956 the British astronomer royal, Richard van der Riet Woolley, announced to the press that "space travel is utter bilge."[21] A year later, the Soviet Union launched *Sputnik I,* the first man-made satellite to revolve around the earth, which kicked off the space race. (And science-fiction writer Jules Verne anticipated space travel one hundred years before it happened in his novel *From the Earth to the Moon.*)

Experts similarly dismissed the inventions of the telephone (1876) and the light bulb (1883). In reviewing Thomas Edison's research on the incandescent light bulb, a committee of the British Parliament proclaimed that the light bulb would be "good enough for our trans-Atlantic friends . . . but unworthy of the attention of practical or scientific men."[22] Another group of British experts concluded that the telephone had no practical value, at least not in their country: "The telephone may be appropriate for our American cousins, but not here, because we have an adequate supply of messenger boys."[23] American experts were similarly uninterested in the invention of the telephone. The large telegraph company Western Union, the most logical candidate to undertake commercial production of the telephone, refused to buy Alexander Graham Bell's patent in 1876 for $100,000. The following meeting notes reveal Western Union's arrogance and lack of foresight:

> Bell's profession is that of a voice teacher . . . yet he claims to have discovered an instrument of great practical value in communication, which has been overlooked by thousands of workers who have spent years in this field. Any telegraph engineer will at once see the fallacy of this plan. The public simply cannot be trusted to handle technical communications equipment. . . . When making a call, the subscriber must give the number verbally to the operator who will have to deal with persons who may be illiterate, speak with lisps or stammer, or have foreign accents or who may be sleepy or intoxicated when making a call. . . . In conclusion the committee feels that it must advise against any investment whatever in Bell's scheme.[24]

Experts also failed to predict electronic computers, even though mechanical computational devices have existed since the early 1800s. As recently as 1950, the dictionary definition of a computer was "a person who computes"—manually, that is, the way it had been done since the invention of counting. Even after the first fully electronic computer was invented in the late 1940s, computer researcher Howard Aiken predicted that the United States would ultimately need only four electronic computers to meet the entire nation's needs, and the British thought they might need only four as well. According to International Data Corp., the worldwide sale of personal computers in 1996 was estimated at 68.4 million units.

Errors in forecasting technology have been large and numerous, with their rate of correct predictions no better than guesswork. Experts have repeatedly failed to foresee breakthrough innovations, the turning points in the evolution of technology. There are no superstars in technology forecasting, no prognosticators who have consistently superior track records. In fact, in 1976 *Futures* magazine reviewed 1,556 technology forecasts and concluded that nonexperts did as well as the experts.[25] The accuracy of technology forecasting has not improved, despite the assertion of experts to the contrary. In analyzing thirty years of technology forecasts, Stephen Schnarrs observed, "There is no evidence that our capacity to foresee the future has improved at all."[26]

Situational bias has continually been a major barrier in envisioning future technology. We have tended, and still tend, to imagine future technologies as mere extensions of things that already exist. Our model for manned flight was the bird. In Greek mythology, Icarus was said to have flown with artificial wings made of feathers and wax, and so thirteenth-century scientist Roger Bacon described his vision of flying machines accordingly: "Artificial wings are made to beat the air like a flying bird."[27] Even the flying machines envisioned by Jules Verne in the late 1800s were propelled by flapping wings, as shown in Figure 6.8.

Situational bias is also a hindrance in envisioning future applications for new technologies, as is evident in names such as the "horseless carriage" and the "wireless." Bell's first patent referred to his invention as "improvements in telegraphy." Guglielmo Marconi believed that his radio invention would only be used to fill in the gaps in the telephone system in areas where it was difficult to put up telephone wires, such as over water. So did the New York Telephone Company in 1915, according to its chief engineer, J. J. Carty: "The results of long-distance tests show clearly that the function of the wireless telephone is primarily to reach inaccessible places where wires cannot be strung. It will act mainly as an extension of the wire system and a feeder to it."[28] Situational bias kept Marconi and his contemporaries from seeing its ultimate use in such applications as radio broadcasting. In fact, the British today still use the word "wireless" to refer to the radio.

Innovations seem to come out of the blue because those most likely to develop a new technology often do not. Contrary to common wisdom, the manufacturers of products do not necessarily invent them. Western Union did not invent the telephone; makers of vacuum tubes did not invent the transistor; makers of mechanical calculators such as IBM did not invent the computer; and the makers of slide rules did not invent the hand-held calculator. In a comprehensive 1988 study of

Figure 6.8 Jules Verne's 1887 vision of birdlike airplanes of the future. (*Source:* UPI/Corbis-Bettman.)

product innovations, MIT professor Eric von Hippel found that innovations usually come from surprising sources.[29] In fact, the source of innovations varies considerably by industry: *manufacturers* have created 92 percent of the innovations in the plastics additives industry, *customers of manufacturers* have created 77 percent of the innovations in the scientific equipment industry, and *suppliers to manufacturers* have created 83 percent of the innovations in the wire-termination-equipment industry (this industry makes machines that attach connectors to wire and cable).

THE HIDDEN PATH OF
TECHNOLOGICAL DARWINISM

A fundamental barrier to forecasting technological change is the unpredictability of the evolution of technology. The path of technological progress is clouded by uncertainty and blocked by unknowns, impasses, and dead ends; only occasionally is it illuminated by serendipitous events. Like most aspects of nature, the evolution of technology is so complex and uncertain that it is almost impossible to foresee breakthrough innovations. As technology historian Martin noted,

> A reasonable forecaster in 1940 would not have predicted the computer; in 1945 he would not have predicted the transistor; in 1950 he would not have predicted the laser; in 1955 he would not have predicted . . . large-scale integration [of computer chips], . . . computer time sharing, on-line real-time systems in commerce, . . . or synchronous communication satellites; in 1960 he would not have predicted holography or satellite antennas on the rooftops; in 1965 he would not have predicted the hand-held calculator or the spread of microcomputers.[30]

Some of the major challenges and perils that act as obstacles to the development of any new technology in its projected path from the lab to the commercial marketplace are illustrated in Figure 6.9. Of the hundreds of millions of potential technologies that are being developed today, most will be stillborn in the lab or will perish somewhere along the evolutionary path. Currently in the United States, there are 33 million patents for a wide variety of technologies, very few of which will ever make it out of the lab and into the market. Of those that do, 80 percent will fail.

Unworkable Concepts

Most technologies in the lab die early as unworkable concepts. The vast majority of technologies that do work in the lab prove to be impractical for commercial applications. The first computers, for instance,

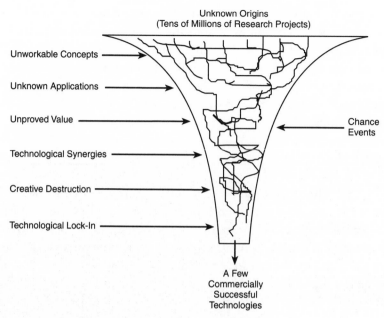

Unknown Origins
(Tens of Millions of Research Projects)

Unworkable Concepts

Unknown Applications

Unproved Value

Chance
Events

Technological Synergies

Creative Destruction

Technological Lock-In

A Few
Commercially
Successful
Technologies

Figure 6.9 Uncertainties in technological evolution.

which were made with many large vacuum tubes, were commercially unviable because they required 100-foot-long rooms to house them. Hot fusion is another example. Although scientists have successfully developed fusion reactors that work like controlled hydrogen bombs in the lab, for decades they have been unable to generate more energy than the fusion reactors consume, making them commercially unviable. Some recently discovered superconducting materials are economically promising except that they are hard to fashion into wires, coils, or other configurations necessary to make them useful. Despite the utopian promise of fusion energy and superconductivity, it is still unknown when and if they will become practical realities.

One of the spookiest scientific discoveries is superfluidity, a property that defies the laws of gravity and friction, and which earned Douglas Osheroff, a physics professor at Stanford University, a Nobel Prize in 1996. Osheroff discovered superfluidity by subjecting an isotope of helium to temperatures near absolute zero, at which point the liquid helium defies gravity by creeping up walls. It also defies resistance and, as Osheroff noted, is "arguably the closest thing to perpetual motion that occurs in nature."[31] Picture this: When you spin a glass of wine and stop, the wine continues to spin for a brief moment until friction brings it to a halt. If you could spin a helium isotope around in a glass and then stop, it would continue spinning forever, as long as it was kept supercooled. Osheroff has obviously found some new property of nature, yet, as he has stated, his discovery has "no foreseeable commercial applications."[32]

Unknown Applications

Innovative technologies often come out of pure research by scientists who begin to pursue a particular line of inquiry with little or no idea of any practical application for their research. Scientists perform such experiments in the hope of making a significant scientific discovery. If they are lucky, their work will lead to published papers and academic acclaim. James Watson and Francis Crick, in their quest to crack the code for DNA—the holy grail of biological research in the 1960s—did not envision that their discovery would lead to such practical uses as infusing tomato DNA with genes from a flounder to make tomatoes frost resistant.

That technologies in the lab have little or no commercial application makes the research being done on them vulnerable to funding cutbacks before any real progress is achieved. In the early 1950s, all three commercial labs conducting basic research that eventually led to the laser—Bell Telephone, Westinghouse, and RCA—curtailed the research because it seemed impractical at the time. The scientists who were then bombarding gas molecules with microwaves in order to understand molecular behavior better did not foresee—and could not have—that their basic research was laying the groundwork for the development of laser technology three decades later. In particular, they could not have foreseen that the technology that came out of their research would revolutionize medical surgery, dentistry, chemical research, navigational systems, measuring devices, recorded music, computer printers, and the telecommunications industry. "The parent device MASER involved an amplification technique so radically different that it could not grow out of previous electronics in any orderly way," explained Charles Townes, who won a Nobel Prize for his early research in laser technology.[33]

Laser-related research continued only at Columbia University, which was sheltered from commercial pressures to turn a quick profit on research. Bell Labs, whose parent company, Bell Telephone, would ultimately greatly benefit from laser technology, resumed its laser research in the mid-1950s but nearly cut funding for it a second time, even when presented with a working model of the device in 1957. This is a clear example of situational bias. As Townes recalled, "Bell's patent department at first refused to patent our amplifier or oscillator for optical frequencies (i.e., visible light), because it was explained, optical waves had never been of any importance to communications and hence the invention had little bearing on Bell System interests."[34] Yet some thirty years later, the laser would link up with fiber-optic cables to create a vastly superior replacement to copper wires. For example, transatlantic cables in 1965 could carry only 138 simultaneous conversations, whereas laser-driven fiber optics can carry 1.5 million.

When technologies are developed to solve a particular problem, it is often difficult to envision how it might otherwise be used. Thomas Newcomen invented the first steam engine in 1705 to pump groundwater out of coal mines in England. His steam engine looked like a pump and acted like a pump, and thus it remained for sixty-one years. Similarly, semiconductor material was first used in 1906 to detect radio waves, and it took more than forty years before it was used to make transistors, and later still to make integrated circuits.

The primitive nature of early technologies also masks their potential uses. Newcomen's steam engine was extremely primitive and delivered its power in reciprocating (back-and-forth) motion well suited to power a pump but little else. It was not until James Watt created gears to convert the engine's reciprocating motion into rotary force in 1764 that the steam engine would be able to power mills, and later trains and steamboats.

When the first electronic computer, with its 18,000 vacuum tubes, was developed, situational bias made it impossible for experts to foresee the vast improvements in and uses for the computer that would evolve over the next fifty years. Early computers, though clunky, were fast compared to people, doing about 30 million calculations a day, equivalent to the effort of 75,000 human number crunchers. The experts believed that computers were actually too fast for humans to use. They thought that the computers would mostly remain idle while slow-thinking humans cooked up something for the machine to do. Computers were developed by academics to do complex mathematical computations, and they had a hard time imagining that the computer would be employed to perform simpler practical tasks such as accounting and payroll processing. Aiken asserted, "If it should ever turn out that the basic logics of a machine designed for the numerical solution of differential equations coincide with the logics of a machine intended to make bills for a department store, I would regard this as the most amazing coincidence that I have ever encountered."[35]

Unproved Value

Once a new technology makes it to the market, there is no guarantee that anyone will buy it. Market flops include lighter-fluid maker Ronson's attempt to replace wax candles with its Varaflame, a metal candle containing butane gas and adjustable flames, just like cigarette lighters. The chemical company giant Du Pont introduced Corfam, a plastic that was intended to replace shoe leather. Though more durable than leather, Corfam shoes were hot, uncomfortable, and expensive. Then there was R. J. Reynold's smokeless cigarette called Premier, with its aluminum flavor capsule and four-page instruction manual—and it was also difficult to light.

Market success depends on customers' perception of value, which can be complex and fickle. Over the past several decades, customers have placed little value on such products as dehydrated foods, plastic houses, sonic wave baths, quadraphonic sound, videotext, and home banking by computer, all of which were predicted to be great market successes. Conversely, who could have predicted the enormous popularity of the video game Nintendo so soon after consumers lost interest in earlier, less imaginative video games?

The costs of switching to a new technology are part of the customer value equation, and if the costs of abandoning an existing technology and gearing up for a new one are high, then the success of the new technology may be delayed by decades or indefinitely. This is why it took ten years for color television to catch on after it was introduced in the mid-1950s, even though most television stations already offered color programming. Widespread use of high definition television (HDTV) may not occur until well into the twenty-first century, if ever.

Customer values are also dynamic. What customers reject in the past, they might desire in the future. It is possible that the increasing use of home computers, online services, the Internet, and home accounting products such as Quicken might resuscitate the currently moribund home banking and videotext technologies.

In particular, the value of a new technology may be unclear because the inventors do not know who the right customers might be. And the right customers may very well change as both the product and the market evolve. When RCA invented the video cassette recorder (VCR), for example, it believed that corporations were the right customers for the expensive device. Matsushita and Sony instead envisioned a mass consumer market, which they pursued by substantially redesigning the VCR to reduce its costs dramatically. Similarly, with continually dropping prices and improved ease of use, the right customer for PCs has changed from hobbyists to businesses to individuals for home use.

Technological Synergies

Superior innovations typically emerge from a combination of different technologies. Israel Dror, from the Israel Institute of Technology, analyzed 630,000 patents issued in the United States from 1975 to 1984 and concluded, "Innovation is essentially a process of coupling."[36] This combining process can take place at any step of the process from the lab to the marketplace. Only when laser and fiber-optic technologies were linked could a vastly superior infrastructure for telecommunication be created. The development of microelectronics technology emerged from the confluence of innovations in crystallography that made it possible to grow near-perfect silicon crystals and new chemical and metallurgical technologies that enabled microscopic circuits to be implanted on the silicon crystal surfaces. The original PC was a novel invention that appealed mostly to computer hackers; the average person had little use for a PC until Lotus produced its versatile 1-2-3 spreadsheet program, which facilitated the simple storage, manipulation, and printing of information. And the marriage of the PC with information systems network technology resulted in the birth of the Internet.

The necessity of synergistic marriage for the creation of new technologies adds great uncertainty to the evolution of technology. Assume, for instance, that the success of technology A depends on its being combined with technology B. What happens if technology B does not emerge at the right time? What if it never gets invented? What if the developers of technology A never discover technology B among the millions of existing technologies? It took twenty years for experts to combine fiber-optic and laser technologies to produce a superior telecommunications system, even though the two technologies had co-existed since the 1960s. It took the confluence of at least five technological innovations to create the first nuclear submarine in 1960: efficient nuclear propulsion, solid rocket fuel for the Polaris missiles, a highly precise navigation system, a lightweight and reliable missile-guidance system, and small, powerful nuclear warheads. Without advances in microelectronics, there would have been little progress in the development of aerospace, computer, and medical-scanning technologies. Without microcircuitry and the silicon chip (unless some other technology had emerged to enable the miniaturization of electronics), there would have been no commercially viable computers (let alone PCs), no manned space travel, and no body-scanning medical devices such as magnetic resonance imaging (MRI) or positron-emission tomography (PET).

Of all the synergistic combinations of technologies that have succeeded, the most fortuitous has been the marriage of the computer and semiconductor technologies, which ultimately gave birth to the inexpensive and powerful PC of today. Both semiconductor and computer technologies originated in the 1800s. The ancestor of the electronic computer technology was Charles Babbage's mechanical computational device, which had 15 million moving parts. The development of semiconductors originated with the detection of radio waves.

In 1945, researchers at the University of Pennsylvania created the first fully electronic computer, called ENIAC (Electronic Numerical Integrator and Computer), which used 17,000 vacuum tubes and nearly 100,000 other electronic components. Based on a fifty-year-old technology, vacuum tubes at the time were massive consumers of electricity, expensive to make, highly prone to failure, and took up considerable space. Without the breakthroughs that occurred in semiconductor technology, the computer might have remained a mere novelty or, worse, an extinct novelty.

In the 1940s, the Bell Telephone Company feared that these faulty vacuum tubes would limit the expansion of its telecommunications system and started exploring semiconductor technology as a possible replacement. This research led to the breakthrough invention of the transistor, which was first put to use in miniature radios by the Sony Corporation. The transistor was applied to computers in 1958, and although it was a huge improvement over vacuum tubes, it still caused computers to suffer from a "tyranny of numbers." The typical computer at the time consisted of 25,000 transistors and hundreds of thousands of other electronic components, all of which had to be manually soldered onto circuit boards, a costly and error-prone process. The computer equipped with only transistors would have remained too expensive, too large, too complex, and too likely to miscompute or break down, and it had many fewer applications than today. In 1956, when 1,000 computers existed in the United States, RCA predicted that there would only be 220,000 computers in existence by the end of the century.

The next breakthrough in semiconductor technology was the integrated circuit, which led to huge improvements in the computer. Instead of soldering hundreds of thousands of individual components onto a circuit board, integrated circuit technology enabled an entire circuit—transistors, wires, and other components—to be made all at the same time on a single silicon chip. The integrated circuit led to the ever-increasing miniaturization and density of computer circuitry and sharply dropping manufacturing costs. From the 1960s to the 1980s, the computational power of these circuits grew a million times, to the point where the entire circuitry for a computer fits on a single small silicon chip. What started as two separate technologies have essentially merged into one; the semiconductor device *is* the computer.

In 1965 Gordon Moore, cofounder of Intel, predicted that the density of transistors on computer chips would double every two years, a prediction that has largely been fulfilled over the past thirty years. As shown in Figure 6.10, the density of transistors on computer chips has grown steadily at an exponential rate; the line in the figure is called the "Moore Curve." The Moore Curve, like life expectancy, is one of those rare sustaining trends that give rise to periods of accurate prediction. Some have speculated that this trend will come to an end as the size of electronic components on a chip approaches the atomic level, but how long that will be is so far an unknown.

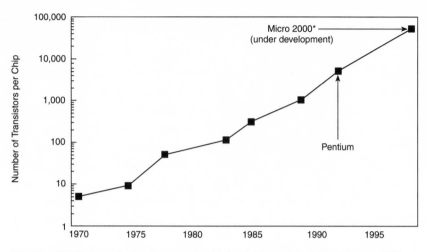

*The Micro 2000 is the next generation computer chip that Intel expects to deliver in the year 2000.

Figure 6.10 Moore's law: Increasing density of microprocessors (number of transistors per microprocessor chip). (*Source of data:* INTEL TECHNOLOGY BRIEFING, Intel's home page on the Internet.)

Creative Destruction

Nineteenth-century economist Joseph Schumpeter called the process of technological innovation "creative destruction," since the creation of new technologies kills off existing ones in a never-ending process of innovation.[37] With today's ever-increasing pace of innovation, Schumpeter's concept is more applicable today than in his time.

Remember those quaint circular plastic disks called "records"? They seem to have become artifacts overnight. Experts predicted that satellite communications would have a promising future, until fiber-optic communications came along. Fax machines, once a fixture of the fast lane, are becoming outmoded by electronic mail and the ability to transmit documents electronically from PC to PC.

A new technology can also be threatened by further advances in existing technologies. The emergence of a new technology can sometimes prompt researchers working on an existing one to improve it so much that the revised old technology becomes superior to the new one. One reason for this is that, according to McGraw-Hill's annual survey on research spending, 80 percent of research and development (R&D) funds are spent on existing technology, as opposed to creating new ones.

Experts predicted, for example, that computer imaging would replace photographic film, but improvements in the silver-halide film technology kept the original technology firmly in place. Although experts predicted that gallium arsenide would replace silicon in making computer chips, silicon technology continues to improve and stay competitive. As Herb Brody noted in *Technology Review,* "We've been hearing for 10 years that silicon is running out of gas. People forget that there are always an army of people working on improving an old technology and only a handful of people working on a new technology."[38]

Technological Lock-In

How sensible is it for railroads in different countries to use tracks with rails of different gauges, or for some countries to use the metric system and others to stick with a nonmetric system, or for some countries to use AC electrical systems and others DC, or for computers to run on the incompatible Macintosh or IBM operating system? These duplicative technical standards create enormous inefficiencies, such as having to write two versions of the same software to accommodate users of IBM-compatible and Macintosh PCs, or having to change trains at a border because the trains on one side cannot run on the tracks across the border. Lock-in occurs when a technology or convention becomes the industry standard before competitors come on the scene; if two or more competing technologies or conventions already coexist, lock-in might occur when the inefficiency of the duplication becomes intolerable, and one of them eventually becomes the industry standard.

The economic theory that market forces ensure that superior technologies ultimately win out over competing inferior ones is clearly not always true; there are too many examples where inferior technologies have become locked in as the industry standard. The strange arrangement of letters on typewriter and computer keyboards, known as QWERTY (so named for the opening sequence in the top row of letters), is a classic example. In 1873, QWERTY was designed intentionally to slow typists down, to keep them from jamming their primitive mechanical typewriters. Now, in spite of QWERTY's obvious disadvantages, we are locked into it because it would be unthinkable to retool the tens of millions of keyboards that exist today and for everyone who uses them to learn a new keyboard configuration.

Remember Betamax? It was introduced at about the same time as the VHS (video home system) format for VCRs and had similar prices and market share. The two technologies coexisted as long as they were used primarily to make home movies, a use that did not necessarily require a single VCR technology. Then video rental stores changed the rules of the VCR game. Not wanting to carry duplicate tape inventory in two different formats, the stores had a strong incentive to settle on a single VCR technology. Competitive moves and random events caused market leadership to vacillate precariously between the two technologies. Eventually VHS gained a slight market share advantage, which tipped competitive forces in its favor, and as VHS moved on a track toward lock-in, Betamax was on a path to obsolescence. As video stores increasingly favored VHS-format tapes, consumers had strong incentive to buy VHS machines, which further reinforced the stores' decisions to carry only VHS tapes. Betamax lost out even though some experts believed that it was the superior technology.

Lock-in creates enormous uncertainty, because it makes it difficult to predict which technologies will win and which will become extinct. As Sante Fe Institute fellow Brian Arthur noted about the Betamax–VHS battle, "It would have been impossible at the outset of the competition to say which system would win."[39] Although Apple Computer started the PC industry and its Macintosh system is still considered to be the best PC operating system, it is on the losing end of a technological lock-in process that is increasingly favoring IBM-compatible PCs equipped with Microsoft's Windows software. By 1995, Apple's share of the PC market had dropped to 7.4 percent, and IBM-compatible computers equipped with Microsoft software had taken over most of the rest of the market.[40] So, which technology are software publishers going to favor for their first (and perhaps only) product release? And when and if software development for Apple computers dwindles, the game will be over.

In hindsight, it is easy to see how lock-in occurred in the PC market. In the early days of the industry, Apple and IBM competed neck and neck and had different advantages. IBM had the largest number of corporate customers; Apple had the Macintosh operating system, which was far superior to Microsoft's DOS operating system, used on all IBM PCs. Incredibly, Apple had a ten-year product advantage with Macintosh's easy-to-use, point-and-click graphical user interface, which ended when Microsoft introduced its Macintosh knockoff called Windows.

IBM clones changed the rules of the game, which Microsoft's founder Bill Gates anticipated when he negotiated his original contract with IBM. The advent of the low-cost "computer on a chip" created a new industry when companies began making low-cost knockoffs of the IBM PC installed with Microsoft's DOS operating system. The clone manufacturers copied IBM's PC because Apple refused to license its innovative Macintosh software until 1995—far too late. For years, the makers of IBM clones have flooded the market with cheap IBM-compatible PCs. However, although the IBM technology is becoming the industry standard, it has not helped IBM itself, which lags in PC market share. The only clear winners in the business are Microsoft and Intel (which makes the microprocessors found in most PCs).

Chance Events

Chance events large and small play a huge role in the evolution of different technologies and, again, interfere with our ability to predict technology winners and losers. World War II deferred the development of semiconductors while hastening the development of such technologies as aerospace, nuclear power, computers, and radar. And wartime interest in radar technology eventually led to the development of the laser. Government spending on research and development, dependent on the vagaries of the political process, is another influence. Currently, for example, the U.S. Congress wants to cut R&D spending and redirect what is left to more practical projects that could lead to new products and jobs. In 1994, Congress instructed the National Science Foundation to spend 60 percent of its $2 billion budget on "projects relevant to national needs." These changes in R&D spending will influence the evolution of different technologies over the next few decades in ways that we cannot possibly predict.

Even small events can have big consequences in the evolution of technology and on who will be the winners and losers in the market. In 1980, IBM, to speed up the introduction of its first personal computer to go on the market, decided to use Microsoft's DOS operating system, which it had coincidentally acquired from the Seattle Computer company just before that for a mere $50,000. According to Microsoft's

Bill Gates, the timing of the deal with IBM was "tense, because there was a forty-eight-hour period after . . . I had officially offered to license Q-DOS (the forerunner of Microsoft DOS) to IBM that we didn't really own it."[41] The key to Microsoft's eventual success, however, was the clause in the IBM contract (for which they negotiated hard) that enabled them to sell Microsoft DOS to other parties in addition to IBM. The rest is history. Randall Stross, author of *The Microsoft Way*, called the IBM deal "a whopping dollop of luck."[42]

How many times a day do total strangers exchange views and perhaps business cards on an airplane—perhaps an engineer with a hot new idea and a venture capitalist seeking new investment opportunities? What new synergistic thinking results when the two scientists in different fields are relocated to adjacent lab stations? The evolution of technology from concept to commercial success is one big game of chance, and, much like the evolution of life, it is hard to predict future innovations.

PROCEED WITH EXTREME CAUTION

The main difference between technology forecasting and science fiction is that the former is sold under the pretense of being factual. The poor track record of technology forecasters prompted science and philosophy author Anthony O'Hear to conclude, "Insofar as such predictions can not be made with any certainty, technological forecasting is largely a bogus and fraudulent enterprise. . . . With technological forecasting, we are always in a state of multiple ignorance regarding both initial conditions and relevant laws."[43] There are several additional reasons to be skeptical about such predictions.

No college degrees or accreditation exist for technology forecasting; the practitioners are all self-anointed experts. The tools they use are weak and have not changed for decades. Using an extrapolation technique such as the S-curve is naive because it assumes that the forecaster knows, for any technology, the total market size and how well the technology has penetrated it. Imagine using such trends in 1960 to predict computer sales in the 1990s; the errors would be in the thousands of percent. Extrapolating trends does not take into account the many fortuitous events that occur in the evolution of a technology that could accelerate its development or eliminate it. And, of course, extrapolating trends could apply only to existing technologies and could not possibly anticipate innovations that come out of the blue.

The Delphi method has proved to be of little help in foreseeing future innovations. How could such an organized bull session with experts whose thoughts about the future are clouded with situational bias envision the hugely uncertain path that future technologies will take? The mysterious pronouncements of the Oracle of Delphi might have been just as helpful.

Businesses, investors, and governments are best advised to discount long-term technology forecasts heavily. As MIT professor James Utterback has suggested regarding technology forecasts, "The illusion of knowing what's going to happen is worse than not knowing."[44] Don't rely on technology-forecasting firms. Herb Brody, in *Technology Review,* said of these firms: "Over the past decade, outfits like these have foretold billion dollar markets for artificial intelligence, videotext, and virtually every other new technology that laboratories have reported."[45] In a surprising admission, a research director at one of these forecasting firms confided, "The higher my [forecast] numbers, the more reports I can sell."[46]

Do not believe the media either. The press cannot resist stories about radically new technologies and how they will change our lives. Remember, though, that Schnarrs determined that 80 percent of the technology forecasts carried by the media were wrong. In particular, do not believe reported corporate pronouncements of promising scientific discoveries, as companies are sometimes overeager to sell their stock. Running such stories adds greatly to their perceived validity, but the mass media lack the time and knowledge to check the validity of scientists' claims of new discoveries. In fact, Rustum Roy, a science professor from Pennsylvania State University, advises readers to be cautious about announced innovations. He suggests that potential investors should first demand to see a working example of the innovation and then ask themselves "If it's really [commercially] interesting would you talk about it?"[47]

Betting the ranch on predictions of promising new technologies, especially those early in their evolution, should be avoided at all costs. The odds of success are extremely low, and there is no need to rush, because new technologies take many years of refinement before they are ready to enter the commercial marketplace. When you consider the vast uncertainties in the evolution of technology, perhaps Bell Labs was not so foolish after all in being reluctant to fund early laser research. The track record clearly shows that the companies on the leading edge—also called the bleeding edge—do not necessarily turn out to be the winners. The United States has led the way in developing technological breakthroughs, while Japan has led the way in their commercial production.

Technology forecasts cannot be used to justify business ventures. I have been amazed at how many managers in both the private and the public sectors plug technology forecasts into their proposals for new investment. Most of these forecasts, just reams of meaningless statistics, will be wrong.

When confronted with a host of tantalizing long-term technology forecasts, keep in mind the following guidelines:

- It can take decades for a new technology to become a commercial success. (The Battelle Institute estimates nineteen years, on average.)
- The applications for radically new technologies are completely unknown, and it is difficult to gauge whether and how they will be commercially successful.
- Do not expect customers to abandon their current technology quickly; change is financially and psychologically painful.
- Trends usually take surprising twists and turns, making extrapolation very error prone.
- When change is predicted, conditions can remain the same for a surprisingly long time—or can change rapidly.
- Forecasts are highly colored with situational bias, and the general thinking of the moment will most likely change in the future.

The uncertain evolution of technology suggests some guidelines could be useful. First, it would be helpful for government and industry to work together to set technical standards. It is enormously wasteful for competitors to fight it out, spending tens or hundreds of millions of dollars to resolve which technology will prevail as the industry standard.

R&D is more efficiently spent on developing innovative products and enhancements within the context of industry standards.

Next, governments should not be in the business of predicting winning technologies of the future, directly or indirectly. Nathan Rosenberg, a Stanford University economist and technology specialist, advises, "The pervasiveness of uncertainty [of technology evolution] suggests that the government should ordinarily resist the temptation to play the role of a champion of any one technological alternative, such as nuclear power, or any narrowly concentrated focus of research support."[48] On this point, Japan has gotten it all wrong. Its efforts to forecast emerging technologies and to funnel resources to predicted areas of promise have proved to be an erroneous exercise that consumes enormous resources with no payoff. In fact, Japan's micromanagement of R&D might well stifle diversity and creativity, which are key influences on technological innovation. In contrast, the loosely directed American system continues to work well; the United States leads the world in producing Nobel laureates and has made most of the major scientific discoveries of the twentieth century. We are just not quite as good at making and selling the things we invent.

To the extent that the government is in the business of doling out money for R&D grants, it makes the most sense to provide a large number of smaller grants than fewer large ones, because innovations emerge from such unknown and diverse efforts. As Rosenberg has further suggested, "It would seem to make a great deal of sense to manage a deliberately diversified research portfolio, a portfolio that is likely to illuminate a range of alternatives in the event of a reordering of social or economic priorities or the unexpected failure of any single, major research thrust."[49]

Big projects might well be a colossal waste of money. The demise of the U.S. supercollider project in autumn 1993 was probably a good thing; the $11 billion savings from shutting the project down can fund numerous smaller-scale research projects. Although the majority of such projects are likely to go nowhere, a few of them might give birth to breakthroughs that will spur the United States' industrial competitiveness decades hence. In retrospect, how much did the United States gain from the massive space program of the 1960s, aside from boasting rights of beating the Soviets to the moon? I have always heard that the billions spent on the program yielded new technologies as a by-product; however, after two decades, the only one that has come to the light is Tang, the powdered orange drink. I hope we got something more for our money.

As you will see in the next chapter, technology forecasts have shaped visions of future society, in the form of both science fiction and serious attempts at social prediction.

7

The Futurists

"Socioquake! These are bizarre times. . . . These changes will strike deeper than social shakeups have in the recent American past."
"A new civilization is emerging in our lives, and blind men everywhere are trying to suppress it."
"A spectre is haunting Europe."

Futurists predict societal change. Those who have become famous often employ fear and intrigue to sell their visions of future societies. Consider the startling quotations above from three famous social forecasters of the past and present. The first quote is from Faith Popcorn, a for-hire social-trend spotter; the next is from Alvin Toffler, the icon of futurology; the last is from Karl Marx and Friedrich Engels, social visionaries with revolutionary spirit (their "spectre" refers to communism).

In a survey conducted in 1990, 115 professors, writers, and leaders in the study of the future, were asked: "In the world today, who do you see as contributing ideas about the future that are especially significant, fresh, and profound?"[1] The top ten winners in this futurist popularity contest were:

1. Alvin Toffler, author of *Future Shock*.
2. Mikhail Gorbachev, former head of the former Soviet Union.
3. David Suzuki, television host and author of *Inventing the Future*.
4. Marilyn Ferguson, author of *Aquarian Conspiracy*.
5. Hazel Henderson, author of *Politics of the Solar Age*.

6. John Naisbitt, author of *Megatrends 2000.*
7. Peter Drucker, management guru and futurist author of *America's Next Twenty Years* (and noted for his statement, "Forecasting is not a respectable human activity").
8. Arthur C. Clarke, author of *2001: A Space Odyssey.*
9. Gene Roddenberry, originator of the TV show *Star Trek.*
10. Nelson Mandela, president of South Africa and former apartheid dissident.

An interesting mix. But what makes a futurist, a futurist? As a predictor of societal change, the moniker embraces an eclectic group of sociologists, authors, political figures, novelists, media celebrities, and numerous others who crank out thousands of books, papers, and speeches on future lifestyles, attitudes, work life, family structure, wars, revolutions, and every other imaginable aspect of society.

THE INFIRM FOUNDATIONS
OF SOCIAL SCIENCE

To the extent that there is any science in social prediction, it lies in the social science fields of sociology and political science, although in 1913, French mathematician Henri Poincaré noted that sociology is the "science with the greatest number of methods and the least results."[2] Of the 19,000 sociologists in the United States, 75 percent are university professors and researchers who are highly educated and trained and increasingly equipped with advanced statistical knowledge, which they use to uncover patterns and relationships in the ebb and flow of social behavior—and to make predictions.[3] According to Michael Hechter, a professor at Oxford University, "Sociology is no less committed to prediction than are its sister disciplines: from its very beginnings, the attainment of predictive knowledge was one of the field's principal rationales."[4] But always nipping at the heels of the social sciences has been the question: Are scientific predictions possible in these disciplines?

If society is a complex system that is affected by almost everything, including popular attitudes and beliefs, economic conditions, technological advances, population trends, political events, wars, the weather, and all of these forces are unpredictable, then society itself must be unpredictable.

The notion of society as an unpredictable complex system was introduced in the 1930s by Karl Popper, a philosopher of natural and social science. Born in Vienna in 1902, Popper has lectured and taught at many leading universities around the world, receiving honorary degrees at thirteen of them. Since the publication in 1935 of his first book, *The Logic of Scientific Discovery,* he has written and published several more, including collections of his papers and lectures on society and the evolution of history, such as *The Open Universe: An Argument for Indeterminism* (1982). Although the Sante Fe Institute is credited with originating the "new science" of complexity in the 1980s, Popper had some of the same notions about complexity fifty years earlier:

> There is no doubt that the analysis of any concrete social situation is made extremely difficult by its complexity . . . a complexity due to the fact that social life is a natural phenomenon that presupposes the mental life of individuals . . . which in its turn presupposes biology, which again presupposes chemistry and physics. The fact that sociology comes last in this hierarchy of sciences plainly shows us the tremendous complexity of the factors involved in social life.[5]

In his discussion and analysis of complexity, Popper even used some of the same terminology as modern complexity theorists, as when he pointed out among society's "most important features . . . the emergence of novelty."[6] He also introduced the concept of the adaptability of complex systems: "It cannot be doubted that [a society] does learn, in so far as it is partially conditioned by its past."[7]

Popper was adamant that "scientific predictions" were impossible in social sciences. Since neither proved laws of nature that invariantly determine the future course of some phenomenon nor a detailed knowledge of one's starting point (also called initial conditions) exist with much reliability in social sciences, social prediction cannot be "scientific" in the way that we can predict with great accuracy the path and future location of heavenly bodies. As Popper noted, "There can be no prediction of the course of human history by scientific or any other rational methods. . . . We must reject the possibility of social science that would correspond to theoretical physics."[8]

A number of factors have a negative effect on the social sciences' ability to predict. For social prediction to be scientifically possible, there would have to be laws that govern the behavior of not only the society in question but of all its individuals as well. People learn and adapt, which means that the dynamics of a society evolve, so that what was true in the past may no longer be true in the future. For example, Leon Trotsky observed from the Austrian rebellion in 1848 that although the Austrian people were courageous enough to topple the government, they were not "organized enough to become the successors."[9] But in 1917, the Bolsheviks were well prepared to take over Russia.

Consider how the actions of individuals can change history. For example, contrast the positive impacts of Abraham Lincoln, Winston Churchill, and Rachel Carson with the destructive impacts of Adolf Hitler, Joseph Stalin, and Mao Ze-dong. In an account of recent Russian history, James Coleman, a professor at the University of Chicago, noted that "had Andropov been succeeded by someone other than Gorbachev, the East European governments and the Soviet Union might have remained intact for some time beyond 1989."[10] Would World War I have occurred when and how it did if a lone assassin had not murdered Austria's Archduke Ferdinand while he was visiting Bosnia? Would the French Revolution have occurred if Louis XIV had permitted his finance minister, Robert Jacques Turgot, to implement a number of economic and tax reforms that might have quelled the restless masses? How different would European societies be today if Martin Luther had not nailed his complaints against the Catholic church to a cathedral door in Worms?

Chance and accident also contribute to unpredictability. As historian Samuel Eliot Morison wrote, "America was discovered accidentally by a great seaman who was looking for something else. . . . History is like that, very chancy."[11] Recently it seems that certain elements of American military policy in the Pacific have been shaped by chance events, such as the eruption of Mount Pinatubo in June 1991, which forced the closure of Clark Air Force Base in the Philippines, and the brutal rape of a twelve-year-old girl by U.S. servicemen in Okinawa in September 1995, which led citizens there to vote ten to one to limit the U.S. military presence on their island. Who could have predicted that U.S. relations with Okinawa would have soured?

Social prediction is also subject to the Heisenberg uncertainty principle, which states that the mere act of observing a phenomenon changes it. Thus, social phenomena cannot be predicted because, as Timur Kuran, a professor at the University of Southern California, has noted, "predictions interact with the phenomena they predict. . . . Any social observation may affect what is being observed."[12] For example, the prediction that a candidate will achieve a landslide victory may scare away contenders who might otherwise have won; predictions that society is about to revolt may trigger the event or, conversely, cause government to crack down on dissenters.

That social prediction cannot be scientifically or reliably accomplished should be considered in the context of several corollary principles:

History does not repeat itself. The evolution of society is continually new, novel, and full of surprises, with no recurring cycles. Wars, revolutions, trends, and movements are as different from one another as snowflakes. "One must expect that events of an intrinsically new character will emerge," wrote Popper. "Every single event in social life can be said to be new, in a certain sense. It may be classified with other events; it may even resemble those events in certain aspects; but it will always be unique in a very definite way. . . . Belief in historical destiny is sheer superstition."[13]

Major social trends, movements, and revolutions surprise those closest to the events. They also surprise leading social scientists equipped with what Timur Kuran called "celebrated theories of social change with ostensibly substantial predictive power."[14] The French Revolution was completely unexpected when it came, as Alexis de Tocqueville noted in his book, *The Old Regime and the French Revolution;* Vladimir Lenin thought that he would never live to see the Russian Revolution; and just weeks before returning to Iran to take charge on February 1, 1979, the Ayatollah Khomeini doubted that the regime of Shah Pahlavi would fall. And there are only two groups of people who did not celebrate the fall of the Soviet empire: the Communist party hacks in charge of the Soviet regime and the sociologists who failed to predict it.[15] In reviewing the events of 1989, Kuran stated, "The evidence is overwhelming that virtually no one expected communism to collapse rapidly, with little bloodshed . . . before the end of the 1980s." His research shows that those who were surprised included "journalists, diplomats, statesmen, futurologists, and scholars," and he cites a survey conducted by the Allensbach Institute in Germany in 1990 showing that 76 percent of East Germans were "totally surprised" by the fall of the East German government.[16] Shortly before the fall of communist Eastern Europe, the dissident author from the former Czechoslovakia, Vaclav Havel, counseled his readers to "stop dreaming" about freedom.[17] He went on to become the democratically elected president of the Czech Republic.

Social theories are necessarily weak and ephemeral in their application to social phenomena. As Seymour Lipset, a sociology professor at Stanford University, wrote, "More often than not the trend or problem that concerns us disappears or ebbs away. . . . Generalizations decay. At one time a conclusion describes the existing situation well, at a later time it accounts for rather little."[18]

Social predictions are subjective and, accordingly, susceptible to situational bias, political agendas, and wishful thinking. These forces will become evident throughout this chapter as I introduce social predictions made by scholars, novelists, and other futurists. Recognizing such flaws in social prediction, Popper warned that predictions come with a point of view and that it is important for forecasters to "state this point of view plainly, and always to remain conscious that it is one among many, and that even if it should amount to a theory, it may not be testable."[19]

Social predictions tend to be wrong. Among the many social predictions made over the past century that have not come to pass, Lipset mentions these: Sociologists during the mid- to late 1800s predicted that society in the United States would become more class structured as its capitalist system matured and geographic expansion slowed in the twentieth century, yet Americans' social mobility has stayed about the same. Sociologists predicted that higher education would lead to greater tolerance for minorities; yet during the 1930s and 1940s, Germany had one of the best educated and least tolerant societies in the world. In the 1940s, sociologists predicted that it would be difficult for the U.S. society and economy to reabsorb the soldiers returning from World War II; no such problem occurred. In the 1950s, sociologists predicted that the shift from self-employment to corporate life in the United States would create a more conformist society; rather, extreme nonconformity emerged in the late 1960s and early 1970s. After the anticommunist hysteria fomented by Senator Joseph McCarthy in the mid-1950s seemed to die down, sociologists predicted that divisive political ideology would decline in the United States; today, ideological infighting threatens to splinter the major political parties.

Sociologists predicted that higher education would cause an increase in voter participation in the United States. The opposite has occurred. Sociologists predicted that in the decades after 1970, the growth of industrialization and urbanization would reduce ethnic tensions around the world. Instead, ethnic conflict has erupted in Europe and the United States and has become devastating in the former Yugoslavia, Pakistan, Africa, Cyprus, India, Israel, and Malaysia.[20]

Finally, like economists, sociologists have missed the major turning points in the evolution of history and society during the past hundred years, including the following: most of the revolutions; the emergence of Organization of Petroleum Exporting Countries in 1960; the increased participation of women in the workforce since the 1970s; the rise of religious fundamentalism in the last decades of the twentieth century; the breakup of several African nations, also during these last several decades; and the creation and widespread use of the Internet starting in the 1990s.

Is the term "social science" a contradiction in terms? Certainly not for the social sciences that are making major scientific discoveries about human nature and behavior, such as psychology, but it is a contradiction for those that are involved in social prediction. If the best and brightest in the social sciences cannot predict accurately, then neither can the other futurists, who have no training or formal credentials to support their prophesying.

THE NEWTONIAN SOCIALISTS

Social prediction actually began during the eighteenth and nineteenth centuries in Europe with the work of such leading intellectuals as Marie-Jean Condorcet, Claude Henri de Saint-Simon, Auguste Comte, Alexis de Tocqueville, John Stuart Mill, and Karl Marx. Influenced by physicist Isaac Newton's profound scientific discoveries, they believed that if Newton could predict the paths of planets, surely they could predict social evolution. They believed that social progress was inevitable and that it was as much a law of nature as Newton's laws of motion.

These early social prophets were reacting to the events and conditions of their times. Capitalism, which was concentrating wealth in the hands of business owners, created an enormous urban working class that was forced to toil long hours under dangerous conditions for subsistence wages, and even permitted the exploitation of child labor. Meanwhile, the French and American revolutions and reformist movements pointed to a brighter future with the promise of inevitable social equality. If anything, the social predictions of these men were colored by wishful thinking; historian Robert Heilbroner called them "reformers of the heart rather than the head."[21] Nevertheless, their wishful thinking coincided with a long-term trend of social progress that made many of their predictions look prescient, such as:

- Public education for the masses.
- The equality of women (although Comte thought that women would continue to be confined to domestic life).
- The growth of knowledge and technological progress.
- Birth control and increasing life span.
- Political democracies and freedoms of voting, speech, press, and religion.
- Industrialization.
- Independence of European colonies.
- Social programs for the poor and retired.
- More equitable distribution of income.
- The institution of a global governing organization.
- The growing role of central government.
- The decline in the dominance of organized religion over daily life.
- The decline of the nobility.
- The emergence of sociology as a distinct discipline.

Variously, these reformist philosophers envisioned that social progress would ultimately lead to socialism. Condorcet, Comte, and de Tocqueville foresaw economic equality; Mill predicted full-blown socialism. Mill was the preeminent economist and intellectual of his time.

He had mastered Greek and its great literature by age seven, Latin by age eleven, and all there was to know at the time about political economics by age thirteen. His book *Principles of Political Economy* was the official treatise on economics in his day, and his *On Liberty* remains a classic.

John Stuart Mill's prediction of socialism was based on his "discovery" that although economic laws dictated the nature of production, they said nothing about how the goods and profits from production could get distributed through expropriation, taxation, and subsidization to achieve various social goals. Socialism was thus technically feasible within the confines of established economic theory. He predicted that the state would limit excessive capitalist profits and tax away inheritances, that associations of workers would compete with capitalist owners and beat them at their own game, and that capitalists would vanish, going out of business or selling out to the associations.

Karl Marx went further than Mill by proclaiming that "[the fall of capitalism] and the victory of the proletariat are equally inevitable."[22] Marx believed he had discovered natural laws of history that dictated capitalism's collapse and the rise of socialism and eventually communism. He even believed that the form of socialism that he had elaborated was a new science no less rigorous than Newton's physics. At Marx's burial, his long-time collaborator Friedrich Engels declared, "Just as Darwin discovered the law of evolution in organic nature, so Marx discovered the law of evolution in human history."[23]

Marx's inevitable communism was to come about in four stages. First, there would be the rise of capitalism and the growth of the proletarian class. With efficiencies from technology, factories would grow larger and drive out the craftsmen and other small businesses to the point where the majority of people would become factory-working proletariat: "The small tradespeople, shopkeepers, and retired tradesmen, the handicraftsmen and peasants—all these sink gradually into the proletariat."[24]

In stage two, capitalists would increasingly exploit the proletariat as their companies experienced cycles of depressions and vicious competition shrank profit margins: "This rate must fall continuously. . . . One capitalist kills many [others]."[25] To stay competitive, capitalists would employ labor-saving technology, which would further exploit the workers: "Machinery obliterates all distinctions of labor, and nearly everywhere reduces wages to the same low level."[26] The plight of the proletariat would steadily worsen, with wages falling to subsistence levels, lengthening workdays, increasing unemployment, a quickening pace of work, deteriorating working conditions, and a shortening of life spans. This would create an explosive situation: "What the bourgeoisie therefore produces . . . are its own gravediggers. "[27]

In stage three, the proletariat would take over by forming a central government to run the economy and industry, redistributing the wealth, and bringing about socialism: "The expropriators are expropriated."[28] Socialism would be so economically successful that in the final stage it would evolve into communism. Ironically, Marx was never very clear about what "communism" really means other than it would be classless: "The dictatorship of the proletariat . . . [leads to] the abolition of all classes and to classless society."[29]

Fundamental aspects of Marx's predictions never happened. By the late 1800s, the plight of the working class had improved: working hours decreased, wages increased, and strong union representation emerged. The proletariat did not rise up in arms to wrest control from capitalists. Nor did the capitalist system self-destruct. Instead it was greatly improved by the establishment of economic controls to prevent severe economic depressions, safeguards against unfair competition, and regulations to promote worker safety and pollution control and outlaw child labor. Marx could hardly have imagined that in today's capitalist management theory, employees are valued assets.

Marx also predicted that communism would emerge first in the most advanced countries, such as the United States and those in Europe, whereas it took hold in Russia, China, North Korea, Vietnam, Cambodia, and Cuba, countries with mostly underdeveloped agrarian societies and without a proletarian class of industrial workers. Instead of a "dictatorship of the proletariat," these poor folk just got dictators—some of the worst despots in history, including Stalin, Mao, and Pol Pot. Furthermore, socialism did not yield exceptionally high levels of productivity but rather caused economic stagnation. For the most part, industries behind the iron curtain suffered from primitive technology, dangerous working conditions, unimaginable pollution problems, poor-quality products, and an inability to compete in global markets.

FROM UTOPIA TO TECHNO-TOTALITARIANISM

At the turn of the twentieth century, socialist prophets began to proclaim technology as the key to the utopias they envisioned. Inexorable technological advances would augment the inevitable social progress, they believed, eradicating society's age-old problems of hunger, disease, ignorance, and war. Futurist historian I. F. Clarke described this period as filled with "confident expectation of constant technological progress and steady social improvement."[30] Naturally, these utopias would be run by engineers and intellectuals.

Many of these social prognosticators expressed their visions through the medium of fiction. H. G. Wells, one of the most popular utopian prophets of this era, was known for the visionary ideas he presented in his science-fiction novels. His 1905 novel, *A Modern Utopia,* foretold of a futuristic society run by a self-appointed group of intellectuals called the "samurai" class or the "voluntary nobility," who would flawlessly run society like clockwork. Technology would lead to greater individual freedom and a decline in, or even an end to, warfare. Some high-tech devices would fulfill human material needs by pumping everything from food to furniture through underground pneumatic tubes, while others would control the weather and climate.

Another utopian novelist of this techno-socialist era was Edward Bellamy, a Bostonian who in 1887 wrote the highly popular *Looking Backward from the Year 2000.* The novel is about a man who falls into a comalike sleep in 1887 and awakes to a utopian world in the year 2000, where social ills such as class inequality and ignorance have been eradicated. *Looking Backward* was read by millions, translated into most major languages, inspired the formation of 163 Bellamy Clubs dedicated to spreading the author's vision, and remains a classic to this day. Bellamy characterized his novel as a form of social prediction: "*Looking Backward* . . . is intended, in all seriousness, as a forecast, in accordance with the principles of evolution, of the next stage in the industrial and social development of humanity."[31]

Some of Bellamy's predictions *were* amazingly prescient. By the year 2000, according to *Looking Backward,* women would achieve equality with men, freedom from a totally domestic life, participation in the workforce, and prominence in all professions, trades, and sports. They would also achieve equality in lovemaking: "Girls of the twentieth century tell their love. There is no more pretence of a concealment of feeling."[32] There would be free public education: "Nowadays all persons equally have those opportunities of higher education which in your day only an infinitesimal portion of the population enjoyed."[33]

Bellamy believed that in 2000, laws would ensure worker safety and prohibit the use of child labor: "Health and safety are conditions common to all industries. The nation does not maim and slaughter its workers by thousands, as did the private capitalists and corporations of your day."[34] Everyone would be equipped with "a credit card issued him with which he procures at the public storehouses . . . whatever he desires whenever he desires it."[35] He predicted the use of technological devices that would seem quite familiar today, such as electronic home entertainment equipment, telephones, electric lighting and heating, cars and airplanes, mechanized farm equipment, and computers and keyboards. Because of the last, he wrote, "practically speaking, handwriting has gone out of use."[36]

Looking Backward is an incredibly imaginative futuristic novel and even a great love story. As a prediction, however, Bellamy's vision of what society would become in the year 2000 for the most part is an extreme case of wishful thinking. He predicted that all advanced countries would become socialist by the year 2000 and that the transition would be quick and peaceful; that all personal incomes would be equalized and that no savings was necessary or desired; that everyone would be a vegetarian and retire at age forty-five; that society would have free and limitless energy; that there would be world government and unrestricted immigration; and that the state would run everything and would provide extensive social programs: "No man any more has any care for the morrow, either for himself or his children, for the nation guarantees the nurture, education, and comfortable maintenance of every citizen from the cradle to the grave."[37] Bellamy even had the age-old utopian dream of "there being no legal profession."[38]

Visions of technological utopia continued through the 1930s, epitomized at futuristic world's fairs in Chicago and New York. Staged during the Great Depression, these fairs were geared to inspire consumer confidence in the future of the U.S. society and its capitalist system. The central theme was that happiness in the future would be achieved through capitalism and advanced technology, which would yield much material wealth for all. According to I. F. Clarke, the fairs "presented a modern, twentieth-century technological utopia in which abundance and leisure were the beneficent results of the reduced need for labor."[39] The fairs, however, were small islands of utopian thinking surrounded by vast seas of grim foreboding that only grew as the twentieth century progressed.

After World War I, utopian optimism dwindled, while visions of the techno-society gone bad proliferated, not only in fiction but in drama and the new medium of film. World War I began as a conventional nineteenth-century battle and ended in the unimaginable horror of mass killings achieved through new technological weapons such as tanks, aircraft bombers, and poison gas. Thirty-seven million men were killed, wounded, or missing, a casualty rate of 58 percent. Bertrand Russell described the war as "an imprudent union between human weakness and technological power. . . . Science threatens to cause the destruction of our civilisation."[40] Ever since 1918, there has been a series of calamitous developments that have further fueled predictions of doom, particularly the emergence of Stalinism, Nazism, and other forms of totalitarianism. These, together with the growing incursion of technology into our lives, have inspired various authors and filmmakers to envision a future in which science goes out of control or in which society is oppressed by a techno-totalitarian regime, or both together.

One of the earliest visions of science gone wrong was *Rossum's Universal Robots,* an eerie play written in 1921 by Karel Capek from the former Czechoslovakia, about a highly successful manufacturer of robots located on a remote island sometime in the second half of the twentieth century. The very human-looking robots sell for only $150 "fully dressed" and "can replace two and a half workmen," since "the human machine had to be removed sooner or later."[41] Rossum was a utopian dreamer who thought robots would solve all of humanity's problems: "There will be no poverty. All work will be done by living machines. . . . Everyone will live to perfect himself. . . . He will not be a machine and a device for production. He will be a Lord of creation."[42] The robots become a hot commodity for industry, are then armed with weapons and used as mechanical mercenaries, and eventually outnumber humans one hundred to one on the planet.

One day, the people at the remote robot plant discover that all communication with the rest of the world has somehow ceased. When some news arrives, they find that robots have gone out of control: "The robot soldiers spare nobody in the occupied territory. . . . Rebellion in Madrid against the government. . . . Robot infantry fires on the crowd."[43] The robots take control of all weapons, telegraphs, radio stations, railways, and ships. They even issue a manifesto: "Robots throughout the world: we, the first international organization of Rossum's Universal Robots, proclaim man as our enemy and an outlaw in the universe."[44] The last person on earth asks a robot leader why they killed the rest of humanity, to which the robot replies, "We had learnt everything and could do everything. It had to be! You gave us firearms. In all ways we were powerful. We had to become masters! Slaughter and domination are necessary if you would be human beings. Read History."[45]

The theme of technology run amok has continued in science fiction with Isaac Asimov's novels and with such movies as *2001: A Space Odyssey* (1968), based on a novel by Arthur C. Clarke, and *Blade Runner* (1982), based on a novel by Philip K. Dick. In *2001,* the supercomputer named HAL takes on a life of its (his?) own and kills everyone on board the spaceship except the protagonist, whom HAL tries but fails to kill. When confronted with the lone survivor, HAL merely says, "I can see you're upset, Dave." In *Blade Runner,* dangerous rebel androids are hunted down in a grimly futuristic Los Angeles in the year 2019.

The very real threat of nuclear war and the consequent extinction of the human race—the ultimate scenario of science gone wrong—has spawned many fictional visions of the end of humanity, or at least of society as we know it. To me, the scariest is the movie *On the Beach* (1959), a straightforward story about the last few remaining days of the temporary survivors of a nuclear war. There are no special effects, bizarre plot twists, or aliens from Mars—just a chilling tale of what could very well happen. Having personally met some of the folks who hold the keys for launching nuclear strikes, I see *On the Beach* as less entirely fictional than I used to.

The theme of a techno-totalitarian society has inspired such frightening visions of future society as Aldous Huxley's *Brave New World,* George Orwell's *1984,* Ray Bradbury's *Fahrenheit 451,* and more recently, Margaret Atwood's *The Handmaid's Tale,* novels that have all been turned into movies. One of the earliest movies on this theme is *Metropolis* (1926) by German director Fritz Lang, about a twenty-first-century high-tech society where an advantaged class lives a carefree life of plenty in a futuristic cityscape, made possible by a horribly exploited working class enslaved to high-tech machines and living and working underground, out of sight of the privileged. Hitler enjoyed *Metropolis*—surely for the wrong reasons—and asked Lang to make movies for the Nazi party; Lang's response was to leave Germany for the United States, where he continued his film career.

In 1949, in reaction to the brutal oppression inflicted by Stalinism and Nazism, George Orwell wrote his classic novel *1984,* which remains one of the most chilling visions of techno-totalitarian life. The novel takes place in London, which is under the control of Oceana, one of three totalitarian countries that rule the world and that are constantly at war with each other for the sole purpose of keeping the elite in power. Oceana is run by the all-powerful Party, which came into power after the Revolution overthrew the previous government and outlawed its capitalistic ideology. An enigmatic, unseen leader called Big Brother heads the Party.

The central role of the Party is total control over its subjects' thoughts and behavior. Everywhere signs warn, "BIG BROTHER IS WATCHING YOU," and indeed he is, via telescreens that invade everyone's privacy everywhere. When the "thought police" detect "thought crimes" against the Party, they take the guilty to the Ministry of Love to be tortured, brainwashed, and then executed. The Party tries to prevent seditious thoughts by employing "double think" to indoctrinate the citizens of Oceana, using slogans such as "War Is Peace," "Freedom Is Slavery," and "Ignorance Is Strength." The Party's official language, Newspeak, eliminates all unnecessary words so that thought crimes will be impossible, because people will not have any words to express them.

The utopian visions of the future have so far proved to be grossly exaggerated. Those earlier utopian writers foresaw a kinder, gentler society free of class conflicts and warfare; technology fulfilling material needs for all and creating a leisure society; and governments and societies run by a benevolent intelligentsia. However, since the days when they envisioned such utopian futures, mankind has continued to demonstrate his dark side with two world wars and the continual eruption of local wars in many areas of the world, from Vietnam to central Africa. Although technology has significantly contributed to our welfare—through advances in medical technology, for example—it has not fulfilled the promise of creating a uniformly wealthy leisurely society, and in fact has frequently put people out of work or 'deskilled' their jobs, or both.

Although the dismal visions of the future have been similarly exaggerated, they continue to provide legitimate warnings of the potential dangers of technology and totalitarianism. For the first time in our history, we now have several ways to annihilate our species quickly and thoroughly, including nuclear warfare, virulent infectious microorganisms (some bred through genetic engineering), and chemical weapons of unparalleled toxicity. (On a positive note, robots have not threatened to revolt against us, so far.) Totalitarian governments are as threatening today as when Orwell wrote *1984*. More than half the world's people live in nondemocratic societies dominated by communist regimes, right-wing dictators, despots, military juntas, and theocratic dictatorships. Before the fall of the communist regimes in the Soviet Union and its Eastern European satellites, about 30 percent of the world lived in totalitarian states that were as frightening as Orwell's *1984*—a figure that has since dropped to 24 percent. But there is no reason to expect that a totalitarian government could not arise again in Russia. As science-fiction writer Arthur Clarke once said, "The future isn't what it used to be."

FUTUROLOGY

Although every social forecaster in this chapter could be called a futurist, some of them specifically refer to themselves as such. A diverse group of social scientists, engineers, authors, humanists, and others are devotees of the "futurology movement." The inner circle consists of prominent members of the World Future Society in Washington, D.C., and the Association Internationale Futuribles in Paris, who, through articles and speeches, achieve a sense of solidarity in pursuing a more or less common purpose. Included in this group are such well-known social prophets as Alvin Toffler (author of *Future Shock*), Daniel Bell (Harvard professor of sociology and author of the popular book, *The Coming of the Post-Industrial Society*), Marvin Cetron (coauthor of *American Renaissance: Our Life at the Turn of the 21st Century*), and Joseph Coates (author of *Future Work*).

Coates calls himself "a futurist in business, industry, and government."[46] He has observed that although futurists come from diverse backgrounds, they share the following beliefs about their practice of futurology:

1. There is no single future. . . . [T]he objective therefore becomes to identify and describe a useful range of alternatives. . . .
2. We can see those alternative futures. . . .
3. We can influence the future. . . . [and]
4. We have a moral obligation to use our capability to anticipate and to influence the future."[47]

Although this is an accurate statement of how most futurists regard their movement, it is not necessarily what they actually do. For example, most futurists argue strongly for a single vision of the future, as opposed to a variety of alternatives, and most of their prophecies are expressed as indisputable assertions beginning with the overly confident words, "There will be."

The modern practice of futurology started with H. G. Wells, when he began writing nonfictional predictions of the future. The turning point in his writing career was the 1901 publication of his book *Anticipations of the Reaction of Mechanical and Scientific Progress upon Human Life and Thought.* Enormously popular and translated into several languages, *Anticipations,* said Wells, was the "first attempt to forecast the human future."[48] He followed up *Anticipations* with other futurist books, such as *The Outline of History,* which in 1905 sold more than 2 million copies in the United States and the United Kingdom. A year later, the Samurai Press (named after the Samurai class who ran society in Wells's novel *A Modern Utopia*) was founded in England to spread his futuristic ideas and to promote the doctrine of social progress. Wells became the most famous prophet in the first half of the twentieth century and was sought out by publishers and journalists for his predictions until his death in 1946.

Like his futurist successors, Wells made as many brilliant calls as forecasting blunders. As I. F. Clarke observed: "His forecasts were—and were not—as good as the rest of the field."[49] His best calls were in regard to the application of technology to society. Years, and in some cases decades, before they happened, he envisioned that the automobile would lead to increased suburbanization and that future warfare would be fought with tanks, bombers, intercontinental missiles, and atomic bombs. Wells also is credited with coining the phrase "atomic bomb" in his 1914 novel, *The World Set Free: A Story of Mankind,* in which his account of a future nuclear war is, in some details, chillingly prophetic:

> They went to war in a delirium of panic, in order to use their bombs first. China and Japan had assailed Russia and destroyed Moscow, the United States had attacked Japan, India was in anarchistic revolt with Delhi, a pit of fire spouting death and flame. . . . Most of the capital cities of the world were burning: millions of people had already perished.[50]

However, Wells also made many erroneous predictions involving future technology and society's fate, among them that eugenics would continually improve humanity through selective breeding to weed out criminal and other undesirable elements and to control population; that French would become the dominant world language, because so many leading scientific and literary books were published in French earlier in the century; and that central governments would run industry and end what he believed to be exploitive free enterprise. When the world was on the verge of World War II, he became increasingly pessimistic, and in his 1939 *The Fate of Man* he envisioned that the imminent war would throw the world into the dark ages, with no one surviving unscathed. Wells made his last prediction in 1946, the year he died: "Homo sapiens, as he has been pleased to call himself, is in his present form played out."[51]

By the 1920s, it became fashionable for famous people from all disciplines to dabble in futurology, including industrialist Henry Ford, economist John Maynard Keynes, founder of psychoanalysis Sigmund Freud, and politician Winston Churchill. In the 1920s, Ford declared that "quadrupeds are out," explaining, "We don't need horses. We've got the tractor. We've got the automobile. We don't need cows—we can make synthetic milk. We can make meat substitutes out of soy beans and coconuts—you can hardly taste the difference. We don't need sheep. We will be able to make wool out of synthetic things—it'll be better than wool."[52] Although Ford was correct in predicting our ability to produce these goods technologically, he failed to anticipate our continued preferences for natural foods and fabrics.

In 1919, Keynes made what is perhaps the most insightful—and responsible—prediction covered in this book. After serving as an official representative to the Paris Peace Conference in 1919 during which the terms of settlement for World War I were set, Keynes came away shocked at the vengeful and shortsighted nature of the settlement. In his book *The Economic Consequences of the Peace,* Keynes warned of the dangers that would arise from the fact that "the Treaty includes no provision for the economic rehabilitation of Europe—nothing to make the defeated Central Empires into good neighbors."[53] He correctly predicted that a combination of starvation and hyperinflation inflicted on Germany and its former allies would ultimately lead to social upheaval throughout Europe: "Men will not always die quietly. . . . In their distress [they] may overturn the remnants of organization, and submerge civilization itself."[54] This is precisely what happened to Germany under the burden of paying war reparations and continuing to suffer the effects of its destroyed economy. Although he anticipated the potential for a dictator to emerge from such a desperate situation, Keynes, unlike more recent futurists, made no hard-and-fast predictions of what would happen, instead questioning, "But who can say . . . in what direction men will seek at last to escape their misfortunes."[55]

In his book *The Future of an Illusion* (1928), Freud predicted that "the greater the number of men to whom the treasures of [scientific] knowledge become accessible, the more widespread is the falling-away from religious belief," which he called an "inevitable transition."[56] Although he gave no specifics as to when and where this will happen, he explicitly declared that religion is a "lost cause."[57] The *New York Times* reviewed Freud's book in an article headlined, "Religion Doomed Freud Asserts/Says It Must Give Way Before Science." Freud was right in predicting that science would create major challenges to established religious beliefs; the big bang theory and Darwin's theory of evolution provide explanations for how the world began and for how life on earth arose that are very different from those in the Judeo-Christian Bible, and advances in genetic engineering continue to peel back the mysteries of life. Freud was also right in predicting a decline in religious beliefs since his time until the middle of the twentieth century, although the reasons for the decline are complicated and cannot be attributed just to advances in science. Freud was wrong, however, in thinking that science would completely supplant religious beliefs, which still remain strong among a sizable portion of the world's population today.

In 1932, while serving as a member of the British Parliament, Winston Churchill wrote a curious article for *Mechanics Illustrated*, called "Fifty Years Hence," which is an interesting combination of insightful predictions and amusing miscalls of technological and social changes that he thought might take place by the year 1982. Churchill foresaw the enormous potential of atomic energy but believed that it would enable us to control the climate. Churchill correctly envisioned great advances in material sciences that would yield material "thirty times stronger than the best steel [of his day]," but such advanced materials have yet to produce a "six hundred horsepower [engine] weighing twenty pounds and carrying fuel for a thousand hours in a tank the size of a fountain pen."[58] He predicted the invention of teleconferencing technology that would link together people who live in cities with those who live in remote places, but erroneously concluded that "the cities and the countryside would become indistinguishable. Every home would have its garden and its glade."[59] He correctly anticipated advances in biological sciences that would enable doctors to administer growth hormones, for example, but he predicted some silly applications of genetic engineering, such as, "We shall escape the absurdity of growing a whole chicken in order to eat the breast or wing, by growing these parts separately under a suitable medium."[60] He also predicted that "the breeding of human beings and the shaping of human nature" would be common practices by the year 1982.[61]

After 1940, the futurist movement really started to take shape. German sociologist Ossip Flechtheim coined the term "futurology" in 1942, and in 1948 the Rand Corporation was founded as a private think tank funded primarily by the U.S. Air Force. Rand hired Herman Kahn as a senior physicist to work on how game theory, systems analysis and other new techniques might be applied to military strategy. Kahn achieved national prominence when he wrote *On Thermonuclear War* (1960), a book on the probability of another world war in the nuclear age. He left the Rand Corporation in 1961 to found his own futurist think tank, the Hudson Institute, specializing in issues of national security and public policy. After writing another book on nuclear war, *Thinking the Unthinkable* (1962), he collaborated on his first book of futurist prediction, *The Year 2000* (1967) (whose predictions on technology were discussed in Chapter 6) and became the first popular contemporary futurist. (He followed that up in 1976 with another collaborative book of futurist prediction, *The Next 200 Years*.) The World Future Society was founded in 1965 and quickly grew, but its membership peaked at 50,000 in the 1970s and dropped to about 30,000 in the 1990s. The World Future Society states that its purpose is to "serve as a neutral clearinghouse for ideas about the future, which include forecasts, recommendations, and alternative scenarios. These ideas help people to anticipate what may happen in the next five, 10, or more years ahead. When people can visualize a better future, then they can begin to create it."[62]

Two currently active futurists are Daniel Bell, author of *The Post-Industrial Society,* and Alvin Toffler, who in addition to *Future Shock,* wrote *The Third Wave.* Bell's *Post-Industrial Society* is Marxist-inspired prophecy with an elitist twist. Bell introduced his predictions in a paper he wrote in spring 1962, "The Post-Industrial Society: A Speculative View of the United States in 1985 and Beyond." In his book he extended the time frame to about 2003 and a couple of decades beyond. Bell predicted that in the postindustrial society, there would be an equalization of wages in industrialized countries such as the United States, Japan, the Soviet Union, and the nations of Western Europe; welfare benefits for all; and, most important, government would run most aspects of the economy and free enterprise would end: "The autonomy of the economic order (and the power of the men who run it) is coming to an end."[63]

Bell's elitist twist is that this strong future government would be run by scientists and other intellectuals, like H. G. Wells's samurai class. A determinist, like Karl Marx, Bell spoke of the "inexorable influence of science"[64] and asserted that "the emerging ethos of science is the emerging ethos of the post-industrial society."[65] Bell also predicted a "dictatorship of the profs" instead of the proletariat (perhaps some situational bias was involved): "The university increasingly [will become] the primary institution of the post-industrial society . . . [and will serve] as the source for the specialized intellectual personnel needed in government and public organizations."[66]

Bell based his utopian vision on the assumption that postmodern society would have the mathematical and scientific tools to predict and control the evolution of technology, economy, and society: "The development of new forecasting and mapping techniques makes possible a novel phase in economic history—the conscious, planned advance of technological change, and therefore the reduction of indeterminacy about the economic future. . . . The aggregate patterns could be charted as neatly as the geometer triangulates the height and the horizon."[67] Thus, herds of intellectuals would be needed to run the government: "By making decisions more technical, it brings the scientist or economist more directly into the political process."[68] In his "dream of ordering the mass society," Bell's inexorable utopian vision contains shades of *1984*.[69]

As we approach the end of the twentieth century, there are few signs of the postindustrial society that Bell predicted. However much they would like to, intellectuals in governments do not run industries, at least in democratic countries, and in the United States today, Democrats and Republicans in the executive and legislative branches are trying to downsize the federal government and have at least curtailed its growth: government employment as a percentage of total employment has shrunk from 17.8 percent in 1970 to about 16.8 percent today.[70] Bell did predict that the manufacturing sector of the economy would decline, but it leveled out at about 20 percent in 1990 instead of dropping to the 5 percent he had forecast. Although growth in scientific and technical jobs continues to outpace the growth in general employment, these jobs today represent merely 3.2 percent of the total workforce. Finally, contrary to Bell's prediction, elected officials in the United States are sharply curtailing government involvement in controlling, assessing, or predicting technology.

In certain respects similar to Bell's *Post-Industrial Society,* Alvin Toffler's *The Third Wave* bolstered his image as an icon of futurology. In *The Third Wave,* Toffler predicted broad social changes that would occur now that the first two waves—the agricultural and industrial revolutions—are history. This "Third Wave," which he says began in 1955, is now little more than a decade away from being complete.[71] Thus, his prophecy covers the same ground as Bell's vision of postindustrial society.

Characteristic of Toffler's writing, he starts off sensationally, promising more radical change than his Third Wave vision can deliver:

> Humanity faces a quantum leap forward; it faces the deepest social upheaval and creative restructuring of all time. . . . This is the meaning of the Third Wave . . . [which] will sweep across history and complete

itself in a few decades. . . . Tearing our families apart, rocking our
economy, paralyzing our political systems, shattering our values, the
Third Wave affects everyone . . . and provides the backdrop against
which the key power struggles of tomorrow will be fought."[72]

The Third Wave would "demassify" work, shifting employment
from the large factory to smaller plants and to the home; it would end
the trend toward increasing specialization; humans would design their
own evolution through eugenics; advanced nations would splinter into
smaller countries along racial, language, or other shared traits; minority
parties would come together to form "temporary modular parties" that
would gain control of government; and interest in religion would
increase.

With few exceptions, Toffler's predictions have been dead wrong
so far. Economies of scale in manufacturing still exist, favoring large production plants that can take advantage of high-cost technology. The return to cottage industries has not happened, although there has been a
rise in remote sales, service, and consulting workers operating out of
their homes, and, using personal computers, e-mail, and faxes, a large
number of workers of all types are doing some of their work at home.
Increased specialization is a fact of life today, given that it takes ever
longer to get to the frontier of established knowledge, as any student in
any specialty like medicine will surely attest. Despite the fact that genetic tinkering with human evolution is becoming increasingly possible, the debatable ethics of such developments has already generated a
sizable opposition. Some splintering of nations has occurred in places
such as the former Yugoslavia and Soviet Union—confederations of diverse groups that were artificially cobbled together—but in fact, in Europe a voluntary confederation is in the works. Finally, special-interest
groups have sought power by influencing the major parties rather than
by creating their own new ones.

Although Toffler predicted that the Third Wave could "turn out to
be the first truly humane civilization in recorded history," the news of
the world each day unfortunately continues to dispel Toffler's prediction.[73] In particular, there is little evidence of a major resurgence of interest in religion in developed countries since he wrote *The Third Wave*.

The 1996 *Statistical Abstract of the United States* shows that religious
belief has remain unchanged over the past fourteen years. The number

of persons attending a church or synagogue on a weekly basis was 40 percent in 1980 and 42 percent in 1994, and church and synagogue membership was 69 percent in 1980 and 68 percent in 1994. The *Gallup Poll Monthly* in 1994 shows that the percentage of people claiming that religion was at least fairly important in their lives was 86 percent in 1980 and 88 percent in 1994, a statistically insignificant difference.

Futurist chronicler Burnham Beckwith describes Toffler's ideas about the future as follows: "Third Wave trends are imaginary, minor, or temporary. . . . Where he offered no evidence of a new Third Wave trend, Toffler resorted to pure wishful thinking or conjecture."[74] Despite his dismal track record, Toffler remains a leading icon of futurology and is still highly influential, especially with Speaker of the House Newt Gingrich, who has known Toffler since the 1970s and recently proclaimed that *The Third Wave* is "one of the great seminal works of our time."[75]

THE TREND SPOTTERS

The last group of social forecasters are the commercial trend spotters: people who search for emerging societal trends and sell their "discoveries" to businesses and governments. The mini-industry of trend spotting includes major opinion-polling firms such as Gallup and Yankelovich and gurus such as John Naisbitt and Faith Popcorn.

Naisbitt makes a living searching for emerging lifestyle trends and changes in the popular psyche. He sells his trend forecasts in his quarterly newsletter, *John Naisbitt's Trend Letter*, the cover of which carries the headline "10 Powerful Trends" and the statement, "Companies who ignore or resist these trends will fail."[76] Naisbitt has written a series of futurist books, beginning with the popular *Megatrends 2000* (1982), which made him famous. In it, Naisbitt put forth ten trends that he believed would shape our futures. When the book came out, it seemed enormously valuable for planners of all types and for the masses curious about life in the future. Looking back, however, it is clear that three of Naisbitts' megatrends were long-term trends that were already well established before he wrote his book and that the other seven trends never materialized.

The three long-term, persistent trends that Naisbitt included among his predictions were pretty safe bets: the growth of an information society, increasing globalization, and north-to-south migration in the United States. Although the term "information society" is especially nebulous, it is fair to say that information technology has had an increasing influence on commerce and society since the electronic computer was invented more than forty years ago—something that would have been obvious in 1982, as Naisbitt himself attested when he referred to "the information industry that is already here."[77] Naisbitt, however, greatly overstated the impact of information technology: "The restructuring of America from an industrial to an information society will easily be as profound as the shift from an agricultural society to an industrial society."[78] The changes in industry, labor, and the nature of work in the United States over the past forty years have in fact caused less social upheaval than occurred when farmers quit their fields to become urban factory workers. Another info-society miscall was Naisbitt's optimistic view on robotics: "In the United States, the guest workers will be robots."[79] Although by now robotic machines are used in many industries, the number of them is not enormous. According to the *U.S. Statistical Abstract,* there are only 50,000 robots in the United States compared to a workforce of 131 million, a 0.04 percent penetration.

Naisbitt's forecast of increasing globalization also was an easy call. When he made his prediction, international trade was booming; U.S. trade with other countries had increased fivefold in the previous ten years. His prediction of north-to-south-migration is similarly obvious, given the long-term trend of U.S. industry moving south in search of lower-cost labor, cheaper operating costs, and better weather. Indeed, the southern and western regions of the United States have grown much faster than the Northeast, but the Northeast did not become the disaster area that Naisbitt predicted, as when he asserted, "In about ten years, colleges in the Northeast will have a hard time finding students."[80] In fact, the Northeast has continued to grow and today has more than its share of high-tech industries; its prestigious colleges are now harder to get into than when Naisbitt wrote *Megatrends.*

Naisbitt was wrong in his analysis of high-tech versus "high-touch" trends. Consider the following "high-touch" predictions he made: "The utilization of electronic cottages will be very limited. . . . [P]eople want to go to the office; people want to be with people. . . . Computer buying will never replace the serendipity and high-touch of shopping for what we want to be surprised about. . . . [T]eleconferencing is so rational, it will never succeed."[81] Naisbitt was right in assuming that these high-tech alternatives would not take over, but he was wrong in envisioning that they would not become popular. Contrary to his prediction, these high-tech alternatives are growing in use where they make economic sense and are convenient. For example, anyone who occasionally travels six hours on an airplane to attend a two-hour meeting can greatly appreciate the value of teleconferencing.

When Naisbitt declared, "The big-business mergers and the big-labor mergers have all the appearances of dinosaurs mating," he obviously failed to foresee the proliferation of mergers and acquisitions in the 1980s that increased—and have continued—throughout the 1990s.[82] According to Securities Data, the number of mergers and acquisitions increased 170 percent between 1983 and 1995, jumping from 3,385 to 9,124 deals. This increase in deals has also included mergers of some of the largest U.S. companies, such as Chase Manhattan Bank and Chemical Banking; Martin Marietta and Lockheed; Westinghouse Electric and CBS; and AT&T and McCaw Cellular Communications. His conviction that "centralized structures are crumbling all across America" and that "the decentralization of America has transformed politics, business, our very culture" has been proved wrong, with big government in the United States admittedly still unpopular but mostly still intact today.[83]

The problem with Naisbitt's assertion that "the 'Old Boy Network' is elitist; the new network is egalitarian" is that the old-boy network is alive and well and retains most of the power, as almost any female worker today would surely confirm.[84] His belief that "since there is so much diversity everyplace else in American culture, ethnics are not so much noticed as different as they are in tune with the country's general mood and values" is contradicted by the ethnic conflicts that continue to emerge.[85] Despite these mispredictions, Naisbitt has created a Megatrends franchise, publishing the books *Megatrends 2000, Megatrends for Asia,* and *Megatrends for Women;* marketing experts at companies like Procter & Gamble would call this "product line extension."

Although Naisbitt remains popular, in recent years he has been overshadowed by trend-spotting guru Faith Popcorn. *Fortune* magazine called Popcorn "the Nostradamus of marketing"; *Newsweek* noted she was "one of the most interviewed women on the planet"; *New Repub-lic* called her "a piece of work."[86] Popcorn has written two books, in-cluding her best-selling *The Popcorn Report: Faith Popcorn on the Future of Your Company, Your World and Your Life* (1991). She is the CEO of Brain Reserve, a $20 million trend-spotting consulting and publishing firm with many blue-chip Fortune 500 clients whose loyalty "borders on the evangelical."[87] More recently, she has extended her trend-prediction "expertise" into the political arena, helping governors, sena-tors, and congressmen win votes.

Popcorn claims to have an IQ of 180 (genius starts at 140) and that her predictions are 95 percent accurate. She told the *New Yorker,* "I'm trying to think of a trend that I've missed—it would be more credible if I could think of one."[88] She says that she divines her vision of the fu-ture by regularly reviewing three hundred newspapers, conducting ex-tensive consumer interviews, and tapping a panel of 2,500 experts in many fields.[89] Her most famous prediction is for the trend she dubbed "cocooning" in 1991: "The impulse to go inside when it just gets too tough and scary outside. To pull a shell of safety around yourself, so you're not at the mercy of a mean, unpredictable world. . . . Hiding . . . a full-scale retreat into the last controllable environment—your own digs. And everybody was digging in. . . . Cocooning is about insulation and avoidance, peace and protection, coziness, and controls—a sort of hyper-nesting."[90] The word *cocooning* has become so popular that it has been added to the *American Heritage Dictionary.*

A quick perusal of the 1996 *Statistical Abstract of the United States* re-veals that cocooning is nonsense. The premise that people are hiding out in their homes just is not happening. From 1989 to 1994, eating and drinking places have increased their revenues by 25 percent, and amuse-ment parks, recreational facilities, and museums have increased theirs by 61 percent. The number of pleasure trips made per year is up 21 per-cent. Participation has gone up in sports clubs by 22 percent, at bowl-ing alleys by 5 percent, and at race tracks by 2 percent. Even sales of tickets at movie theaters are up 20 percent, despite the formidable com-petition from video rentals and cable TV subscriptions.

According to Popcorn's prediction of a "Save Our Society (S.O.S.)" trend, the 1990s were going to be the "Decency Decade, dedicated to the three critical E's, Environment, Education, and Ethics."[91] The ev-idence shows that this has not happened. At best, the 1990s have shown little change over the late 1980s with respect to Popcorn's three E's. In fact, the data available to discern whether Americans have become more environmentally conscious in the 1990s are conflicting and inconclusive. In November 1994, according to the National Wildlife Foundation, voters elected "the most explicitly anti-environmental Congress in history"; however, that Congress was unable to pass adverse environmental legislation or cut the budgets of the Environmental Protection Agency or the Interior Department.[92] A 1996 consumer poll sponsored by the National Wildlife Foundation showed that 49 percent of U.S. voters believe that environmental regulations do not go far enough, an increase of 8 percent over a similar poll conducted in 1994 (but note that 49 percent is not even a simple majority).[93] Conversely, a biannual survey conducted by the National Opinion Research Center shows that from 1990 to 1994 the percentage of consumers who believe that the government should spend more on the environment has dropped. Jan Larson, who published the results of the survey in *American Demographics,* noted about this downward trend that "Americans seem to age out of their 'green' years."[94] A 1995 study by the Gallup Organization found that the percentage of households making contributions to environmental organizations dropped from 13.4 percent to 11.6 percent between 1989 and 1993. The *Gallup Poll Monthly* shows that the percentage of persons ranking the environment as the most important problem decreased from 8 percent in 1990 to 1 percent in 1996, and that after 1990, that figure has varied year to year in the 1 to 3 percent range. Although the evidence does suggest that Americans are concerned about the environment and want to keep existing safeguards against pollution in place, Popcorn's predicted upsurge in environmental consciousness has failed to happen.

As for Popcorn's prediction about education in the 1990s, there has been no demonstrable increase in Americans' interest in education, notwithstanding President Clinton's pledge to become the "nation's first genuine education President" and his 1997 inaugural speech, where he put forth a plan to improve education.[95] Although total spending on education in the United States as a percentage of the gross domestic product rose slightly between 1989 and 1995, from 7 to 7.3 percent, Congress proposed budget cuts for education in 1995 and 1996. According to a 1995 Gallup Organization study, the percentage of households contributing money to education dropped from 19.1 percent in

1989 to 17.5 percent in 1993. If abilities are any measure of interest, although scholastic aptitude test scores have remained about the same over the 1989 to 1995 period, reading skills have slipped. The National Assessment Governing Board found in 1994 that 30 percent of high school seniors were "non-functional readers," up from 25 percent in 1992. According to a 1996 U.S. Department of Education study, teachers perceived a marked decrease in parental involvement in child education and an increase in disrespect for teachers over the 1990–91 to 1993–94 school years.

What about ethics in the 1990s? A survey conducted in 1996 by *USA Today* shows that Americans' attitudes about ethics have changed very little over the past few years. Charitable giving, divorce rates, and drug use by high school students have remained about the same, and although there has been a decline in the rate of violent crime, there has been an increase in the number of children born out of wedlock.[96]

Some of Popcorn's predictions seem more a function of her own wishful thinking than anything else: "We [will] finally recognize the power, insight, and intuition of children and turn to them for expert advice, placing them on our most important boards, electing them to political office, and making them peace arbitrators" and "You won't see humans driving buses, at supermarket checkouts, or serving up fast (slow) food. They'll be replaced by colonies of androids who can walk your dog or fight your wars."[97]

Popcorn also presents trends that are contradictory, albeit admitting this in her book by saying, "It's inevitable. Trends merely reflect the coming consumer moods, and consumers are people—full of contradictions."[98] For example, while cocooning behind bolted doors, we would also be taking "Fantasy Adventures." While we would be concerned about our health in "Staying Alive," we would be pigging out on our favorite junk food in "Small Indulgences." According to her "Down-Aging" trend, "The skin-care market, with accelerated research in anti-aging technology, will see a new surge in vitality," *but,* "If you're secretly planning a face lift at fifty, you might want to find a doctor who leaves some lines in."[99]

If Popcorn is any kind of genius, it is only for marketing and self-promotion, for she has packaged pure fantasy and successfully sold it to some of the highest-level executives in U.S. industry. In fact, Popcorn got her schooling as a method actress at New York's High School for the Performing Arts and her training in commercial advertising. There is no doubt that her advertising background honed her skills at writing catchy titles and lines, as she herself attests: "I was an extremely good headline writer. That's how I think. I think short." She even confesses to have changed her name from Plotkin to Popcorn for marketing purposes: "It's a name created to cause attention—and it does."[100]

Never have so many given so much for so little. For $15,000 Faith Popcorn will give a speech; for $20,000 subscribers receive the bimonthly *Trendpack* newsletter; and for up to $1 million, her firm will undertake a project for a particular client. In an article in the *New Republic* entitled "Faith Popcorn's CEO Scam," Ruth Shalit declared, "The familiar rap on Faith Popcorn is that she is an old-fashioned scam artist, hoodwinking corporations and journalists."[101] Popcorn and Nostradamus have much more in common than perhaps *Fortune* realized when it called her the "Nostradamus of marketing." Like Popcorn, Nostradamus changed his name for marketing purposes, Latinizing his former name, Notre Dame, to give it more scientific authority. They both influenced the powerful: he the medieval court, she the executive suite. They both captivated their clients with their writing styles: he with mysterious prose, she with catchy sound bites. They both succeeded in selling a lot of baloney to the naive elite.

AN EXCUSE TO DO THE INEXCUSABLE

Much social prediction has been egregiously erroneous forecasts that reveal more about the prophet's psyche than about the future. These predictions are harmless, if you do not mind being naive about overly optimistic visions and needlessly agitated by doomsday prophecy. There is, however, an evil side to social prediction: the misuse of prophecy by demagogues to control the masses in order to achieve their master plan for society, which they claim is "inevitable" or "inexorable." "Self-interest and the quest for power: this, of course, is what false prophecy is and always has been about," wrote Max Dublin, author of *Futurehype: The Tyranny of Prophecy*.[102]

Marx's prophecy became the deadliest prediction in recorded history when it got into the hands of maniacal revolutionaries such as Lenin, Stalin, Mao, and Pol Pot, who used Marx and Engel's vision of the inexorable "specter of communism" as justification for committing crimes against humanity on a scale rivaling those of Hitler. For example, some demographers have estimated that the toll in human lives due to executions and starvation in Soviet Russia was about 40 million killed during the reigns of Lenin and Stalin; the number of millions more killed by other Marxist regimes is unknown. Popper dedicated his book, *The Poverty of Historicism,* accordingly: "In memory of the countless men and women of all creeds or nations or races who fell victims to the fascist and communist belief in Inexorable Laws of Historical Destiny."[103] In the words of sociologist Lipset, "No crueler joke has been played by history than the phenomenon of Marxism becoming the banner of the revolutionary movements to totally nonindustrial societies of Communism holding power in China, Cambodia, Albania, and many other poor, largely agrarian nations."[104] (Marx predicted that communism would emerge from developed industrial nations.)

Hitler used false prophecy in *Mein Kampf* to justify his belief that the Aryan German race was destined to rule because of what he claimed was its racial superiority. *Mein Kampf* sold more than 1 million copies when it came out in 1926 and later became part of the rationale for the murder of 6 million European Jews and hundreds of thousands of other people persecuted by the Nazis.

The United States used a false prophecy called "Manifest Destiny" to justify the takeover of most of the North American continent from Mexico and various Indian tribes during the nineteenth century. According to Manifest Destiny, American colonial states with their superior institutions were destined by God to take over the rest of the continent (and more) at the expense of Native Americans, Mexicans, Canadians, Spaniards, and anyone else who lived in these soon-to-be-expropriated lands. In envisioning an ever-expanding American populace of European descent, New York editor and author John L. O'Sullivan in 1845 wrote, "The fulfillment of our manifest destiny to overspread the continent allotted by Providence for the free development of our yearly expanding millions. . . . Yes, more, more, more! More our national destiny is fulfilled and . . . the whole boundless continent is ours."[105] The domino theory, a false prediction that the United States used in the 1960s and 1970s to justify its military actions in Southeast Asia during the Vietnam War, was a fundamental reason that 50,000 Americans and millions of Vietnamese lost their lives. It was argued at the time that if the communist regime in North Vietnam were allowed to take over South Vietnam, then all the countries in Southeast Asia and other places would fall to communism, like a series of falling dominoes.

The best way for a society to deflect the dangerous effects of false prophecy is to ensure a high level of education throughout its citizenship and to protect the freedom of all people to dissent. Ignorance is the breeding ground for false prophecy, superstition, bigotry, and other tools of despots, which can and have lured the masses into supporting or even participating in destructive, inhumane actions. Having a strong and clear sense of history is especially important, because false prophecy is typically built on a foundation of distorted historical facts that lend credence to such predictions. Recall that the Truth Department in Orwell's novel *1984* was responsible for continually altering history to serve the Party's needs: "The alteration of the past is necessary . . . to safeguard the infallibility of the Party."[106]

Although Lenin and his fellow Bolsheviks were responsible for initiating history's largest effort to remake an entire society, smaller projects of social engineering have been undertaken on a regular basis by most governments throughout the twentieth century. At least in democratic, free societies, these efforts are well intended, proposed and put into practice in order to correct a social problem or inequity—for example, the liberal social programs in many European countries and the 1930s New Deal and 1970s Great Society programs in the United States. However, the outcomes of such social engineering efforts are unknowable in advance and can yield unintended and counterproductive results.

The cost of failed social programs can be immense, including the destruction of neighborhoods, institutions, and individual initiative, in addition to wasting billions of taxpayer dollars. Lipset warns, "We [sociologists] should be exceedingly modest about using our status as experts to draw conclusions that call for major policy changes."[107] Popper believed that the role of social science is "the modest one of helping us to understand even the more remote consequences of possible actions, and thus of helping us to choose our actions more wisely."[108] As voters, we must question all attempts at broad-scale social engineering.

For years I have wondered why people argue so vigorously about politics, even when they basically share the same desired outcomes, such as general prosperity and full employment. The answer is, There are no laws that specify how these shared social goals can be attained. Consequently, we fall back on our own unfounded pseudotheories about social economics, which reflect our biases, beliefs, and suspicions. To cure poverty, for example, liberals believe in direct transfer of tax proceeds to needy individuals, while conservatives believe that poverty is best attacked by economic growth achieved through tax cuts and healthy free enterprise unencumbered by government. There is no proof that either approach is universally valid.

There is one last potential evil of social prediction: scientific bigotry. Given that people individually and collectively are not very predictable and that social theories are weak, making predictions about the behaviors of various groups of people can be very dangerous. For example, there are many social models used to predict the incidence of crime based on various social, economic, and demographic factors. Even if these models have some statistical significance, they can be used to make false conclusions about classes of people and individuals within them, because not everyone in a particular class will respond to the same situation in the same way.

8

Corporate Chaos

The height of the planning era, the early 1970s, was a time of tremendous confidence in the budding discipline of management science, which seemed to provide the answers to complex management problems for businesses and governments. Planning for the future never seemed clearer. All self-respecting major corporations had sophisticated internal planning departments and were heavy users of economic forecasters, futurists, strategic planners, and corporate models of every type. Corporate planners became so numerous that they were able to support two professional associations: the North American Society for Corporate Planning and the Planning Executives Institute.

General Electric, then generally regarded as the most planning-oriented company in the United States, typified the corporate planning era. After GE had floundered for years in the computer business, its CEO, Reginald Jones, attempted to bring more centralized control over the company by building a strong corporate planning department, which was ultimately staffed with 193 planners, many of whom previously held senior positions at major consulting firms and were leading contributors to the development of strategic analysis theories and planning techniques. GE's elite group of planners exercised considerable influence over operating divisions, kindling resentment among line management charged with running their divisions. The same thing was happening at other corporations.

During the 1970s, governments in Europe were also heavily

involved in planning their economies and industries. The communist governments of Eastern Europe planned their command economies down to the minutest detail, which they had done since coming under the control of the Soviet Union after World War II. Central planners forecasted the national need for all goods and then issued production quotas to the various plants that made them. The planners told each plant how much of their product to sell to whom, how many people to employ, the amount and type of raw materials to buy, and from whom to purchase them. In democratic Western Europe, France took similar measures to plan and control its industries and its overall economy through comprehensive national economic planning.

Even in the early 1960s, the Kennedy administration was heavily planning oriented in running the U.S. government. Henry Mintzberg, a professor of management at McGill University in Montreal and a specialist in strategic planning, noted that "the U.S. government in the heady days of President Kennedy's 1960s ranks up there next to the French experience [in attempting to plan government activities]."[1] Defense Secretary Robert McNamara, one of President Kennedy's "best and brightest" recruited from prestigious universities and think tanks to work in his administration, introduced the sophisticated Planning-Programming-Budgeting System (PPBS) to make important policy decisions—and to run the Vietnam War. PPBS was an elaborate planning system that attempted to link long-term strategic analysis and planning with day-to-day budgetary decisions affecting thousands of government programs. McNamara, for example, treated the Vietnam War as one big optimization problem, relying on statistical formulas such as "kill ratios" and other analytic tools to determine the most efficient use of soldiers and equipment to fight the war. In 1965, President Johnson dictated the use of PPBS in all federal agencies, and from there its use spread rapidly to state and local governments in the United States and then to foreign governments. Aaron Wildavsky, in his authoritative 1974 book, *The Politics of the Budgetary Process,* hailed PPBS as "the major budgetary phenomenon of our time."[2]

PPBS was not the only planning model to capture people's fancy. The most influential suppliers of planning advice during the 1970s were the "strategy boutiques," such as the Boston Consulting Group (BCG). BCG's claim to fame was its growth-share matrix, which boiled all of strategic planning down to the simple notion that winning in business meant becoming the low-cost producer among competitors and becoming the low-cost producer meant achieving the largest market share in the industry. The rationale behind this logic is that the company with the largest market share would have the greatest economies of scale (the biggest plants) and the most experience and learning advantages in making goods or providing services, and therefore the lowest costs.

BCG created a graphic representation of the growth-share matrix, illustrated in Figure 8.1, to indicate which of four strategies the management of a company should employ, depending on which of the four quadrants of the matrix applied to the business. Those in quadrant one (low growth/high market share) were *cash cows* that could be expected to generate an ample cash flow, which should be milked to fund investments. Those in quadrant two (high growth/high market share) were *stars* that should be fed cash so that they could sustain their leadership and become the cash cows of the future when market growth slowed. Those in quadrant three (low growth/low market share) were the *dogs* that should be shot without further question. Those in quadrant four (high growth/low market share) were *question marks;* management either had to invest in them in the hope that they would become stars or give up hope and shoot them like the dogs.

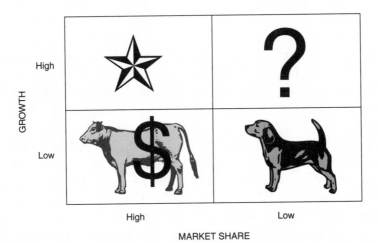

GROWTH

High

Low

High   Low

MARKET SHARE

Figure 8.1   The Boston Consulting Group's growth-share matrix.

THE MANAGEMENT SCIENCE MYTH

The foundations of the planning movement began crumbling in the early 1980s, when the sophisticated strategic-planning efforts failed to prepare Western businesses for the onslaught of global competition, especially Japan's aggressive entry into Western markets with superior, low-cost products. Strategic planning flew out the window as Western businesses frantically cut costs, streamlined operations, and improved product quality.

Hindsight, through research, has shown that planning had little or no effect on corporate profitability. In 1991, Brian Boyd, a corporate planner for Blue Cross and Blue Shield, analyzed the data in twenty-nine independent studies linking the practice of planning and financial performance for 2,496 companies between 1970 and 1988. He concluded, "The overall effect of planning on performance [was] very weak."[3] Despite all of GE's sophisticated strategic planning during that period, its share price remained flat and its price-earnings ratio declined. When Jack Welch took over as CEO in 1984, he quickly dismantled the corporation's much-heralded planning operation, downsizing the corporate planning function, and purging planners from divisional ranks.

According to Wildavsky, PPBS has "failed everywhere and at all times. . . . It produces costly rationales for inevitable failures."[4] The failure of government-run strategic planning, epitomized by the bankrupt command economies and crippled industries of Eastern Europe, was also evident in the most highly developed counties in the West over the past twenty years. In France, national economic planning failed because central planners could not control all the interactions among all the players in its economy, especially private-sector firms, nor could they plan for major shocks like the oil crisis. Actual economic events never went according to the national plan. For the United States, PPBS could not answer the most fundamental strategic questions about the Vietnam War, such as what its mission was or how the war could be won. According to Mintzberg, "The system, the machinery, McNamara and his whiz kids were leading America to its most humiliating debacle ever."[5]

In his seminal book *The Rise and Fall of Strategic Planning,* Mintzberg concluded that strategic planning "does not pay in general. . . . The annual planning process itself was rarely the source of new key issues or radical departures into entirely different product/market realms."[6] In 1984, *Business Week* came to a similar conclusion after analyzing thirty-three strategies it had profiled from 1979 and 1980: "It has become obvious that very few strategies seem to succeed."[7] *Business Week* further concluded that strategic planning failed because it relied on forecasts, calling it "planners' obsession with predicting the unpredictable."[8] Steven Schnaars, author of *Megamistakes,* had this to say from his ten years of research on strategic planning and forecasting: "There are almost no cases of companies that successfully predicted long-term trends and acted upon them."[9]

Not only is nearly everything that a planner would like to know about the future unpredictable—the weather, the economy, capital markets, technological developments, and societal trends—but organizations themselves are unpredictable. Organizations, like economies and societies, are complex systems that behave in subtle and sometimes counterintuitive ways. They are much more highly interconnected than tidy organizational charts and functional compartmentalization would suggest. For example, the retention of customers is a major determinant of an organization's financial viability, and almost everything that an organization does in some way affects its ability to retain customers. Although customer retention obviously depends on the organization's ability to deliver quality goods and services, there are many more subtle causes and linkages. Customer retention can also depend on whether the sales organization builds unrealistic expectations that the organization cannot deliver, whether the billing department makes mistakes, whether customer service representatives are cordial and efficient, and whether the organization maintains a good reputation.

Organizations exhibit nonlinear behavior with many different feedback loops. Some feedback loops amplify events in positive ways, such as the notion that success breeds success, as when a hot product generates enough positive word of mouth and publicity to turn it into a craze. Conversely, vicious cycles can send an organization into a downward spiral that is hard to break, as when negative conditions cause employees to quit, causing morale to plummet, causing more employees to quit. The combined effect of these feedback loops often generates unintended and surprising results.

Also affecting the complexity and unpredictability of organizations is irrational decision making. University of Chicago professor James

March, a specialist in managerial decision making, tells us in his 1994 book, *A Primer on Decision Making,* that rational decision making is an illusion, because decision makers in organizations lack sufficient information, have faulty memories, and tend to rework the facts to support original conclusions. He concluded:

> Decision makers do not consider all consequences of their alternatives. They focus on some and ignore others. Relevant information about consequences is not sought, and available information is often not used. . . . [T]he decision rules used by real decision makers seem to differ from the ones imagined by decision theory. . . . Instead of calculating the "best possible" action, they search for an action that is "good enough."[10]

No one can precisely understand how an organization works, because the links between cause and effect are elusive, and actions can create unintended consequences. The fact that investment newsletters that make buy-and-sell recommendations based on records of legal insider trading fail to beat the market suggests that even corporate executives do not know how their companies will fare in the stock market.[11] Organizations are also subject to the vagaries of chance. Within the short span of a year, a company could lose major clients, see its competitive advantage erode, go from technology laggard to leader, or introduce a winning new product.

W. Edwards Deming, the quality management guru—from the 1950s, when he helped Japan repair its war-torn economy, until he died in 1993—declared that "what is missing is a theory of management."[12] He was right about there being no proved natural laws of management, but wrong in expecting that such laws could ever exist. Philosopher Karl Popper's observation that natural laws of society cannot exist because societies consist of willful humans also applies to organizations, which in reality are microsocieties. Arthur D. Little (ADL) consultants Ranganath Nayak and John Ketteringham, in their 1986 book, *Break-Throughs,* concluded that "the power of the organization to control its destiny is often dwarfed by the resourceful individual's power to rewrite the organization's destiny."[13] Different groups of humans react differently to the same stimulus.

That there are no laws governing the behavior of organizations was known as far back as 1513, when Florentine Niccolò Machiavelli wrote in *The Prince* that organizational and political situations "vary according to circumstances, they cannot be reduced to rule."[14] More recently, MIT professor Peter Senge noted in his popular 1991 book, *The Fifth Discipline,* that "there simply is 'no right answer' when dealing with complexity [in organizations]."[15] With respect to innovation, the ADL researchers found that "breakthroughs have no formula. . . . There isn't a process."[16] Organizational consultant Margaret Wheatley noted in her book, *Leadership and the New Science,* "I know I am wasting time whenever I draw straight arrows between two variables in a cause and effect diagram."[17]

In my own consulting experience, I have witnessed the absence of durable laws and theories in management science that can predict how an organization will respond to change or that can reliably produce successful strategies. In the space of a few years, I have seen conventional wisdom vanish and paradigms for success become formulas for failure. I have seen strategies fail miserably in the United States but succeed handsomely in Europe. Innumerable forces of time, place, and circumstance determine whether strategies, brilliant or otherwise, succeed or fail.

The video game market is a classic case of strategic uncertainty and the failure of conventional wisdom. Video games became a craze in the 1970s but sank in popularity—and sales—in the early 1980s, causing the once stellar Atari, the leading manufacturer of video games in the United States, to lose hundreds of millions of dollars and lay off 7,000 employees. Most business analysts in the 1980s believed that the video game market was forever dead, supplanted by the growing use of personal computers. However, video games once again became a craze when Nintendo introduced its games with superior graphics.

In his authoritative 1973 book, *Management,* Peter Drucker wrote: "Management science has been a disappointment. It has not lived up, so far, to its promise. . . . It would have been more prudent—let alone a little more modest—to speak of 'management analysis' rather than 'management sciences.' "[18] Martin Gimpl and Stephen Dakin wrote more cynically in their *California Management Review* article "Management and Magic":

Is there really any difference between a chief executive asking his strategic planners for scenarios for the future and a Babylonian monarch making similar demands of his astrologer? We suspect not. Both may provide a basis for decisions where there is no rational method, given the current state of technology. But more important, both demonstrate that the leader is competent and knows what to do."[19]

BACK TO THE FUTURE

The absence of consistently valid organizational laws combined with management's insatiable appetite for quick solutions and formulas for success has created a continual procession of management fads from consultants, professors, and authors pushing the next big management concept. Of necessity, these new concepts are short-lived, because they cannot be universally applicable. The latest management fad may help some organizations solve some of their problems some of the time—under the right conditions—but invariably it will fail to fulfill its oversold promises and sink into the dustbin of once-popular notions.

BCG's growth-share matrix, for example, was overly simplistic and in many respects completely misleading, since it did not take into consideration quality, product innovation, corporate culture, leadership, or a multitude of other factors. Even its all-important premise that having dominant market share is the key determinant of productivity has been proved false many times, as demonstrated by the difficulties of such former market leaders as IBM, Sears, and General Motors. James Womack, author of the groundbreaking book *The Machine That Changed the World,* found that Japan's practice of "lean manufacturing," not plant size or economies of scale, explained how the world's most productive automotive plants achieved their cost advantage. While Western manufacturers emphasized high-volume output, economies of scale, and a fix-it-later mentality, Japan's lean manufacturing focused on teamwork and quality.

In 1980, as the growth-share matrix was fading in popularity, Harvard Business School professor Michael Porter emerged with the next big management idea. His popular book *Competitive Advantage* transformed Porter from being a respected academic at Harvard into a highly sought-after strategy guru and the wealthy co-owner of the successful consulting firm, Monitor. In the mid-1980s, I was invited to a business conference to give a keynote speech on strategic planning, and in preparing my speech, I read *Competitive Advantage* in search of a universal theory of strategy that the book seemed to promise. The closest thing to that was what Porter called "Strategy Space," a two-dimensional grid for plotting a company's position relative to its competitors. Unlike BCG's model, however, Porter's grid had no labels. Users of Strategy Space had to invent their own labels; in other words, Strategy Space was essentially a blank piece of paper. But Porter did provide some guidance on how to label the grid axes: "First, the best strategic variables to use as axes are those that determine the key mobility barriers in the industry. . . . Second, . . . it is important to select axis variables that do not move together."[20] *Translation:* Pick the most important variables, and make sure that they are different.

Was this all that the hottest strategy guru of the moment could tell us about the theory of strategy? In fact, many jealous rivals in the field of strategic planning at that time criticized Porter's book for being nothing more than a laundry list of potentially interesting considerations. I now realize that's all that any book on strategy can be, because there can be no universal theory of strategy.

The next big management idea came in 1982, with the publication of *In Search of Excellence,* by Tom Peters and Bob Waterman, the most popular business book ever written, to this day. Peters and Waterman, while working at the consulting firm McKinsey & Company, identified forty-three top-performing corporations and distilled the reasons that they were excellent into eight characteristics, using pithy phrases such as "Stick to Your Knitting."[21] The book created an "excellence" craze that lasted years after its initial publishing and launched Peters's career as a leading management guru, author, and highly paid speaker. But just two years after *In Search of Excellence* was first published, fourteen of the forty-three companies that Peters and Waterman praised for their excellence were floundering, plagued by earnings declines, management turmoil, and tarnished reputations.[22]

What the *Wall Street Journal* called "this decade's hottest management fad" may also have been its shortest-lived: reengineering. Reengineering came on the scene in 1990 with the highly popular *Harvard Business Review* article "Re-engineering Work: Obliterate Don't Automate," by Michael Hammer. Hammer's premise was that businesses could cut costs by 30 percent or more by eliminating a similar percentage of its workforce—that is, by downsizing. Within a few years, nearly every major corporation was doing some sort of reengineering, and in 1994 management consulting firm Bain & Co. ranked reengineering as the topic of most interest to top executives based on its survey of a thousand major corporations. Reengineering backfired, however, when management discovered the downsides to the mass firings of employees. In 1996, Bain's survey ranked reengineering below average in executive interest, causing a mad scramble to promote what the *Wall Street Journal* called "The next big thing."[23]

Ironically, we have recently come full circle, with strategic planning again back in vogue. Such was the theme of the August 26, 1996, *Business Week* cover story entitled, "Strategic Planning."[24] In a 1996 *Harvard Business Review* article, "What Is Strategy?" Michael Porter told us that executives have neglected strategic planning too long during these past few years of cutting costs, improving quality, and streamlining operations. According to a survey conducted by the Association of Management Consulting Firms, "Business strategy is now the single most important management issue and will remain so for the next five years."[25] In fact, many corporations have reestablished 1970s-style planning departments.

Forecasting is also back. Gary Hamel and C. K. Prahalad, in their popular 1994 book, *Competing for the Future,* advised us "to build the best possible assumption base about the future. . . . Industry foresight gives a company the potential to get to the future first and stake out a leadership position. . . . The trick is to see the future before it arrives."[26] This would be a nice idea if foreseeing the future were possible; as the *Economist* noted, "What firms really want to know is what Mr. Hamel and Mr. Prahalad steadfastly fail to tell them: how to guess [the future] correctly."[27]

THE ILLUSION OF CONTROL

Yet another aspect of the complexity of organizations is that they are not directly controllable. Attempting to control an organization usually creates unintended results, much like pushing in on a balloon in one place and having it bulge out somewhere else. It reminds me of the story, perhaps apocryphal, about a factory in the former Soviet Union that was supposed to produce a certain tonnage of nails as dictated by the Soviet government's national plan. Able to produce only a limited volume of nails within the allotted time, the factory succeeded in meeting its production quota only by making foot-long nails; anything smaller would not have weighed enough.

Peter Senge noted in *The Fifth Discipline,* "The perception that someone 'up there' is in control is based on an illusion—the illusion that anyone could master the dynamic and detailed complexity of an organization from the top. . . . Power may be concentrated at the top . . . but that does not mean that they actually exercise control commensurate with their apparent importance."[28] James March observed from his studies of decision making that "organizations are continually changing, routinely, easily, and responsively, but change within them cannot ordinarily be arbitrarily controlled. Organizations rarely do exactly what they are told to do."[29] Similarly, the researchers from ADL concluded the following, regarding attempts to control creativity and innovation: "A manager can't make a new idea spring up within the organization. He cannot create the creative team. . . . The breakthrough leap is something that comes from individual people, not from organizations, and not from anything the organization does to those people."[30]

In fact, organizations do not need to be heavily controlled, because they have the capacity to achieve great things on their own through the process of self-organization. If permitted, organizations readily adapt to changes in the environment, self-renew, create innovations, and solve problems in novel ways. March was perhaps the first to report these positive aspects of organizational complexity, in his 1981 article, "Footnotes to Organizational Change," published in *Administrative Quarterly.* "Organizations," he wrote, "are remarkably adaptive, enduring institutions responding to volatile environments routinely and easily."[31]

The ADL researchers found that innovation and creativity come naturally to organizations of all types:

> The good news is that creativity is more prevalent and more hardy than most people imagine. The evidence of these breakthroughs is that new, extraordinary ideas can emerge from any environment. . . . We have seen breakthroughs that grew from rich soil, but also from barren soil, rocky soil, and no soil at all. Breakthroughs have come from

creative teams that were ignored by their organizations, supported only belatedly by their organizations, misunderstood by their organization, even assaulted by their organization. Breakthroughs can emerge just as readily from no organization at all. As a manager . . . you can get a breakthrough whether you deserve it or not.[32]

Self-organization is a powerful phenomenon that enables organizations at their lowest levels to respond flexibly to emerging threats and opportunities with little management oversight. The ADL study on innovation provides a fascinating window on how self-organization, in the form of what it calls "benevolent conspiracies," takes place deep within organizations to create new products:

[The innovators] learn the system mostly for the purpose of finding its weaknesses, perverting it for their own purposes. They find gaps in schedules, slush funds in budgets, and personnel who have interests compatible to theirs. . . . These conspiracies are usually—and best—kept safely out of sight of management. . . . Without its knowledge, the saboteur [takes] the organization beyond the point of no return.[33]

The development of successful strategies is a form of innovation, which also cannot be controlled. Mintzberg has studied the process of strategy development and has concluded that novel strategies do not normally come from logical analysis but rather from the intuition of visionary executives and intuitive employees buried deep in the organization where they are closest to solving clients' problems. Mintzberg's following note on strategy development is surprisingly similar to the ADL findings on innovation:

Strategies grow initially like weeds in a garden, they are not cultivated like tomatoes in a hot house. . . . Strategies can take root in all kinds of places, virtually anywhere people have the capacity to learn and the resources to support that capacity. . . . Such strategies become organizational when they become collective, that is when the patterns proliferate to pervade the behavior of the organization at large. . . . To manage this process is not to preconceive strategies but to recognize their emergence and intervene when appropriate.[34]

The ADL researchers provided the following assessment of how control stifles organizational creativity and innovation:

If as a manager, you make the development of breakthroughs a corporate mission and begin to pontificate on your strategies to attain this objective, the creative people in your organization will immediately recognize you as the worst sort of pompous ass and will retire to their recreation rooms and garages to work on their ideas as far as possible from the cheerleading scrutiny of Big Brother. . . . It seems true, in many cases, that the only role management can play without confusing the development of a new idea is to stand by and observe."[35]

Efforts to control the development of strategies through formal planning exercises have the similar effect of stifling creativity. A survey published in 1985 by *Long Range Planning* found that 60 percent of CEOs and even 40 percent of chief planning officers agreed that the planning department had "a somewhat negative impact on managerial innovativeness."[36] Ironically, planning kills the thing it aspires to create: a strategy. Mintzberg concluded that planning is a process for gaining central control and that the term "strategic planning" has "proved to be an oxymoron."[37]

THE FUTURE DOES NOT EXIST

The future is totally unpredictable. Organizations are unpredictable. Efforts to control organizations are futile, even harmful to organizations. Planning stifles strategic thinking. What is to be done? Do we give up planning for the future? Surprisingly, there is much that can be done to help organizations succeed in the future. Let's start by examining exactly what we mean by "future," "opportunity," and "vision."

The Future

Most people would define the "future" as something or sometime that is going to happen. But it does not follow to think that the future is some predetermined sequence of events. For each of us, an infinite number of possible futures could emerge, and it is impossible to predict which one will. The pathway into the future is unknowable; it consists of innumerable crossroads, branches, detours, accidents, and reversals. What happens today influences what happens tomorrow, which in turn influences what happens the next day, and so on.

The often quoted notion that "anything is possible" is only half right. Almost anything is reasonably possible in the remote future. But over, say, a ten-year period, what is possible in the future is somewhat constrained by what exists in the present. As shown in Figure 8.2, the realm of future possibilities fans out from the present into the distant future. For a couple of years ahead, it is reasonable to assume that the future will much resemble the present.

The history of manned space travel provides a good illustration of how the realm of future possibilities changes over time. The cold war fueled the space race between the United States and the Soviet Union, with each trying to demonstrate its ideological and military superiority. The crowning achievement of this enormous investment in space travel was the U.S.'s landing on and successfully returning from the moon in 1969, thus fulfilling the mission that President Kennedy announced to the U.S. Congress in 1961: "I believe that the aim of this nation should be to land a man on the Moon and return him safely to Earth before the end of the decade."[38] The 1972 Apollo mission to the moon, however, has so far been the end of the line for human travel into deep space. After that, the U.S. government sharply curtailed its investment in space exploration, focusing on more modest ventures such as unmanned space probes and the recyclable space shuttle program.

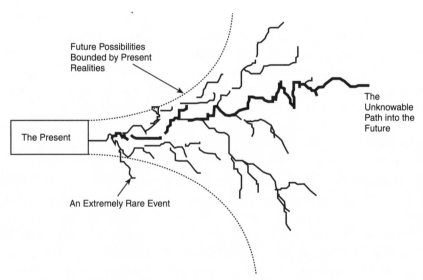

Figure 8.2   The realm of future possibilities.

In 1968, at the height of the U.S. space program, Americans were first entertained by the movie *2001: A Space Odyssey,* about a U.S. space mission to the planet Jupiter in the year 2001. In 1968, a trip to Jupiter by the year 2001 was certainly within the realm of future possibilities, and it is hard to imagine what we might have achieved in space technology if the United States had maintained the 1960s level of funding and research on space travel over the past thirty years. For better or worse, we did not, and now traveling to Jupiter by the year 2001 is nearly outside the realm of future possibilities. Ironically, though, the United States and Russia are currently collaborating to put a permanent space station in orbit around the earth, whereas collaborative East-West space ventures were outside the realm of future possibilities during the cold war.

Opportunity

We do know that whether an organization thrives or even continues to exist in the future depends on its continual pursuit of opportunities to gain advantages relative to its competition. But large or small, opportunities exist more in the present than the future. Assume that Figure 8.3 represents the realm of current opportunities, where the height of the terrain indicates competitive fitness: the higher an organization is on the terrain relative to its competitors, the greater is the likelihood of its survival. Greater competitive fitness for an animal could mean larger size, hunting in packs, or night vision; for an organization it could mean higher productivity, product innovation, or a superior sales force. Organizations, like species, must continually climb to greater heights to survive in a competitive world.

Assume that, in Figure 8.3, Hill C is the hill of conventional wisdom, where an organization can take small steps toward its summit to attain slight but well-known competitive advantages. Beyond Hill C is Mount Breakthrough (Mt. B, for short)—a discontinuity, an innovation, and a quantum leap in competitive advantage over Hill C. In football, for example, Hill C might be the pursuit of better blocking and tackling, which have traditionally yielded a few more inches per play, while Mt. B might be the introduction of the forward pass into the game in 1906. Until then, football had been purely a running game, where a gain of three yards was a major, hard-fought step toward victory. St. Louis

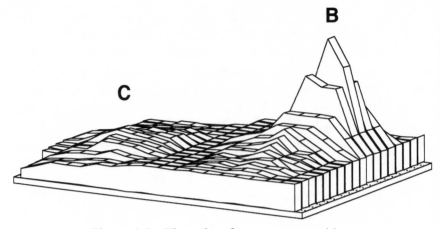

Figure 8.3   The realm of current opportunities.

University's football team trained heavily on the forward pass when it was legalized in 1906 and beat competitors 402 to 11 points during that season.

Organizations are typically run by conventional thinkers who pursue proved opportunities that are sure to yield a slight gain in competitive advantage. These conventional thinkers are like myopic climbers on the side of Hill C, oblivious to Mt. B. To gain the summit of Hill C, myopic climbers need only make sure that every step they take is an uphill step, which a blind climber could do just as well.

Vision

The Mt. Bs of the world are invisible to most people, because such breakthroughs are outside the realm of conventional thinking and often counterintuitive. For example, getting to Mt. B requires climbing down Hill C, and climbing downhill does not seem to make much sense to the conventional thinker and may well be painful. This downhill climb in sports is called "positive regression"; it means that the acquisition of a new, superior technique usually causes a diminution of overall skill until the new technique is adequately learned. Anyone who plays golf or tennis and takes an occasional lesson to learn better skills knows how frustrating positive regression can be. Your game degrades for months before you emerge as a better player. Positive regression for organizations might mean abandoning traditional practices that provided a competitive advantage, in favor of a new, innovative approach that might cause a deterioration in short-term financial performance.

There are rare individuals who speak of Mt. B–type opportunities. We call them dreamers or fools until they prove that the opportunities they see actually exist, and then we call them visionaries. However, these visionaries did not foresee the future; rather, they envisioned a superior way of doing things. These envisioned opportunities exist in the present, even though it might take several years to develop them fully. Hindsight creates the illusion of entrepreneurial clairvoyance; but, in fact, the visionary helped shape the future, not foresee it.

Every move on the competitive map of opportunities changes the pathway into the future and opens a new realm of possible futures. For example, Wal-Mart, Home Depot, and Toys 'Я' Us have so thoroughly revolutionized mass merchandising that, in addition to nearly causing the demise of Main Street businesses, they have completely changed the rules of the retailing and the realm of future possibilities. In reflecting on how the growth of the Internet affected his company and competing companies, Microsoft CEO Bill Gates observed, "Every new change forces all the companies in an industry to adapt their strategies to that change."[39]

Clearly the future is not some fixed entity that awaits us in time; the only thing that is real is the present. The first implication of this is that an organization must be adaptable to an ever-changing environment, as Drucker advised in his book *Management:* "The question that faces the strategic decision-maker is not what his organization should do tomorrow. It is 'What do we have to do today to be ready for an uncertain tomorrow?' "[40] Ralph Stacey, author of *Managing the Unknowable,* similarly suggested: "By focusing our concern on present issues that have long-term consequences, we actually deal with the long term in a more realistic and creative way."[41]

The nonexistence of a single, fixed future also implies that organizations and their leaders can change how the future unfolds by influencing which of the infinite pathways in the realm of future possibilities become realities. In his book *If It Ain't Broke . . . Break It,* motivational speaker Robert Kriegel observed that successful leaders "know that the future isn't found; it is invented. It is shaped by people with the vision, courage, and wisdom to think beyond the boundaries of the known."[42]

That the future is moldable is a powerful concept. If an organization does not try to shape the evolution of its future environment, then it will be overtaken by other organizations that shape the future to give themselves a competitive advantage.

THRIVING IN THE FUTURE

Although there is no explicit formula for designing a successful strategy, there are some guidelines for developing an organization that is likely to create one. Following them can result in an organization that is stronger and more adaptable than its competitors and better able to deal with future uncertainty. These guidelines for shaping the future are based on six success-oriented bioevolutionary properties.

Self-Organization

Self-organization requires two essential ingredients: empowerment and guiding principles. Empowerment provides the freedom, training, and tools to accomplish great things at the lowest levels of the organization; guiding principles focus these self-initiated efforts on what needs to be done to achieve the organization's goals. Empowerment and guiding principles are both complementary and countervailing forces. As Margaret Wheatley has noted, "The two forces that we have always placed in opposition to one another—freedom and order—turn out to be partners in generating viable, well-ordered, autonomous systems."[43]

Empowerment requires giving authority, skills, and freedom to employees at all levels to do their jobs; it is especially important for the front-line employees who perform the important tasks of providing goods and services and satisfying customers. Without empowerment, self-organization gets too constrained; employees have to stick to the rule books and do exactly as told by their supervisors. They lack the freedom and trust to act creatively in aiding customers or clients, solving problems, and generating new ideas. Empowerment comes in many forms, including delegation of responsibility, involvement in task forces, participation in making organizational decisions, and the use of self-directed teams—work groups of about ten employees that run their day-to-day operations without a supervisor.

Guiding principles, the second ingredient to self-organization, include a few meaningful statements about an organization's strategic direction and its organizational and cultural values, which have been variously called mission statements, strategic intent, theories of the business, value statements, and business philosophy. Peter Drucker concluded that without a vision statement, "decision-makers in the business, all the way up and down, will decide and act on the basis of different, incompatible, and conflicting theories of the business. They will pull in different directions without even being aware of their divergences."[44] Margaret Wheatley observed; "If we allow autonomy at the local level, letting individuals or units be directed in their decisions by guideposts . . . , we can achieve coherence and continuity."[45] Of course, these visionary and cultural statements must be meaningful to employees to work. They must state what the business is about, what it seeks to become, what behaviors are sought. Kriegel suggests that a vision statement should "resonate with . . . employees' dreams."[46] The vision statements must also be specific, but not so detailed as to be overly controlling—"visions that inspire but do not describe," as Wheatley recommended.[47]

Perhaps the most successful case in which self-organization prevailed during a highly unpredictable event was D-Day, the World War II invasion of the Normandy coast. According to historian Stephen Ambrose, the empowerment of the Allied troops at all levels and the straightforward mission of cracking the German defenses (the guiding principle) were the prime reasons that the Allied forces succeeded during D-Day. In his book *D-Day,* Ambrose came to the following conclusions based on hundreds of interviews with D-Day veterans:

> But for all the planning, strategizing, and deception, in the end the success or failure in Operation Overlord [D-Day] came down to a relatively small number of junior officers, noncoms, and privates or seamen in the American, British, and Canadian armies. . . . It all came down to a bunch of eighteen-to-twenty-year-olds. They were magnificently trained and equipped and supported."[48]

Winston Churchill called D-Day "the most difficult and complicated operation ever to take place."[49] The invasion was prepared for with a two-year planning exercise that involved 175,000 soldiers, 5,333 ships of all types, 11,000 airplanes, and 50,000 tanks, bulldozers, and other vehicles. In spite of the massive planning exercise, not much went according to plan during D-Day, except perhaps the tides. The weather caused paratroopers to be dropped in the wrong places and hindered aerial bombing of the Germans' coastal defenses. After the invaders left their landing craft, the top brass back in their ships and in England could do nothing but watch as the troops acted on their own. The Allied invaders adapted to horrific and unpredicted battle conditions, doing what was needed at all levels of command to achieve their mission.

Hitler had a completely different organizational model. He believed that Germanic discipline and total control from the top would easily conquer the democratically bred Western forces, especially those from the United States who had never seen military action. In his view, as described by Ambrose, "totalitarian fanaticism and discipline would always conquer democratic liberalism and softness," and Germany's greatest military asset was "the unquestioning obedience expected of Wehrmacht personnel from field marshal down to private."[50]

Hitler's concept of command backfired during D-Day. Although he and his forces had the capability to defeat the Allied invasion, his subordinates were paralyzed. His air force, navy, and nearby tank forces failed to counterattack during D-Day when the Allied forces were most vulnerable. According to Ambrose:

> The performance of the Wehrmacht's high command, middle ranking officers, and junior officers was just pathetic. The cause is simply put: they were afraid to take the initiative. They allowed themselves to be paralyzed by stupid orders coming from far away that bore no relation to the situation on the battlefield. Tank commanders who knew where the enemy was and how and when he should be attacked sat in their headquarters through the day, waiting for the high command in Berchtesgaden to tell them what to do. . . . The men fighting for democracy were able to make quick, on-site decisions and act on them; the men fighting for the totalitarian regime were not."[51]

Intelligence

Organizational intelligence is the collective intelligence of the organization as a whole, with all its connections, exchanges of knowledge, and group inspiration. It involves much more than hiring a bunch of smart people (although it starts there). Anyone who has participated in highly productive brainstorming exercises knows that the collective brilliance of the group is far greater than that of the most intelligent person in the room.

Nature confers great competitive advantages on intelligent life forms and on smart organizations. Intelligent life forms more quickly and flexibly adapt to changing environments and learn to capitalize on new opportunities and avoid pitfalls. The same is true of intelligent organizations, be they corporations, governments, associations, or armed forces.

The *American Heritage Dictionary* defines intelligence as "the capacity to *acquire* and *apply* knowledge." To keep in touch with its environment and internal workings, organizations must acquire a tremendous amount of external and internal information. Customer information is vital for an organization to know what it needs to do to satisfy clients with new products and improved service. In his 1991 book, *The Customer Driven Organization,* Richard Whiteley advised, "Saturate your company with the voice of the customer," and then he provided a long list of ways for organizations to collect information from clients, including things like visiting client sites to examine how products get used and conducting client forums to get feedback on changing needs in the market place.[52] Employees are also a treasure trove of ideas for creating new products and improving processes.

The acquisition of knowledge is useless, however, if the information does not get to the right places in the organization where it can be best put to use. The most obvious right place is senior management; if they are to play any meaningful role in running the company, they must know what is going on with respect to employees, customers, and competitors. However, some executives are so isolated from the flow of vital information they remind me of a brontosaurus that does not react quickly enough to evade a tyrannosaurus's biting its tail, because it takes too long for the pain signals to travel through its long tail and neck to reach its brain. Beyond senior management, there are no specific right places to which to direct information; it is impossible to tell in advance who might need what information when in order to resolve any number of problems. The only answer is to share information broadly across all levels and organizational boundaries.

Being kept in the dark has been a top-ranked grievance in every employee survey I have seen. Building an open culture is the key to maximizing the free flow of information. Organizations with open cultures operate on a first-name basis, encourage considerable informal interaction across all levels, and often place executives close to the operations they manage (sometimes even in cubicles just like the people they work with). Toyota's auto plants keep all employees informed about plant operations using lighted electronic display panels to post daily production targets, cars produced that day, breakdowns, personnel shortages, and other operational data. "Every time anything goes wrong anywhere in the plant," Womach observed, "any employee who knows how to help runs to lend a hand."[53]

In contrast, organizations with closed cultures tend to be hierarchical, formal, and secretive. Layers of middle management and privileges such as remote offices, executive dining rooms, and reserved parking spots insulate top executives from the people they manage. Many organizations operate like the CIA, withholding vital information from employees in fear that it might fall into the wrong hands or because employees "don't need to know"—the all-time worst excuse for withholding information.

Organizational learning is greatly enhanced by sharing information across different levels and functions, and these new information connections result in a cross-fertilization of organizational thinking that often leads to new ideas. As Margaret Wheatley noted, "Knowledge is generated anew from connections that weren't there before."[54] Employing cross-functional teams to solve problems, having employees from different backgrounds work together, and using new forms of electronic communication all significantly augment the exchange of information, even in secretive organizations. In this respect, the impact of e-mail, electronic bulletin boards, and other forms of electronic communication has been especially fruitful. In their book *Connections,* Lee Sproul and Sara Kiesler, professors at Boston University and Carnegie-Mellon, respectively, wrote that electronic communications "do not simply cross space and time; they also can cross hierarchical and departmental barriers, change standard operating procedures, and reshape organization norms. They create entirely new options in organizational behavior and structure."[55]

If all this newly acquired and shared information does not change traditional beliefs and result in some form of behavioral change, then learning has not happened and organizational intelligence does not exist. Many organizations are highly resistant to new information that challenges current beliefs or threatens its sacred cows. If management cannot countenance hearing such information, it will be left in the dark whenever crises arise; if it is wed to winning formulas of the past, it will get blindsided by the competition. In most organizations, the naysayers vastly outnumber the innovators; they kill new ideas with negative criticism, such as falsely protesting, "We've tried that before and it failed." Ironically, naysayers usually believe that they are helping the organization avoid mistakes, when in fact they are stifling its learning and intelligence.

Every organization has the capacity to learn, but it is the speed of learning that separates the winners from the losers. Arie De Geus, head of planning for Royal Dutch/Shell, has concluded that "the ability to learn faster than your competitors may be the only sustainable competitive advantage."[56] For organizations, as with humans and other higher life forms, the quicker the ability to learn, the greater the intelligence and the greater the likelihood of thriving in the future.

Organizations learn quickest by taking risks and acting fast, like an infant stumbling through an unknown world and occasionally getting bruised while learning at an enormous rate. In fact, organizational intelligence increases with the number of mistakes its employees make, because mistakes cause everyone to go back to the drawing board with new insights and a fresh outlook. Tom Watson, Jr., past CEO of IBM, describing his attitude toward problem solving, said, "Solve it, solve it quickly, solve it right or wrong. If you solved it wrong, it would come back and slap you in the face and then you could solve it right."[57] Ironically, risk avoidance is in itself a significant risk, because it diminishes learning.

Natural Reflexes

Although an organization cannot predict its future, it can prepare itself for the otherwise unexpected surprise events. The human pain system, for example, has natural reflexes developed over eons of evolution that cause the body to react quickly and without thought to resolve a potentially harmful situation. For the same reasons, the military continually conducts maneuvers to familiarize the troops with all types of foreign terrain and battle conditions. The same is true with fast-moving sports. For example, when you play at the net in tennis, your opponent may smash a ball at you so quickly that you have no time to think about what to do. Essentially, you have to prepare for such a situation and respond reflexively when it arises.

Managements can anticipate possible future situations by simply asking "what-if" questions (e.g., If situation X happens, what will be the impact on my organization, and how should I respond?). Some corporations have made great use of what-if questions. In 1984, when the price of oil was $28 a barrel, Royal Dutch/Shell worked out a number of scenarios concerning what it would do if the price of oil were cut in half, then considered a doomsday scenario. Yet by April 1986, the price of oil fell to $10 a barrel. According to the company's head of planning, "The fact that Shell had already visited the world of $15 oil helped a great deal in that panicky spring of 1986."[58]

Scenario development is a great managerial tool so long as it is restricted to simple what-if questions. Taken to an extreme, however, the development of elaborate scenarios comes too close to full-fledged prediction. When that happens, managements are asked to choose among several highly detailed futures, none of which may ever come to pass. Melvyn Goetz, Westinghouse's director of corporate development, observed that this "still leaves you with having to choose which scenario you need to prepare for—and what if you guess wrong?"[59]

Mutation

Occasionally and significantly, accidents happen in nature that provide a quantum leap in competitive advantage that could not otherwise be attained through slow evolutionary growth. Similarly, small random changes in a home-grown cohesive organization may produce highly beneficial results. There are many sources of potentially beneficial organizational mutation, such as tolerating pockets of seemingly mutinous behavior, selectively hiring high-level executives from outside the company's industry, and exploring the inner workings of unrelated industries and corporations that may yield important analogies. For example, my research for this book was greatly helped by a few random acts by friends and relatives, who gave me books about subjects that at first seemed to have no relevance to this book. Several of these books proved to be highly relevant and introduced me to new perspectives, which I doubt I would have discovered through my normal methodical research approach.

Symbiosis

Nature has conferred some advantages on life forms that, unwittingly or otherwise, help each other in a process called symbiosis. A typical example of symbiosis is the bird eating tiny insects off the back of the hippopotamus; the bird gets a meal, and the hippo gets relief from pests. Environmental friendliness also applies to organizations, which can be greatly helped by maintaining strong, mutually beneficial relationships with all types of fellow inhabitants. Recently, enlightened businesses have discovered the advantages of building strong partnerships with suppliers, as opposed to considering them to be vendors only as good as their latest price. These partnerships can lead to mutually beneficial process improvements and provide a source of creative new product ideas.

Competitive Challenges

Life forms that thrive in highly competitive environments evolve to become tough and resilient, such as the highly adaptive animals on Africa's Serengeti Plain. In contrast, life forms that thrive in protected niches, insulated from competition, tend to become weak and threatened by extinction, as did several species of flightless birds on remote Pacific islands, including the dodo and the kiwi. Lacking land-based predators, these species eventually lost their ability to fly, because flying conferred no advantages in either getting food or avoiding predators. The dodo bird thrived until humans, dogs, rats, and other carnivores invaded their protected habitat and hunted them to the point of extinction in the late seventeenth century.

Competitively challenged organizations also evolve to become tough and resilient, while protected organizations (such as nationalized industries and government agencies) do not stand a chance in competing against world-class rivals. Federal Express and other commercial couriers now far outperform the once-protected and monopolistic U.S. Postal Service. State-run companies in Eastern Europe and the former Soviet Union were protected from global competition for decades and have evolved into nightmares of commerce, hampered by high-cost–low-quality production, and therefore unable to compete in global markets, while continuing to maintain unsafe conditions and to inflict massive pollution on the environment.

THE MURKY WORLD OF LEADERSHIP

It is probably obvious that much of the preceding discussion of the six principles is full of apparent contradictions and half-truths: coherence is good, but so is mutation; mistakes are good; risk should not be eliminated because it is a source of innovation; and planning thwarts strategic thinking. But these principles are only counterintuitive to Western management thinking whose orientation is toward planning, control, linear logic, and the cause-and-effect relationships of management science. What they exemplify is the notion of yin and yang, the complementary forces that pervade all things in life and combine to make them a vibrant whole.

One of the most important roles leaders have is to build empowered and intelligent organizations that are capable of self-organizing and creatively adapting to an uncertain, ever-changing environment. Despite the proved advantages of employee empowerment, easing up on control and micro-management requires intestinal fortitude. Since the great majority of Western businesses are heavily control oriented, only 7 percent of employees at major companies work in teams; the rest toil under the traditional command-and-control management. Ironically, the U.S. military, the bastion of command and control, has embraced the concept of empowerment to enable its troops to self-organize during chaotic battle conditions. As Army Chief of Staff General Gordon Sullivan noted, "We are trying to change this organization to do things we can't even predict." He advises his officers that they should be prepared for "leadership roles in a world that is violent, uncertain, complex, and ambiguous."[60]

Beyond building an organization that is *responsive* to the future, leaders have a critical role in "making things happen," molding their organizations' futures to every extent possible. Making things happen starts with setting forth a strategic vision. However, such a task cannot be delegated to corporate planning departments, nor can a vision be bought from a strategy consultant. As Henry Mintzberg noted, "The notion that an effective strategy can be constructed by someone in an ivory tower is totally bankrupt."[61] The leader must either be a visionary or—as is more probable—be smart and intuitive enough to adapt strategic ideas from inside or outside the organization, perhaps from the creative efforts of a single office or from an analogous situation in a completely unrelated industry. Either way, the leader must be sufficiently immersed in the business to develop strong intuitive insights. Successful leaders spend considerable time visiting clients and meeting employees at all levels. For example, Home Depot's top executives spend 25 to 40 percent of their time visiting stores and talking to customers and employees, and the senior management at Intuit, the successful maker of the financial planning software program Quicken, spends several hours a month manning the customer service phones. Tom Peters advises leaders to find out what is happening in their business through a process that he calls "management by walking around."[62] Baseball legend Yogi Berra once said, "You can observe a lot by watching."

After a strategic vision is given its initial form, it can be handed off to staff planners to be developed into a full-blown written strategic plan. The strategic plan is an important communications tool that explains the past, present, and possible future; it provides meaning and purpose to employees and makes them feel more secure to take day-to-day risks.

The real test of a leader's skill is the ability to guide and influence all the employees to fulfill the strategic vision that has been developed, knowing that directly controlling them is not possible. As March observed, "Typically, it is not possible to lead an organization in any arbitrary direction that might be desired, but it is possible to influence the course of events."[63] The idea of leading through influence is an ancient notion and is the essence of political acumen.

The most potent way to influence organizational behavior is to alter its structural components, such as reporting relationships, incentives and rewards, company procedures, and profit-center configurations. Doing so, however, changes the rules of the organizational game. And, of course, there is no way of predicting how employees will respond to structural changes, which may induce unintended organizational behavior. Leaders must rely on their intuitive skills to determine which structural changes will bring about the desired results.

Peter Senge, James March, Ralph Stacey, Margaret Wheatley, and other authorities on managing and complexity speak of influencing organizations by manipulating their "leverage points," small structural changes made at the right time and place that produce huge changes in organizational behavior. They all concur with March that "the effectiveness of leadership often depends on being able to time small interventions so that the force of natural organizational processes amplifies the interventions."[64] None of them, however, says much about how to find these leverage points and how to manipulate them, and even Peter Senge admits, "The only problem is that high-leverage changes are usually highly nonobvious to most participants in the system. . . . This is what makes life interesting."[65] Leaders must rely on their intuition to find leverage points and know to use them to achieve their aims.

Machiavelli advised his Prince that good luck was not required to attain goals, but rather "a certain fortunate cunning," and that "the craftiness to turn men's minds has accomplished great things."[66] James March, in his 1977 book *Ambiguity of Leadership,* advised leaders to employ such Machiavellian political tactics as enrolling the participation of the opposition because it will "reduce the aspirations of oppositional leaders"; overloading the opposition with multiple agendas, because they can't reject them all at once; and reinterpreting history, because "the legitimacy of history as a basis for current action is fairly strong."[67]

March also suggested the use of persistence. Leaders are likely to get their agendas approved sooner or later if they persist, because past decisions are not final and situations eventually change: "Things change; people involved change, environments change, ideas change."[68] As Greek philosopher Plutarch observed during the first century A.D., "Perseverance is more prevailing than violence; and many things which cannot be overcome when they are together, yield themselves up when taken little by little."[69]

The keys to leading complex organizations into an unknown future all point to the fact that an effective leader must have a strong sense of intuition. Intuition is critical in developing strategic vision, playing politics, restructuring organizations, and, perhaps most important, judging people. This is the central theme of Roy Rowan's book, *The Intuitive*

Manager. Rowan interviewed many highly successful corporate executives and concluded that having strong intuitive capabilities was the most important personal skill for effective leaders: "Since management is an inexact science, frequently defined as the art of making decisions with insufficient information, even the most deliberate boss is sometimes forced to act prematurely on nebulous inner impressions. . . . The higher up an executive moves, the more often he or she will be forced into making intuitive long-range, nonlogical decisions."[70]

Although leaders cannot control their organizations or predict the future, they can build highly responsive organizations that adapt well to future changes. Most important, leaders can play a significant role in shaping their organizations' future. In this context, leadership is a much more vital function than is implied by the traditional image of the all-powerful leader in control of everything. The leader's job is also more subtle, complex, and challenging than management science would ever have us believe.

9

The Certainty
of Living in an
Uncertain World

C harles Richter, the inventor of the earthquake-measuring
Richter scale, said that "only fools, liars, and charlatans predict
earthquakes."[1] That evaluation can be applied to most other
forecasts as well. It is pretty clear that unless you are a fisherman or an
astronomer, predictions beyond the shortest of intervals are of not much
value to your day-to-day life. The movements of tides and celestial
objects are predictable long into the future, but they are the very rare
exceptions; almost everything else that touches our lives is filled with
uncertainty, and becomes less predictable as we try to look weeks,
months, and years into the future. Chaos pervades many of the important aspects of our physical world, such as weather, climate, droughts,
erosion, floods, mudslides, volcanic eruptions, and earthquakes. Complexity drives our biological and social world, including such phenomena as ecosystems, disease, politics and government, societies,
economies, and the organizations in which we work. The only certainty
is that we are destined to live in an unpredictable world filled with endless uncertainty. To help cope with this inescapable fact of life, here are
two questions to consider:

1. How can we sort the wheat from the chaff in terms of evaluating predictions?
2. What lessons does complexity theory offer on how to live in this uncertain world?

THINKING CRITICALLY

The preceding chapters show how vulnerable we are to false prophets. We fear uncertainty and seek the counsel of those who profess to know what the future will bring. We are innately gullible. Our minds are oriented to believe rather than to question, we attribute meaning to chance events, and we are driven by herd instinct and swayed by what we perceive to be voices of authority. On top of this, we are continually flooded with predictions that affect so many aspects of our lives, such as whether to buy common stocks, snowblowers, and survival kits, which political candidates to vote for, and what business decisions to make for the organizations in which we work. As we get ever closer to the end of the twentieth century, we are certain to be barraged by twenty-first-century predictions.

Our only self-defense against futurists and predictors from all quarters of society, and their barrage of forecasts, is to think for ourselves in a critical and objective manner about their forecasts. To begin with, our first reaction to any forecast should be informed skepticism. Next, we should ask the following five questions to assess the credibility of the forecast:

1. Is the forecast based on hard science?
2. How sound are the methods used to make the projection?
3. Does the forecaster have credible credentials?
4. Does the forecaster have a proved track record?
5. To what extent is my belief in a particular forecast influenced by my own personal beliefs and wishful thinking?

Science

Forecasts are often purported to be scientific. But a truly scientific forecast is one based on equations derived from proved laws of nature that specify how a phenomenon at point A in the present will progress to some point B in the future. For example, Newton's laws of motion and gravity enabled scientists to predict with great precision several years in advance that comet Shoemaker-Levy 9 would collide with the planet Jupiter in 1994. Among the things that affect our day-to-day lives, however, there are only a few kinds of events that can be predicted using scientific forecasts, like the tides and short-term weather.

Scientific forecasts for social systems such as economies and stock markets are impossible for the same reason: there are no proved natural laws underlying the behavior of social systems. Social scientists might make predictions based on their theories, but such theories are not laws of nature and do not stand the test of the scientific method. At best, these result in forecasts that are not much better than simple, naive guesses.

Methods

Rather than relying on science, forecasters frequently make predictions merely by extending past trends into the future, implicitly presuming that the future will look just like the past. In rare instances, long-term trends emerge that give rise to periods of reliable predictions many years into the future. For example, the Moore Curve has been used to project the increasing density and power of integrated circuits since 1965, and life expectancy in the developed world has steadily increased throughout the twentieth century, making actuarial projections quite accurate. However, although predictions based on these persistent trends need to be taken seriously, we should be careful to consider that these trends will some day cease to continue and possibly even reverse themselves. In fact, most trends follow the S-shaped growth curve shown in Figure 6.5, going through three distinct periods of birth, rapid growth, and maturity, where growth slows, stops, or even declines. But because one can never know when these three periods of a trend will happen, predictions based on trends can be highly inaccurate.

Predictions based on cycles are almost sure to be erroneous because very few phenomena are governed by regular periodic cycles. Events and phenomena may ebb and flow, giving the illusion of cyclical behavior, but they do not rise and fall with any regularity such that the time interval from peak to peak and valley to valley is constant over time. One interesting exception is the regular three- to four-year population cycle of

Soay sheep mentioned in Chapter 5. This rare exception occurs because the Soay sheep population is part of a relatively simple complex system involving only sheep and grass, with no migration and just the right birthing cycle. But when we look at human societies, that social systems operate in cycles is complete myth; there are no natural laws driving the behavior of social systems, because human behavior is unpredictable, and without natural laws there can be no fixed cycles.

Dismiss purported cycles used in predictions of calamities (unless they are based on astronomy). As shown in Figure 9.1, such prophets of doom first proclaim the existence of a cycle and then show how the cycle is turning down, ushering in a new era of calamity. False prophets have routinely used such faulty forecasting methods to predict recessions, stock market crashes, and returning ice ages.

Credentials

We should be very careful in assessing the validity of a prediction on the basis of the forecaster's presumed credibility. Our minds look for simple clues to gauge forecasters' credibility, such as their association with a prestigious institution, their résumé, and their appearance, reputation, and conviction. We are especially convinced when the media claim, directly or indirectly, that a particular prediction has merit. One strange recent case shows how so many people could become so thoroughly persuaded by false prophecy.

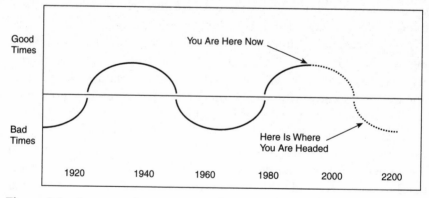

Figure 9.1   A commonly erroneous prediction based on imagined regular cycles.

In autumn 1989, earthquake prognosticator Iben Browning predicted that on December 3, 1990 (plus or minus forty-eight hours), a devastating earthquake would strike New Madrid, Missouri, very near the epicenter of an 1811 earthquake classified as the most severe to strike North America in recorded history. As December 3 approached, the town of New Madrid was seized by mass panic. Schools and factories closed; shopping centers taped up their windows; many residents left town, and others called the American Red Cross in tears of hysteria; and rumors spread that the town's reservoir had dropped fifteen feet (and New Madrid does not even have a reservoir). Radio and television media invaded New Madrid from as far away as Poland to cover the impending disaster. But the earthquake never happened. Browning had convinced everyone otherwise, including highly credible media such as the *New York Times.*

The building of Browning's credibility explains how everyone was fooled. The press referred to him as "Dr. Browning" and described him as a Ph.D. specializing in earthquake prediction, with a great track record. Also, David Stewart, a Ph.D. in geophysics at Southeast Missouri State University's Earthquake Information Center, attested that Browning's prediction was sound and said, "Here's a man who has hit several home runs."[2] As it turns out, Browning's Ph.D. is in zoology, his stated profession is actually "business consulting," and his backer Stewart is a believer in the use of psychic powers to predict earthquakes.

Track Records

Perhaps foremost in establishing the credibility of forecasters is their track records. For example, Browning's reputation significantly hinged on his purportedly excellent track record in earthquake prediction. The *New York Times,* for example, reported that Browning "is known to have predicted the 1989 San Francisco earthquake a week in advance."[3] This prediction was later shown not to have been all it was claimed to be.

Track records are not easy to judge, especially when they involve vague forecasts that fail to mention the whens, hows, whos, and wheres in their predictions. Vagueness gives the forecaster enough maneuverability after the fact to claim success when none is due. Perhaps the all-time master of vague predictions was Nostradamus, the sixteenth-

Original Nostradamus Prophecy	Recent Interpretation
When the sepulcher of the great Roman shall be found,	A Russian spacecraft will crash on America.
The next day after a pope shall be elected,	Two people killed.
	The leader Yeltsin will hardly listen to
Who shall not be much approved by the Senate,	the acrimony.
	A fool shown up by bloodshed.
Poisoned, his blood in the sacred chalice.	

Figure 9.2   Example of an original Nostradamus prophecy and a recent interpretation of it.

century seer, who himself confessed that his predictions "cannot generally be understood until they have been fulfilled."[4] Figure 9.2 shows a typical Nostradamus prediction, with its vague imagery, and a recent 1991 interpretation of it by Nostradamus devotees V. J. Hewett and Peter Lorie as a prediction of events that were supposed to occur on August 4, 1994 (and, of course, they did not).[5]

The most important aspect of evaluating forecasters' track records is to assess whether they demonstrate any skill beyond naive guessing (as in merely flipping a coin). For example, although *The Old Farmer's Almanac* claims that its weather predictions are accurate 80 percent of the time, that track record actually does not demonstrate any forecasting skill, because the simple use of seasonal averages to predict future temperatures would result in accurate forecasts 85 percent of the time.

Using these criteria, we can see that Browning's track record does not hold up. His purportedly successful prediction of the 1989 San Francisco earthquake was in fact a very nebulous forecast: "On the 16th of October [1989], plus or minus a few days, according to my predictions of weather, there should be a volcano or two and certainly some big earthquakes."[6] *But he did not specify where.* Although the San Francisco earthquake struck on October 17, 1989, Browning never mentioned California in his prediction, let alone San Francisco. Furthermore, earthquakes strike and volcanoes erupt every day somewhere on the planet, so Browning's prediction of "some big quakes" was a sure bet. As Richard Kerr wrote in an article in *Science* magazine debunking

Browning's ostensibly successful track record, "His claimed 5-year-long record of prediction success was no better than chance."[7]

Another challenge in assessing track records is that some forecasters revise history to make their predictions conform to supposed real outcomes. In order to control the minds of its oppressed citizens, the government of the former Soviet Union blatantly retold history to make world events conform to Marx's prediction that communism would prevail over capitalism. A more benign instance of retelling history involves the 1974 book *The Jupiter Effect,* in which the authors prophesied that the 1982 alignment of the planets would trigger a violent earthquake along the San Andreas Fault that "will herald one of the greatest disasters of modern times."[8] When the predicted 1982 calamity failed to occur, the authors wrote a new book, *The Jupiter Effect Revisited,* in which they claimed that their prophecy was fulfilled in the eruption of Mount St. Helens in 1980: "The 'Jupiter Effect' did happen—almost as forecast—but it came two years early, in 1980."[9]

Personal Biases

One of the biggest challenges in assessing the validity of a prediction is to question whether our own judgment about the prediction is clouded by personal beliefs and predispositions. Is our belief in a prediction a function of hearing what we want to hear? For example, the chronic pessimist is much more likely to believe an economist who issues a negative forecast. Our propensity to believe in predictions consistent with our own beliefs is often exploited by charlatans using what is called the Barnum effect, named in honor of the master showman and trickster who advised other tricksters to "have a little something in it for everyone."[10] This tactic is central to the art of astrology, where the believability of predictions or personality analysis is enhanced by including general observations in which customers can see themselves.

QUE SERA, SERA?

Paradoxically, our future lives are more influenceable than predictable. Although one can never really know how one's life will evolve, it is surely possible to influence the evolution of one's life to achieve certain aims. If there is something to be gained by heeding the message, "What shall be, shall be," it is that we should not take ourselves so seriously in the light of the fact that our futures will be filled with uncertainty and, in large part, shaped by chance events and luck. In spite of that, we can choose to lead lives that flexibly adapt to unforeseen changes, and ambitious and motivated individuals can influence their futures by striving to make things happen.

Notes

CHAPTER 1: THE SECOND OLDEST PROFESSION

1. Isaac Asimov, *Future Days* (New York: Random House, 1970), p. 11.
2. Ravi Batra, *The Great Depression of 1990* (New York: Simon & Schuster, 1987), p. 25.
3. Peter F. Drucker, *Management: Tasks, Responsibilities, Practices* (New York: HarperBusiness, 1973), p. 124.
4. I. F. Clarke, *The Pattern of Expectation* (New York: Basic Books, 1979), p. 193.
5. Batra, *Great Depression,* p.17.
6. Ibid., pp. 17, 20.
7. Paul R. Ehrlich, *The Population Bomb* (New York: Ballentine, 1971).
8. Jeff Jacoby, "Riches Rain on Doctor Doom," *Boston Globe,* February 2, 1995, p. 13.
9. Alvin Toffler, *Future Shock* (New York: Random House, 1970), p. 11.
10. George H. Gallup, Jr., and Frank Newport, "Belief in Paranormal Phenomena Among Adult Americans," *Skeptical Inquirer* 15(2) (Winter 1991): 137.
11. Daniel Gilbert, "How Mental Systems Believe," *American Psychologist* (February 1991): 107.

CHAPTER 2: WHEN CHAOS RAINS

1. The source for the amount of damage from Hurricane Bob is Richard A. Wood, *The Weather Almanac* (New York: Gale Research, 1996), p. 63.
2. Ian Stewart, *Does God Play Dice?* (Cambridge, UK: Basil Blackwell, 1989) p. 132.
3. *Boston Globe,* February 5, 1978, p. 46.
4. Louis W. Uccelini, Paul J. Kocin, Russell S. Schneider, Paul M. Stokols, and Russell A. Dorr, "Forecasting the 12–14 March 1993 Superstorm," *Bulletin of the American Meteorological Society* (February 1995): 183.
5. J. Neumann, "Great Historical Events That Were Significantly Affected by the Weather," *Bulletin of the American Meteorological Society* (November 1975): 1167; and R. R. Palmer and Joel Colton, *A History of the World,* 3d ed. (New York:

Alfred A. Knopf, 1965), pp. 8, 111. Neumann's essay is the first in an interesting series in the *Bulletin* on how weather has changed history.

6. J. Neumann and H. Flohn, "Great Historical Events That Were Significantly Affected by the Weather: Part 8, Germany's War on the Soviet Union, 1941–1945," *Bulletin of the American Meteorological Society* (June 1987): 620.

7. U.S. Department of Commerce, *Benefit-Cost Analysis for the Modernization and Associated Restructuring of the National Weather Service* (Washington, D.C.: Government Printing Office, July 1992), p. 54.

8. Albert Lee, *Weather Wisdom: Facts and Folklore of Weather Forecasting* (New York: Congdon & Weed, 1976), p. 160.

9. Ibid.

10. Richard Lewinsohn, *Science, Prophecy and Prediction* (New York: Harper & Brothers, 1961), p. 179.

11. John Zarocostas, "Transport Sector Saves Millions with Weather Data, Experts Say," *Journal of Commerce,* October 17, 1994, p. 3B.

12. "What Is a Meteorologist? A Professional Guideline," *Bulletin of the American Meteorological Society* (January 1991): 61.

13. A brief discussion of the weather equations can be found in James Gleick, *Chaos: Making a New Science* (New York: Viking Penguin, 1987), pp. 23–25.

14. Stephen H. Kellert, *In the Wake of Chaos* (Chicago: University of Chicago Press, 1993), p. 121.

15. Gleick, *Chaos,* p. 17.

16. Ibid., p. 322, n. 20.

17. S. Dunlop and F. Wilson, *The Larousse Guide to Weather Forecasting* (New York: Larousse and Co., 1982), p. 118.

18. American Meteorological Society, "Policy Statement: Weather Forecasting," *Bulletin of the American Meteorological Society* (August 1991): 1275.

19. Steven Zubrick, meteorologist, NWS Forecast Office, Washington D.C., telephone interview with the author, January 15, 1997.

20. James Lee, science operations officer, NWS Forecast Office, Taunton, Mass., personal interview with the author, February 17, 1995.

21. Charles A. Doswell III, "More Thoughts on the Future of Weather Forecasting," Internet home page.

22. Ibid.

23. Harold Brooks, "The Possible Future Role of Humans in Weather Forecasting," Internet home page.

24. Doswell, "More Thoughts."

25. Zubrick, interview.

26. Weather accuracy statistics were provided by the National Weather Service on December 2, 1996.

27. Richard A. Kerr, "Upgrade of Storm Warnings Paying Off," *Science,* October 15, 1993, p. 331.

28. AMS, "Policy Statement," p. 1273.

29. Debi Iacovelli, "Inside the Hurricane Center," *Weatherwise* (June–July 1994): 28.

30. "Hurricane Detection, Tracking, and Forecasting," *Bulletin of the American Meteorological Society* (July 1993): 1377.

31. Ibid., p. 1379.

32. Ibid., p. 1380.

33. Mark DeMaria, telephone interview with the author, January 15, 1997.

34. AMS, "Policy Statement," p. 1274.

35. Ibid.

36. Donald L. Gilman, "Long-Range Forecasting: The Present and the Future," *Bulletin of the American Meteorological Society* (February 1985):159.

37. Robert E. Livezey, "Variability of Skill of Long-Range Forecasts and Implications for Their Use and Value," *Bulletin of the American Meteorological Society* (March 1990): 301. Note that Livezey states that the official measure of forecast skill is 6 percent, which according to the skill formula translates into a 4 percentage point advantage over random chance.

38. Douglas H. Hoyt, "The Probability of Correct Climate Forecasts in the Absence of Any Forecasting Skill," *Bulletin of the American Meteorological Society* (October 1983): 1172; and Anthony G. Barnston and Robert E. Livezey, "The Probability of Correct Climate Forecasting in the Absence of Any Forecasting Skill," *Bulletin of the American Meteorological Society* (July 1985): 847.

39. Bob Sheets, quoted in Peter Catalano, "Hurricane Alert!" *Popular Science* (September 1995): 66.

40. Catalano, "Hurricane Alert!"

41. William Gray, *Early August Updated Forecast of Atlantic Seasonal Hurricane Activity for 1995,* (Colorado State University, August 4, 1995).

42. Gary McWilliams, "The Farmers' Almanacs Start a Storm," *Business Week,* December 12, 1994, p. 48.

43. Climate Prediction Center, Internet home page: caps.wwb.noaa.gov:80/products/assessments/assess 95/temp.htmL.

44. Sherrin Wight, telephone interview with the author, January 8, 1997.

45. All recent versions of *The Old Farmer's Almanac* include this note on its forecasting methodology.

46. Judson Hale, *The Best of the Old Farmer's Almanac* (New York: Random House, 1992), p. 4.

47. Ibid., p. 42.

48. Ibid., p. 15.

49. Wight, interview.

50. Sandi Duncan, telephone interview with the author, January 9, 1997.

51. Lucas McFadden, telephone interview with the author, January 8, 1997.

52. Hale, pp. 4, 54.

53. Duncan, interview.

54. McFadden, interview.

55. Kate Bohner Lewis, "Take a Bow Lee Iacocca," *Forbes,* November 21, 1994, p. 198.

56. "The Old Farmer's Almanac," Internet home page.

57. Lewis, "Take a Bow Lee Iacocca," p. 198.

58. Catalano, "Hurricane Alert!" p. 66.
59. Ibid.
60. Doswell, "More Thoughts."

CHAPTER 3: THE DISMAL SCIENTISTS

1. John Bartlett and Justin Kaplan, *Bartlett's Familiar Quotations* (Boston: Little, Brown, 1992), p. 413.
2. Gene Koretz, "A D+ for Dismal Scientists?" *Business Week,* September 25, 1995, p. 25; Dana Weschler Linden, "Dismal Days for the Dismal Science," *Forbes,* April 22, 1996, p. 65.
3. Robert Heilbroner, *The Worldly Philosophers* (New York: Touchstone, 1992), p. 322.
4. William Greider, *Secrets of the Temple* (New York: Simon & Schuster, 1987), p. 12.
5. *Economic Report of the President* (Washington, D.C.: U.S. Government Printing Office, 1996), p. 265.
6. U.S. Congress, *The Congressional Budget Office: Responsibilities and Organization* (Washington, D.C.: U.S. Government Printing Office, 1976), p. 1.
7. Michael Belongia, *Are Economic Forecasts by Government Agencies Biased? Accurate?* (St. Louis: Federal Reserve Bank of St. Louis, November–December 1988), p. 22.
8. Ken Militzer, "The Business Economist at Work: The Chief Economist at AT&T," *Business Economics* (January 1990): 45.
9. The twelve studies used to judge economic forecast accuracy are: Victor Zarnowitz, "An Analysis of Annual and Multiperiod Quarterly Forecasts of Aggregate Income, Output and Price Level," *Journal of Business* 52(1) (1979): 31; Steve Swidler and David Ketcher, "Economic Forecasts, Rationality, and the Processing of New Information over Time," *Journal of Money, Credit, and Banking* (February 1990): 65; Stephen McNees and John Ries, "The Track Record of Macroeconomic Forecasts," *New England Economic Review* (November–December 1983): 5; Charles Nelson, "A Benchmark for the Accuracy of the Econometric Forecasts of GNP," *Business Economics,* April 1, 1984, p. 413; Stephen McNees, "An Assessment of the 'Official' Economic Forecasts," *New England Economic Review* (July–August 1995): 17; Stephen McNees, "How Large Are Economic Forecast Errors?" *New England Economic Review* (July–August 1992): 33; Roy A. Batchelor and Pami Dua, "Forecaster Ideology, Forecasting Technique, and the Accuracy of Economic Forecasts," *International Journal of Forecasting* (June 1990): 3; Roy A. Batchelor and Dua Pami, "Product Differentiation in the Economic Forecasting Industry," *International Journal of Forecasting* (1990): 313; Stephen McNees, "The Uses and Abuses of 'Consensus' Forecasts," *Journal of Forecasting* (August 1991): 703; "The Accuracy of World Economic Projections for Major Industrial Countries," *World Economic Outlook* (May 1992): 88; "How Accurate Are

Economic Outlook Projections?" *Economic Outlook* (June 1993): 49; and Stephen K. McNees, "How Large Are Economic Forecast Errors?" *New England Economic Review* (July–August 1992): 25.

10. Zarnowitz, "Analysis," p.1.

11. Ibid., p. 13.

12. Stephen McNees, "An Assessment of the 'Official' Economic Forecasts," *New England Economic Review* (July–August 1995): 17.

13. *Economist,* July 27, 1991, p. 61.

14. Zarnowitz, "Analysis," p. 31.

15. Swidler and Ketcher, "Economic Forecasts," p. 65.

16. Robert Pindyck and Daniel L. Rubinfeld, *Econometric Models and Economic Forecasts* (New York: McGraw-Hill,1976), p. 432.

17. Zarnowitz, "Analysis," p. 23.

18. McNees and Ries, "Track Record," p. 5.

19. Batchelor and Dua, "Product Differentiation," p. 3.

20. McNees, "How Large Are Economic Forecast Errors?" p. 34, and McNees and Ries, "Track Record," p. 12.

21. McNees and Ries, "Track Record," p. 5.

22. Nelson, "Benchmark," p. 52.

23. "Garbage In, Garbage Out," *Economist,* June 3, 1995, p. 70.

24. Batchelor and Dua, "Product Differentiation," p. 313.

25. McNees, "Uses and Abuses," p. 703.

26. *World Economic Outlook* (May 1992): 88.

27. OECD, *Economic Outlook* (June 1993): 49.

28. Ronald Baily, "Them That Can, Do, Them That Can't, Forecast," *Forbes,* December 26, 1988, p. 94.

29. David Altany, "New Jobs for the Number Crunchers," *Industry Week,* April 20, 1992, p. 76.

30. Stephen Durlauf, telephone interview with the author, January 15, 1997.

31. Heilbroner, *Worldly Philosophers,* p. 55.

32. John Cassidy, "The Decline of Economics," *New Yorker,* December 2, 1996, p. 53.

33. Charles Morris, "It's Not the Economy, Stupid," *Atlantic Monthly* (July 1993): 50.

34. *Boston Globe,* October 5, 1996, p. 1.

35. Joseph P. Martino, "Does the Kondratieff Wave Really Exist?" *Futurist* (February 1985): 25.

36. Mitchell Waldrop, *Complexity* (New York: Touchstone, 1992), p. 141.

37. Simon Caulkin, "Chaos Inc.," *Across the Board* (July–August 1995): 34.

38. Waldrop, *Complexity,* p. 147.

39. Morris, "It's Not the Economy," p. 49.

40. Zarnowitz, "Analysis," p. 12.

41. Robert Kuttner, "The Poverty of Economics," *Atlantic Monthly* (February 1985): 78.

42. Heilbroner, *Worldly Philosophers,* p. 322.

43. Durlauf, interview.

44. Morris, "It's Not the Economy," p. 49.

45. Paul Magnusson, "Need an Economic Forecast," *Business Week,* September 13, 1993, p. 38.

46. Ibid.

47. "Pick a Number," *Economist,* September 13, 1992, p. 18.

48. Stephen Sharf, "Forget the Forecasters," *Ward's AutoWorld* (July 1989): p 17.

49. Peter Drucker, *The Practice of Management* (New York: Harper & Row, 1954), p. 89.

50. William Rukeyser, "Pardon Me, But Is This Armageddon," *Fortune,* February 6, 1995, p. 84.

51. *Economist,* June 2, 1990, p. 80.

52. Jay Forrester, "Economic Conditions Ahead, Understanding the Kondratieff Wave," *Futurist* (June 1995): 16.

53. Rukeyser, "Pardon Me," p. 85.

54. Peter Drucker, *Management: Tasks, Responsibilities, Practices* (New York: HarperBusiness, 1973), p. 123.

55. L. McTier Anderson, "The 'Dismal Science' Revisited," *Business Horizons* (May-June 1992): 3.

56. Waldrop, *Complexity,* p. 328.

57. Durlauf, interview.

CHAPTER 4: THE MARKET GURUS

1. Mitchell Waldrop, *Complexity* (New York: Touchstone,1992), p. 269.

2. James Lorie and Mary Hamilton, *The Stock Market—Theories and Evidence* (Homewood, Ill.: Richard D. Irwin, 1973), p. 75.

3. Martin S. Fridson, *Delusions and Confusion* (New York: Wiley, 1996), p. 162.

4. Ibid., p. 155.

5. William F. Eng, *The Technical Analysis of Stocks, Options and Futures* (Chicago: Probus Publishing, 1988), p. 3.

6. Ibid., p. 233.

7. Burton G. Malkiel, *A Random Walk Down Wall Street* (New York: Norton, 1990), p. 141.

8. Ibid., p. 136.

9. Eng, *Technical Analysis,* p. 345.

10. Martin Douglas, "Money and Metaphysics: New-Age Wall Street," *New York Times,* January 30, 1994, p. C-1.

11. Eng, *Technical Analysis,* p. 351.

12. Ibid., p. 356.

13. Malkiel, *Random Walk,* p. 151.

14. Ian M. D. Little and A. C. Rayner, *Higgledy Piggledy Growth Again* (Oxford: Basil Blackwell, 1966), and Richard A. Brealey, "The Character of Earnings Changes," paper presented to the Seminar on the Analysis of Security Prices (University of Chicago, May 1967).

15. Eugene F. Fama, "Efficient Capital Markets: A Review of Theory and Empirical Work," *Journal of Finance* 25 (1970): 383.

16. Gene G. Marcial, *Secrets of the Street* (New York: McGraw-Hill, 1995), p. 5.

17. "Insider Trading," *Business Week,* December 12, 1994, p. 71.

18. John Kenneth Galbraith, *The Great Crash of 1929* (Boston: Houghton Mifflin, 1954; reprinted in 1988), pp. 84–85.

19. James B. Stewart, "Calling the Crash: Pessimistic Predictions by Analyst at Shearson Make Her a Star," *Wall Street Journal,* October 28, 1987, p. 35.

20. Jeffrey M. Laderman, "But What Have You Done for Us Lately," July 26, 1993.

21. *New York Times,* February 28, 1988, p. III-10.

22. Daniel Kadlec, "Garzarelli Wears Celebrity Well," *USA Today,* February 2, 1994.

23. Daniel Dorfman, "'Go Go Garz' Puts on the Breaks," *USA Today,* July 25, 1994.

24. Daniel Kadlec, "World-Class Market Forecasts Questioned," *USA Today,* September 3, 1994, p. 3B.

25. Ibid.

26. Jeffrey M. Laderman, "What Made Elaine Shout 'Sell,' " *Business Week,* August 12, 1996, p. 75.

27. "The Granville Market Letter," *Financial World,* March 1, 1981, p. 44.

28. Ibid., p. 132.

29. Malkiel, *Random Walk,* p. 179.

30. John Bogle, chairman of Vanguard, telephone interview with the author, February 7, 1997.

31. "Market Plunge Caught Strategists Off Guard," *USA Today,* April 7, 1994, p. 3B.

32. Malkiel, *Random Walk,* p. 180.

33. Bogle, interview.

34. Malkiel, *Random Walk,* p. 178.

35. John McDonald, professor, Stanford Graduate School of Business, telephone interview with the author, February 6, 1997.

36. Peter Lynch, *One Up on Wall Street* (New York: Penguin Books, 1989), pp. 78, 74, 73.

37. Michael C. Jensen, "Problems in Selection of Security Portfolios: The Performance of Mutual Funds in the Period 1945–1964," *Journal of Finance* 23(2) (1968): 389.

38. Richard A. Ippolito, "Efficiency with Costly Information: A Study of Mutual Fund Performance, 1965–1984," *Quarterly Journal of Economics* (February 1989): 1.

39. Vanguard commentary on index funds.

40. Stephen A. Berkowitz, Louis D. Finney, and Dennis E. Logue, *The Investment Performance of Corporate Pension Plans—Why They Do Not Beat the Market Regularly* (New York: Quorum Books, 1988).

41. Malkiel, *Random Walk,* p. 173.

42. Jensen, "Problems in Selection of Security Portfolios," p. 415.

43. Lynch, *One Up on Wall Street,* pp. 122–24, 129–130, 139.

44. McDonald, interview].

45. Bogle, interview.

46. David Dreman, "Chronically Clouded Crystal Balls," *Forbes,* October 11, 1993, p. 178.

47. David Dreman, "Flawed Forecasts," *Forbes,* December 9, 1991, p. 342.

48. Scott E. Stickel, "Reputation and Performance Among Security Analysts," *Journal of Finance* (December 1992): 1811.

49. J. C. Cragg, and Burton G. Malkiel, "The Consensus and Accuracy of Some Predictions of the Growth of Corporate Earnings," *Journal of Finance* (March 1968): 67.

50. "Answers to Commonly Asked Questions," *Value Line Selection and Opinion,* April 28, 1995, p. 8117.

51. Fisher Black, "Yes, Virginia, There Is Hope: Tests of the Value Line Ranking System," *Financial Analysts Journal* (September–October 1973): 10.34.

52. *Value Line Investment Survey,* April 28, 1995, p. 8117.

53. Mark Hurlbert, "Proof of Pudding," *Forbes,* December 10, 1990, p. 316.

54. Robert S. Kaplan and Roman Weil, "Kaplan and Weil Rejoinder," *Financial Analysts Journal* (September–October 1973): 14.

55. Cheng F. Lee, "Value Line Investment Survey Rank Changes and Beta Coefficients," *Financial Analysts Journal* (September–October 1987): 70.

56. Gur Huberman, and Shmuel Kandel, "Market Efficiency and Value Line's Record," *Journal of Business* 63 (1990): 208.

57. Fridson, *Delusions,* p. 12.

58. Ibid., p. 114.

59. Ibid., p. 119.

60. "A Conversation with Benjamin Graham," *Financial Analysts Journal* (September–October 1976): 20.

61. Fridson, *Delusions,* p. 167.

62. Debbie Galant, "Financial Follies," *Institutional Investor* (January 1995): 139.

63. Lynch, *One Up on Wall Street,* p. 34.

64. Waldrop, *Complexity,* p. 274.

65. Kevin Kelly, "Cracking Wall Street," *Wired Online* (1993): article number 2.07.

66. "Chaos–Predictions That Arcane Mathematics Can Give the Bulls and Bears a Run for the Money," *Discover* (March 1993): 82.

67. Tony Vaga, *Profiting from Chaos* (New York: McGraw-Hill, 1994), p. 168.
68. John L. Casti, *Complexification* (New York: Harper Perennial, 1995), p. 107.
69. "Chaos Under a Cloud," *Economist*, January 13, 1996, p. 69.
70. Fridson, *Delusions*, p. 147.
71. Warren Weaver, *Lady Luck: Theory of Probability* (Garden City, N.Y.: Anchor Books, 1963), p. xx.
72. Bogle, interview.
73. "A Conversation with Benjamin Graham," p. 20.
74. Lynch, *One Up on Wall Street*, p. 60.
75. Malkiel, *Random Walk*, p. 50.
76. Ibid., p. 201.
77. Bogle, interview.
78. David S. Fondiller, "Repent, Sinners," *Forbes*, June 19, 1995, p. 240.

CHAPTER 5: CHECKING THE "UNCHECKED POPULATION"

1. Larry Ephron, *The End: The Imminent Ice Age and How We Can Stop It!* (Berkeley, Calif.: Celestial Arts, 1988).
2. William and Paul Paddock, *Famine—1975! America's Decision: Who Will Survive?* (Boston: Little, Brown, 1967), pp. 61, 141.
3. Greg Burns, "The New Economics of Food," *Business Week*, May 20, 1996, p. 78.
4. Jared Diamond, "Easter's End," *Discover* (August 1995): 63.
5. Nathan Keyfitz, "The Limits of Population Forecasting," *Population and Development Review* (December 1981): 583.
6. William H. McNeill, *Plagues and Peoples* (Garden City, N.Y.: Anchor Press, Doubleday, 1976).
7. Nancy Duin and Jenny Sutcliffe, *A History of Medicine* (New York: Simon & Schuster, 1992), p. 36.
8. Ibid., p. 100.
9. Ibid., p. 62.
10. Bureau of the Census, *Projections of the Population of the United States, By Age and Sex: 1972 to 2020* (Washington, D.C.: U.S. Government Printing Office, 1972), p. 8.
11. Keyfitz, "Limits," p. 583.
12. Bureau of the Census. *Current Population Reports* (Washington, D.C., U.S. Government Printing Office, March 1994), p. 25.
13. Stanley Smith, "Tests of Forecast Accuracy and Bias for County Population Projections," *Journal of the American Statistical Association* (December 1987): 993.
14. Dennis Ahlburg and Kenneth Land, "Population Forecasting: Guest Editors' Introduction," *International Journal of Forecasting* 8 (1992): 294.

15. Michael Stoto, "The Accuracy of Population Projections," *Journal of the American Statistical Association* (March 1983): 13.

16. Stanley Smith and Terry Sincich, "Forecasting State and Household Populations," *International Journal of Forecasting* 8 (1992): 504.

17. Nathan Keyfitz, "On Future Population," *Journal of the American Statistical Association* (June 1972): 361.

18. McNeill, *Plagues*, p. 291.

19. David Jeremiah with C. C. Carlson, *Escape the Coming Night: An Electrifying Tour of Our World as It Races Toward Its Final Days* (Dallas: Word, 1990), p. 73.

20. Jack Van Impe, "The AIDS Cover-UP," TV Soundtrack (Troy, Mich., 1986).

21. Russell Chandler, *Doomsday: The End of the World* (Ann Arbor, Mich.: Servant Publications, 1993), p. 154.

22. W. Meade Morgan and James W. Curran, "Acquired Immunodeficiency Syndrome: Current and Future Trends," *Public Health Reports* (September–October 1986): 459; and U.S. Department of Health and Human Services, *HIV/AIDS Surveillance Report* (Washington, D.C.: U.S. Government Printing Office, December 1994), p. 25.

23. David E. Bloom and Sherry Glied, "Projecting the Number of New AIDS Cases in the United States," *International Journal of Forecasting* 8 (1992): 339.

24. Ibid.

25. Ahlburg and Land, *Population Forecasting*, p. 291.

26. Stoto, "Accuracy," p. 14.

27. Dennis A. Ahlburg and James W. Vaupel, "Alternative Projections of the U.S. Population," *Demography* (November 1990): 639.

28. John Hedderson, "Theories of Fertility Norms: A Consolidation," *Population Review* (January 1980): 32.

29. Charlotte Phelps, "Wives' Motives and Fertility," *Journal of Economic Behavior and Organization* 27 (1995): 47.

30. Bureau of the Census, *Current Population Reports,* July 9, 1947, p. 5.

31. Bureau of the Census, *Current Population Reports and Population Estimates,* February 14, 1949. p. 6.

32. House of Representatives, Committee on the Judiciary, *Impact of Illegal Immigration on Public Benefit Programs and to the American Labor Force* (Washington, D.C.: U.S. Government Printing Office, 1996), p. 2.

33. "Tucson or Bust," *Economist,* May 20, 1995, p. 29.

34. John Nielsen, "5 Billion and Ticking," *Stanford* (March 1995): 50.

35. Robert Heilbroner, *The Worldly Philosophers* (New York: Touchstone, 1992), p. 78.

36. Ibid., p. 90.

37. William Petersen, *Malthus* (Cambridge, Mass.: Harvard University Press, 1979), p. 55.

38. James Bonar, *Malthus and His Work* (New York: Augustus Kelley, 1967), pp. 1–2.

39. Heilbroner, *Worldly Philosophers,* p. 7

40. Ed Ayres, Worldwatch Institute, telephone interview February 20, 1997.

41. Ibid.

42. Donella Meadows, Dennis Meadows, Jorgen Randers, and William Behrens III, *The Limits to Growth* (New York: Universe Books, 1970), p. 9.

43. Ibid., p. 23.

44. Donella Meadows, Dennis Meadows, and Jorrgen Randers, *Beyond the Limits* (Post Mills, Vt.: Chelsea Green Publishing Co., 1992), p. xv.

45. H. S. D. Cole, Christopher Freeman, Marie Hahoda, and L. L. R. Pavitt, *Thinking About the Future: A Critique of* The Limits to Growth (London: Sussex University Press, 1973).

46. Rachel Carson, *Silent Spring* (Boston: Houghton Mifflin, 1962), p. xii.

47. Lewis Regenstein, *How to Survive in America the Poisoned* (Washington, D.C.: Acropolis Books, 1982), p. 276.

48. Michael Lemonick, "The Ice Age Cometh?" *Time,* January 31, 1994, p. 79.

49. American Meteorological Society, "Policy Statement on Global Warming," *Bulletin of the American Meteorological Society,* January 1, 1991, p. 57.

50. Thomas Moore, "Global Warming: A Boon for Humans and Other Animals," Internet article, March 20, 1995.

CHAPTER 6: SCIENCE FACT AND FICTION

1. I. F. Clarke, *The Pattern of Expectation* (New York: Basic Books, 1979), p. 3.

2. Ibid., p. 202.

3. Ibid., p. 197.

4. Patrick Barrett, "The Good and the Bad Die Young," *Marketing,* July 11, 1996, p. 16; David Wolfe, "Why Marketing Executives Aren't Thinking Straight," *Advertising Age,* November 7, 1994, p. 34.

5. B. Bowonder and T. Miyake, "Technology Forecasting in Japan," *Futures* (September 1993): 759.

6. Reuven R. Levary and Dongchui Han, "Choosing a Technological Forecasting Method," *Industrial Management* (January–February 1995): 14.

7. Fred Woudenberg, "An Evaluation of Delphi," *Technological Forecasting and Social Change* (September 1991): 131.

8. Levary and Han, "Choosing a Technological Forecasting Method," p. 18.

9. Joseph F. Coates, "Why Forecasts Fail," *Research Technology Management* (July–August 1993): 5.

10. Steven P. Schnaars, *Megamistakes: Forecasting and the Myth of Rapid Technological Change* (New York: Free Press, 1989), p. 10.

11. Ibid., p. 20.

12. Shlomo Maital, "Caution: Oracles at Work," *Across the Board* (June 1993): 52.

13. Robert Hutchins, "A Bill for the Development and Control of Atomic Energy, 79th Congress 2nd Session 1946" (Washington, D.C.: U.S. Government Printing Office, 1947), p. 102.

14. Stephen L. Del Sesto, "Wasn't the Future of Nuclear Energy Wonderful?" in Joseph J. Corn, *Imagining Tomorrow* (Cambridge: MIT Press, 1987), p. 58.

15. M. Thring, "A Robot in the House," in Nigel Calder, *The World in 1984* (Baltimore: Penguin Books, 1964), p. 38.

16. Herman Kahn and Anthony J. Wiener, *The Year 2000: A Framework for Speculation on the Next Thirty Years* (New York: Macmillan, 1967), p. 94.

17. Herb Brody, "Great Expectations: Why Technology Predictions Go Awry," *Technology Review* (July 1991): 41.

18. Kahn and Wiener, *The Year 2000,* p. 89.

19. James Martin, *Future Developments in Telecommunications* (Englewood Cliffs, N.J.: Prentice-Hall, 1977), p. 9.

20. Ibid., p. 12.

21. Ibid., p. 9.

22. Ibid.

23. Ibid., p. 12.

24. Ibid., p. 11.

25. Schnaars, *Megamistakes,* p. 32.

26. Ibid., p. 4.

27. Clarke, *Pattern of Expectation,* p. 3.

28. Rupert W. Maclaurin, *Invention in the Radio Industry* (New York: Macmillan, 1949), p. 92.

29. Eric Von Hippel, *The Sources of Innovation* (Oxford: Oxford University Press, 1988), p. 3.

30. Martin, *Future Development,* p. 12.

31. David Salisbury, "His Beaker Runneth Over," *Stanford* (January–February 1997): 27.

32. Ibid., p. 28.

33. Charles H. Townes, "Quantum Electronics and Surprise in Development of Technology," *Science,* February 16, 1968, p. 699.

34. Ibid., p. 701.

35. Corn, *Imagining Tomorrow,* p. 197.

36. Israel Dror, "The Process of Technology Evolution, Multi-Technology as the Driving Force," *Technology Forecasting and Social Change* 44 (1993): 49.

37. Alfred Kleinknecht, *Innovation Patterns in Crisis and Prosperity* (New York: St. Martin's Press, 1987), p. 201.

38. Brody, "Great Expectations," p. 42.

39. W. Brian Arthur, "Positive Feedbacks in the Economy," *Scientific American* (February 1990): 92.

40. *ComputerWorld,* December 26, 1994, p. 76.
41. Brent Schlender, "Bill and Paul Talk," *Fortune,* October 2, 1995, p. 76.
42. Randall Stross, *The Microsoft Way* (Reading, Mass.: Addison-Wesley, 1996) p. 8.
43. Anthony O'Hear, *An Introduction to the Philosophy of Science* (Oxford: Oxford University Press, 1989), p. 221.
44. Brody, "Great Expectations," p. 43.
45. Ibid., p. 41.
46. Ibid.
47. Philip E. Ross, "Show Me a Piece," *Forbes,* June 19, 1995, p. 230.
48. Nathan Rosenberg, "Uncertainty and Technological Change," paper presented at the Conference on Growth and Development (Stanford University, June 1994), p. 27.
49. Ibid.

CHAPTER 7: THE FUTURISTS

1. Allan Tough, "Intellectual Leaders in Futures Studies—A Study," *Futures* (May 1991): 436.
2. John Bartlett and Justin Kaplan, *Bartlett's Familiar Quotations* (Boston: Little, Brown, 1992), p. 565.
3. *Encyclopedia of Careers and Vocational Guidance* (Chicago: J. G. Ferguson Publishing Co., 1993), p 377.
4. Michael Hechter, "Symposium on Prediction in the Social Sciences," *American Journal of Sociology* (May 1995): 1520.
5. Karl R. Popper, *The Poverty of Historicism* (Boston: Beacon Press, 1957), pp. 4, 139.
6. Ibid., p. 11.
7. Ibid., p. 10.
8. Ibid., p. 158.
9. Leon Trotsky, *1909* (London: Penguin, 1971), p. 71.
10. James Coleman, "Comment on Kuran and Collins," *American Journal of Sociology* (May 1995): 1618.
11. Samuel E. Morison, *The Oxford History of the American People* (New York: Oxford University Press, 1965), p. 23.
12. Timur Kuran, "The Inevitability of Future Revolutionary Surprises," *American Journal of Sociology* (May 1995): 1540.
13. Popper, *Poverty of Historicism,* p. vii.
14. Kuran, "Inevitability," p. 1528.
15. Hechter, "Symposium," p. 1520.
16. Kuran, "Inevitability," p. 1528.
17. Ibid.
18. Seymour M. Lipset, "Futurology," *Across the Board* (May 1980): 17.

19. Popper, *Poverty of Historicism*, p. 152.

20. Lipset, "Futurology," p. 24.

21. Robert Heilbroner, *The Worldly Philosophers* (New York: Touchstone, 1992), p. 322.

22. Karl Marx and Friedrich Engels, *The Communist Manifesto* (London: Penguin Books, 1848, republished in 1967), p. 94.

23. Heilbroner, *Worldly Philosophers*, p. 170.

24. Marx and Engels, *Manifesto*, p. 88.

25. Burnham P. Beckwith, *Ideas About the Future* (Palo Alto, Calif.: Beckwith, 1986), p. 63.

26. Marx and Engels, *Manifesto*, p. 89.

27. Frederic L. Bender, *Karl Marx: The Communist Manifesto* (New York: Norton, 1988), p. 66.

28. Heilbroner, *Worldly Philosophers*, p. 161.

29. Marx and Engels, *Manifesto*, p. 34.

30. I. F. Clarke, "All Our Yesterdays," *Future* (April 1992): 251.

31. Edward Bellamy, *Looking Backward from the Year 2000* (Mattituck, N.Y.: Amereon Ltd., 1887), p. 273.

32. Ibid., p. 217.

33. Ibid., p. 176.

34. Ibid., p. 5.

35. Ibid., p. 68.

36. Ibid., p. 43.

37. Ibid., p. 70.

38. Ibid., p. 167.

39. Joseph J. Corn, *Imagining Tomorrow* (Boston: MIT Press, 1987), p. 114.

40. I. F. Clarke, "The Future Is Not What It Used to Be," *Futures* (September 1993): 794, and "Rediscovering Original Sins," *Futures* (May 1992): 390.

41. Karel Capek, *Rossum's Universal Robots* (New York: Doubleday Page & Co., 1930), p. 199.

42. Ibid., pp. 202, 203.

43. Ibid., p. 212.

44. Ibid., p. 230.

45. Ibid., p. 242.

46. Joseph F. Coates and Jennifer Jarratt, "Exploring the Future: A 200-Year Record of Expanding Competence," *Annals of the American Academy* (July 1992): p. 12.

47. Ibid., p. 140.

48. Beckwith, *Ideas*, p. 85.

49. I. F. Clarke, "Factor Four: The Assessment of Coming Things," *Futures* (October 1991): 866.

50. I. F. Clarke, "Factor Three: Science and Fiction," *Futures* (July–August 1991): 644.

51. I. F. Clarke, "20th Century Future-Think," *Futures* (April 1992).

52. John Cote Dahlinger and France Spartz Leighton, *The Secret Life of Henry Ford* (Indianapolis: Bobbs-Merrill, 1978), p. 171.

53. John Maynard Keynes, *The Economic Consequences of the Peace* (New York: Harcourt, Brace and Howe, 1920), p. 226.

54. Ibid., p. 228.

55. Ibid., p. 251.

56. Sigmund Freud, *The Future of an Illusion* (New York: Norton, 1928), p. 38.

57. Ibid., p. 53.

58. Winston Churchill, "Fifty Years Hence," *Popular Mechanics* (March 1932): 390.

59. Ibid., p. 395.

60. Ibid., p. 396.

61. Ibid., p. 397.

62. *The Art of Forecasting* (Washington, D.C.: World Future Society, 1993), p. 4.

63. Daniel Bell, *The Coming of Post-Industrial Society* (New York: Basic Books, 1973), p. 373.

64. Ibid., p. 378.

65. Ibid., p. 376.

66. Ibid., pp. 246, 247.

67. Ibid., pp. 26, 33.

68. Ibid., p. 43.

69. Ibid., p. 33.

70. U.S. Department of Commerce, *Statistical Abstract of the United States* (Washington, D.C.: Government Printing Office, 1996).

71. Alvin Toffler, *The Third Wave* (New York: Morrow, 1980), p. 26.

72. Ibid.

73. Ibid., p. 27.

74. Beckwith, *Ideas,* p. 253.

75. Paul Gray, "Inside the Minds of Gingrich's Gurus," *Time,* January 23, 1995, p. 20.

76. John Naisbitt, *John Naisbitt's Trend Letter* (New York: Global Network, 1995), cover.

77. John Naisbitt, *Megatrends* (New York: Warner Books, 1982), p. 13.

78. Ibid., p. 18.

79. Ibid., p. 74.

80. Ibid., p. 217.

81. Ibid., p. 46.

82. Ibid., p. 87.

83. Ibid., p. 97.

84. Ibid., p. 197.

85. Ibid., p. 244.

86. Ruth Shalit, "The Business of Faith," *New Republic,* April 18, 1994. p. 23; Andrew Serwer, "Trend Surfing in the U.S.A.," *Fortune,* April 15, 1965, p. 14; and Annetta Miller, "Putting Faith in Trends," *Newsweek,* June 15, 1987, p. 46.

87. Shalit, "Business of Faith," p. 23.

88. "Talk of the Town," *New Yorker,* July 7, 1986, p. 22.

89. Shalit, "Business of Faith," p. 24.

90. Faith Popcorn, *The Popcorn Report: Faith Popcorn on the Future of Your Company, Your World, Your Life* (Garden City, N.Y.: Doubleday, 1991), p. 27.

91. Ibid., p. 86.

92. Mark Van Putten, "Values That Americans Hold Dearly," *National Wildlife* (December–January 1996): 8.

93. Ibid.

94. Jan Larson, "Burning Issues," *American Demographics* (November 1996): 44.

95. Chester E. Finn, Jr., "Will They Ever Learn," *National Review,* May 29, 1995, p. 27.

96. Patricia Edmonds, "Morality Issues Matter More, Especially in This Election Year," *USA Today,* August 6, 1996, p. 4A.

97. Popcorn, *Popcorn Report,* p. 188.

98. Ibid., p. 58.

99. Ibid., p. 25.

100. Joe Treen, "Search for Tomorrow," *People Weekly,* December 2, 1991, p. 109.

101. Shalit, "Business of Faith," p. 23.

102. Max Dublin, *Futurehype: The Tyranny of Prophecy* (New York: Dutton, 1991), p. 16.

103. Popper, *Popcorn Report,* Dedication.

104. Lipset, "Futurology," p. 23.

105. James M. McPherson, *Battle Cry of Freedom* (New York: Ballantine Books, 1988), p. 48.

106. George Orwell, *1984* (New York: Signet Classic, 1950), p. 175.

107. Lipset, "Futurology," p. 17.

108. Popper, *Poverty of Historicism,* p. 343.

CHAPTER 8: CORPORATE CHAOS

1. Henry Mintzberg, *The Rise and Fall of Strategic Planning* (New York: Free Press, 1994), p. 117.

2. Aaron Wildavsky, *The Politics of the Budgetary Process,* 2d ed. (Boston: Little, Brown, 1974), p. 186.

3. Brian K. Boyd, "Strategic Planning and Financial Performance: A Meta-Analytical Review," *Journal of Management Studies* (July 1991): 353.

4. Wildavsky, *Politics,* p. 205.

5. Mintzberg, *Rise and Fall,* pp. 200, 205.

6. Ibid., p. 97.

7. "The New Breed of Strategic Planner," *Business Week,* September 17, 1984, p. 63.

8. Ibid., p. 65.

9. Steven P. Schnaars, "Where Forecasters Go Wrong," *Across the Board* (December 1989): 38.

10. James G. March, *A Primer on Decision Making* (New York: Free Press, 1994), p. 9.

11. According to the *Hurlbert Financial Digest's* July 1996 LT Performance Ratings, the two newsletters it tracks that make buy and sell suggestions according to the number of shares bought and sold by corporate outsiders and reported to the Securities and Exchange Commission did not outperform the S&P 500 market index throughout the entire period that *Hurlbert Financial Digest* tracked them. Over the ten years that *Hurlbert* has tracked *The Insiders* (ending July 1996), it produced an average annual return of 12.6 percent, while the S&P 500 Index yielded 13.8 percent; and over the three years that *Hurlbert* has tracked *Vickers Insiders' Portfolio* (ending July 1996), it produced an average annual return of 14.3 percent, while the S&P 500 Index yielded 17.2 percent.

12. Michael D. McMaster, *The Intelligence Advantage* (Boston: Butterworth-Heinemann, 1996), p. xx.

13. P. Ranganath Nayak and John M. Ketteringham, *Break-Throughs* (New York: Rawson Associates, 1986), p. 349.

14. Niccolò Machiavelli, *The Prince* (New York: Bantam Books, 1981), p. 41.

15. Peter M. Senge, *The Fifth Discipline; The Art and Practice of the Learning Organization* (Garden City, N.Y.: Currency Doubleday, 1990), p. 63.

16. Nayak and Ketteringham, *Break-Throughs,* pp. 343, 357, 358.

17. Margaret J. Wheatley, *Leadership and the New Science* (San Francisco: Berrett-Koehler Publishers, 1992), p. 43.

18. Peter F. Drucker, *Management: Tasks, Responsibilities, Practices* (New York: Harper Business, 1973), pp. 507, 508.

19. Martin L. Gimpl and Stephen R. Dakin, "Management and Magic," *California Management Review* (Fall 1984): 125.

20. Michael E. Porter, *Competitive Strategy; Techniques for Analyzing Industries and Competitors* (New York: Free Press, 1980), p. 152.

21. Thomas J. Peters and Robert H. Waterman, Jr., *In Search of Excellence* (New York: Harper & Row, 1982), p. 292.

22. "Who's Excellent Now?" *Business Week,* November 5, 1984, p. 77.

23. Joseph B. White, "The Next Big Thing," *Wall Street Journal,* November 26, 1996, p. 1.

24. John Byrne, "Strategic Planning," *Business Week,* August 26, 1996, p. 46.

25. Ibid.

26. Gary Hamel and C. K. Prahalad, *Competing for the Future* (Boston: Harvard Business School Press, 1994), p. 79.

27. "The Vision Thing," *Economist,* September 3, 1994, p. 67.

28. Senge, *Fifth Discipline,* p. 290.

29. James G. March, "Footnotes to Organizational Change," *Administrative Science Quarterly* 26 (1981): 563.

30. Nayak and Ketteringham, *Break-Throughs,* p. 349.

31. March, "Footnotes," p. 564.

32. Nayak and Ketteringham, *Break-Throughs,* p. 343.

33. Ibid., pp. 346, 349.

34. Mintzberg, *Rise and Fall,* p. 287.

35. Nayak and Ketteringham, *Break-Throughs,* pp.345, 348, 357, 358.

36. Mintzberg, *Rise and Fall,* p. 180.

37. Ibid., p. 321.

38. Michael Rycraft, *The Cambridge Encyclopedia of Space* (Cambridge: Cambridge University Press, 1990), p. 55.

39. John Byrne, "Strategic Planning," *Business Week,* August 26, 1996, p. 48.

40. Drucker, *Management,* p. 125.

41. Ralph D. Stacey, *Managing the Unknowable* (San Francisco: Jossey-Bass, 1992), p. 99.

42. Robert J. Kriegel, *If It Ain't Broke . . . Break It!* (New York: Warner Books, 1991), p. 273.

43. Wheatley, *Leadership,* p. 95.

44. Drucker, *Management,* p. 77.

45. Wheatley, *Leadership,* p. 95.

46. Kriegel, *If It Ain't Broke,* p. 42.

47. Wheatley, *Leadership,* p. 116.

48. Stephen E. Ambrose, *D-Day* (New York: Simon & Schuster, 1994), p. 25.

49. Ibid.

50. Ibid., p. 579.

51. Ibid.

52. Richard C. Whiteley, *The Customer-Driven Company* (Reading, Mass.: Addison-Wesley, 1991), p. 15.

53. James P. Womack, Daniel T. Jones, and Daniel Roos, *The Machine That Changed the World* (New York: Harper Perennial, 1990), p. 99.

54. Wheatley, *Leadership,* p. 113.

55. Lee Sproul and Sara Kiesler, *Connections: New Ways of Working in the Networked Organization* (Cambridge, Mass.: MIT Press, 1991), p. ix.

56. Arie P. De Geus, "Planning as Learning," *Harvard Business Review* (March–April 1988): 71.

57. Thomas J. Watson, Jr., "The Greatest Capitalist in History," *Fortune,* August 31, 1987, p. 28.

58. De Geus, "Planning," p. 73.

59. Anne B. Fisher, "Is Long-Range Planning Worth It?" *Fortune,* April 23, 1990, p. 284.

60. Lee Smith, "New Ideas from the Army," *Fortune,* September 19, 1994, p. 204.

61. Mintzberg, *Rise and Fall,* p. 256.

62. Thomas Peters and Nancy Austin, *A Passion for Excellence* (New York: Random House, 1985), p. 8.

63. March, "Footnotes," p. 575.

64. Ibid.

65. Senge, *Fifth Discipline,* p. 64.

66. Machiavelli, *Prince,* p. 39, 62.

67. Michael D. Cohen and James G. March, *Leadership and Ambiguity* (Boston: Harvard Business School Press, 1974), p. 208.

68. Ibid., pp. 209, 215.

69. John Bartlett and Justin Kaplan, *Bartlett's Familiar Quotations* (Boston: Little, Brown, 1992), p. 575.

70. Roy Rowan, *The Intuitive Manager* (Boston: Little, Brown, 1986), pp. 4, 169.

CHAPTER 9: THE CERTAINTY OF LIVING IN AN UNCERTAIN WORLD

1. *Scientific American* (December 1992): 52.

2. William Robbins, "Midwest Quake Is Predicted; Talk Is Real," *New York Times,* August 20, 1990, p. 10.

3. Ibid.

4. James Randi, *The Mask of Nostradamus* (New York: Charles Scribner's Sons, 1990), p. 33.

5. V. J. Hewitt and Peter Lorie, *Nostradamus, The End of the Millennium* (New York: Simon & Schuster, 1991), p. 106.

6. William Robbins, "In Quake Zone, a Forecast Sets Off Tremors," *New York Times,* December 1, 1990, p. 11.

7. Richard A. Kerr, "The Lessons of Dr. Browning," *Science* (August 1991): 622.

8. John R. Gribbin and Steven H. Plagemann, *The Jupiter Effect* (London: Macmillan, 1974), p. 105.

9. John R. Gribbin and Steven H. Plagemann, *The Jupiter Effect Reconsidered* (New York: Vintage Books, 1982), p. xiii.

10. Christopher C. French, Mandy Fowler, Katy McCarthy, and Debbie Peers, "Belief in Astrology," *Skeptical Inquirer* (Winter 1991): 166.

Bibliography

"The Accuracy of World Economic Outlook Projections for the Major Industrial Countries." *World Economic Outlook,* May 1992.

Ahlburg, Dennis, and Land, Kenneth. "Population Forecasting: Guest Editors' Introduction." *International Journal of Forecasting* 8 (1992): 289–298.

Ahlburg, Dennis A., and Vaupel, James W. "Alternative Projections of the U.S. Population." *Demography* (November 1990): 639.

Altany, David. "New Jobs for the Number Crunchers." *Industry Week,* April 20, 1992, p. 76.

Ambrose, Stephen E. *D-Day.* New York: Simon & Schuster, 1994.

American Meteorological Society. "Policy Statement: Weather Forecasting." *Bulletin of the American Meteorological Society* (August 1991): 1275.

American Meteorological Society. "Policy Statement on Global Warming." *Bulletin of the American Meteorological Society,* January 1, 1991, p. 57.

Anderson, L. McTier. "The 'Dismal Science' Revisited." *Business Horizons* (May–June 1992): 3–5.

"Answers to Commonly Asked Questions." *Value Line Selection and Opinion,* April 28, 1995, p. 8117.

"Apocalypse Soonish." *Economist,* June 2, 1990, pp. 79–80.

The Art of Forecasting. Washington, D.C.: World Future Society, 1993.

Arthur, W. Brian. "Positive Feedbacks in the Economy." *Scientific American* (February 1990): 92–99.

Asimov, Isaac. *Future Days.* New York: Random House, 1970.

Bailey, Ronald. "Them That Can, Do, Them That Can't, Forecast." *Forbes,* December, 26, 1988, pp. 94–100.

Barnston, Anthony G., and Livezey, Robert E. "The Probability of Correct Climate Forecasting in the Absence of Any Forecasting Skill." *Bulletin of the American Meteorological Society* (July 1985): 847–848.

Barreby, David. "Chaos Hits Wall Street." *Discover* (March 1993): 76–84.

Barrett, Patrick. "The Good and the Bad Die Young." *Marketing,* July 11, 1996, p. 16.

Bartlett, John, and Kaplan, Justin. *Bartlett's Familiar Quotations.* Boston: Little, Brown, 1992.

Batchelor, Roy A., and Dua, Pami. "Forecaster Ideology, Forecasting Technique, and the Accuracy of Economic Forecasts." *International Journal of Forecasting* (June 1990): 3–10.

————. "Product Differentiation in the Economic Forecasting Industry." *International Journal of Forecasting* (1990): 311–316.

Batra, Ravi. *The Great Depression of 1990*. New York: Simon & Schuster, 1987.

Beckwith, Burnham P. *Ideas About the Future*. Palo Alto, Calif.: Beckwith, 1986.

Bell, Daniel. *The Coming of Post-Industrial Society*. New York: Basic Books, 1973.

Bellamy, Edward. *Looking Backward 2000–1887*. Mattituck, NY: Amereon Ltd., 1887.

Belongia, Michael. *Are Economic Forecasts by Government Agencies Biased? Accurate?* St. Louis: Federal Reserve Bank of St. Louis, November–December 1988.

Bender, Frederic L. *Karl Marx: The Communist Manifesto*. New York: Norton, 1988.

Berkowitz, Stephen A.; Finney, Louis D.; and Logue, Dennis E. *The Investment Performance of Corporate Pension Plans—Why They Do Not Beat the Market Regularly*. New York: Quorum Books, 1988.

Black, Fisher. "Yes, Virginia, There Is Hope: Tests of the Value Line Ranking System." *Financial Analysts Journal* (September–October 1973): 10–14.

Bloom, David E., and Glied, Sherry. "Projecting the Number of New AIDS Cases in the United States." *International Journal of Forecasting* 8 (1992): 339–365.

Bonar, James. *Malthus and His Work*. New York: Augustus Kelley, 1967.

Bowonder, B., and Miyake, T. "Technology Forecasting in Japan." *Futures* (September 1993): 757–775.

Boyd, Bryan K. "Strategic Planning and Financial Performance: A Meta-Analytical Review." *Journal of Management Studies* (July 1991): 353–374.

Brealey, Richard A. "The Character of Earnings Changes." Paper presented to the Seminar on the Analysis of Security Prices, University of Chicago, May 1967.

Brody, Herbert. "Great Expectations: Why Technology Predictions Go Awry." *Technology Review* (July 1991): 39–44.

Brooks, Harold. "The Possible Future Role of Humans in Weather Forecasting." Internet home page.

Bureau of the Census. *Current Population Reports*, July 9, 1947.

————. *Current Population Reports*, March 1994.

————. *Current Population Reports and Population Estimates*, February 14, 1949.

————. *Projections of the Population of the United States, By Age and Sex: 1972 to 2020* (Washington, D.C.: U.S. Government Printing Office, 1972).

Burns, Greg. "The New Economics of Food." *Business Week*, May 20, 1996, pp. 78–84.

Byrne, John. "Strategic Planning." *Business Week*, August 26, 1996, pp. 46–52.

Capek, Karel. *Rossum's Universal Robots*. New York: Doubleday Page & Co., 1930.

Carson, Rachel. *Silent Spring*. Boston: Houghton Mifflin, 1962.

Cassidy, John. "The Decline of Economics." *New Yorker*, December 2, 1996, pp. 50–60.

Casti, John L. *Complexification*. New York: Harper Perennial, 1995.

Catalano, Peter. "Hurricane Alert!" *Popular Science* (September 1995): 65–70.

Caulkin, Simon. "Chaos Inc." *Across the Board* (July–August 1995): 33–36.

Chandler, Russell. *Doomsday: The End of the World.* Ann Arbor, Mich.: Servant Publications, 1993.

"Chaos—Predictions That Arcane Mathematics Can Give the Bulls and Bears a Run for the Money." *Discover* (March 1993): 82.

"Chaos Under a Cloud." *Economist,* January 13, 1996, p. 69.

Churchill, Winston. "Fifty Years Hence." *Popular Mechanics* (March 1932): 390–397.

Clarke, I. F. "All Our Yesterdays." *Futures* (April 1992): 251–259.

———. "Factor Four: The Assessment of Coming Things." *Futures* (October 1991): 860–867.

———. "Factor Three: Science and Fiction." *Futures* (July–August 1991): 637–644.

———. "The Future Is Not What It Used to Be." *Futures* (September 1993): 792–800.

———. *The Pattern of Expectation.* New York: Basic Books, 1979.

———. "Rediscovering Original Sins." *Futures* (May 1992): 388–396.

———. "20th Century Future-Think," *Futures* (April 1992).

Coates, Joseph F., and Jarratt, Jennifer. "Exploring the Future: A 200-Year Record of Expanding Competence." *The Annals of the American Academy* (July 1992): 12–17.

———. "Why Forecasts Fail." *Research Technology Management* (July–August 1993): 4–5.

Cohen, Michael D., and March, James G. *Leadership and Ambiguity.* Boston: Harvard Business School Press, 1974.

Cole, H. S. D.; Freeman, Christopher; Hahoda, Marie; and Pavitt, L. L. R. *Thinking About the Future: A Critique of "The Limits to Growth."* London: Sussex University Press, 1973.

Coleman, James. "Comment on Kuran and Collins." *American Journal of Sociology* (May 1995): 1616–1619.

"A Conversation with Benjamin Graham." *Financial Analysts Journal* (September–October 1976): 20–23.

Corn, Joseph J. *Imagining Tomorrow.* Cambridge, Mass.: MIT Press, 1987.

Cragg, J. C., and Malkiel, Burton G. "The Consensus and Accuracy of Some Predictions of the Growth of Corporate Earnings." *Journal of Finance* (March 1968): 67–84.

Dahlinger, John Cote, and Leighton, France Spartz. *The Secret Life of Henry Ford.* Indianapolis: Bobbs-Merrill, 1978.

De Geus, Arie P. "Planning as Learning." *Harvard Business Review* (March–April 1988): 70–74.

Del Sesto, Stephen L. "Wasn't the Future of Nuclear Energy Wonderful?" in Joseph J. Corn, *Imagining Tomorrow.* Cambridge, Mass.: MIT Press, 1987.

Diamond, Jared. "Easter's End." *Discover* (August 1995): 63–69.

"Disagreeing About the Consensus." *Economist,* July 27, 1991, p. 61.

Dorfman, Daniel. "'Go Go Garz' Puts on the Breaks." *USA Today,* July 25, 1994, p. 5B.

Doswell III, Charles A. "More Thoughts on the Future of Weather Forecasting." Internet home page.

Douglas, Martin. "Money and Metaphysics: New-Age Wall Street." *New York Times,* January 30, 1994, p. C-1.

Dreman, David. "Chronically Clouded Crystal Balls." *Forbes,* October 11, 1993, p. 178.

———. "Flawed Forecasts." *Forbes,* December 9, 1991, p. 342.

Dror, Israel. "The Process of Technology Evolution, Multi-technology as the Driving Force." *Technology Forecasting and Social Change* 44 (1993): 49–58.

Drucker, Peter F. *Management: Tasks, Responsibilities, Practices.* New York: Harper-Business, 1973.

———. *The Practice of Management.* New York: Harper & Row, 1954.

Dublin, Max. *Futurehype: The Tyranny of Prophecy.* New York: Dutton, 1991.

Duin, Nancy, and Sutcliffe, Jenny. *A History of Medicine.* New York: Simon & Schuster, 1992.

Dunlop, S., and Wilson, F. *The Larousse Guide to Weather Forecasting.* New York: Larousse and Co., 1982.

Economic Report of the President. Washington, D.C.: U.S. Government Printing Office, 1996.

Edmonds, Patricia. "Morality Issues Matter More, Especially in This Election Year." *USA Today,* August 6, 1996, pp. 4A–5A.

Ehrlich, Paul R. *The Population Bomb.* New York: Ballantine Books, 1968.

Encyclopedia of Careers and Vocational Guidance. Chicago: J. G. Ferguson Publishing Co., 1993.

Eng, William F. *The Technical Analysis of Stocks, Options and Futures,* Chicago: Probus Publishing, 1988.

Ephron, Larry. *The End: The Imminent Ice Age and How We Can Stop It!* Berkeley, Calif.: Celestial Arts,1988.

Fama, Eugene F. "Efficient Capital Markets: A Review of Theory and Empirical Work." *Journal of Finance* 25 (1970): 383–417.

"Finding Fault: Can Seismologists Predict Earthquakes?" *Scientific American* (December 1992): 52.

Finn Jr., Chester E. "Will They Ever Learn?" *National Review,* May 29, 1995, pp. 26–27.

Fisher, Anne B. "Is Long-Range Planning Worth It?" *Fortune,* April 23, 1990, pp. 281–284.

Fondiller, David S. "Repent, Sinners." *Forbes,* June 19, 1995, p. 240.

Forrester, Jay. "Economic Conditions Ahead, Understanding the Kondratieff Wave." *Futurist* (June 1995): 16–20.

Frederic, L. Bender, *Karl Marx: The Communist Manifesto*. New York: W. W. Norton, 1988.

French, Christopher; Fowler, Mandy; McCarthy, Katy; and Peers, Debbie. "Belief in Astrology." *Skeptical Inquirer* (Winter 1991): 166–172.

Freud, Sigmund. *The Future of an Illusion*. New York: Norton, 1928.

Fridson, Martin S. *Delusions and Confusion*. New York: Wiley, 1996.

Galant, Debbie. "Financial Follies," *Institutional Investor* (January 1995): 139–140.

Galbraith, John Kenneth. *The Great Crash of 1929*. Boston: Houghton Mifflin, 1954.

Gallup, George H., and Newport, Frank. "Belief in Paranormal Phenomena Among Adult Americans." *Skeptical Inquirer* 15(2) (Winter 1991): 137–148.

"Garbage In, Garbage Out." *Economist,* June 3, 1995, p. 70.

Gilbert, Daniel. "How Mental Systems Believe." *American Psychologist* (February 1991): 107.

Gilman, Donald L. "Long-Range Forecasting: The Present and the Future." *Bulletin of the American Meteorological Society* (February 1985): 159–163.

Gimpl, Martin L., and Dakin, Stephen R. "Management and Magic." *California Management Review* (Fall 1984): 125–136.

Gleick, James. *Chaos: Making a New Science*. New York: Penguin Books, 1987.

"The Granville Market Letter." *Financial World,* March 1, 1981, pp. 44–45.

Gray, Paul. "Inside the Minds of Gingrich's Gurus." *Time,* January 23, 1995, pp. 20–21.

Gray, William. *Early August Updated Forecast of Atlantic Seasonal Hurricane Activity for 1995*. Fort Collins, Colo.: Colorado State University, August 4, 1995.

Greider, William. *Secrets of the Temple*. New York: Simon & Schuster, 1987.

Gribbin, John R., and Plagemann, Steven H. *The Jupiter Effect*. London: Macmillan, 1974.

———. *The Jupiter Effect Reconsidered*. New York: Vintage Books, 1982.

Hale, Judson. *The Best of "The Old Farmer's Almanac."* New York: Random House, 1992.

Hamel, Gary, and Prahalad, C. K. *Competing for the Future*. Boston: Harvard Business School Press, 1994.

Hechter, Michael. "Symposium on Prediction in the Social Sciences." *American Journal of Sociology* (May 1995): 1520–1527.

Hedderson, John. "Theories of Fertility Norms: A Consolidation." *Population Review* (January 1980): 32–36.

Heilbroner, Robert. *The Worldly Philosophers*. New York: Touchstone, 1992.

Hewitt, V. J., and Lorie, Peter. *Nostradamus: The End of the Millennium*. New York: Simon & Schuster, 1991.

Hoyt, Douglas H. "The Probability of Correct Climate Forecasts in the Absence of Any Forecasting Skill." *Bulletin of the American Meteorological Society* (October 1983): 1172–1174.

"How Accurate Are Economic Outlook Projections?" *OECD Economic Outlook* (June 1993).

Huberman, Gur, and Kandel, Shmuel. "Market Efficiency and Value Line's Record." *Journal of Business* 63(2) (1990): 187–216.

Hurlbert Financial Digest's LT Performance Ratings. July 1996.

Hurlbert, Mark. "Proof of Pudding." *Forbes,* December 10, 1990, p. 316.

"Hurricane Detection, Tracking, and Forecasting." *Bulletin of the American Meteorological Society* (July 1993): 1377.

Hutchins, Robert. "A Bill for the Development and Control of Atomic Energy, 79th Congress, 2nd Session, 1946." Washington, D.C.: U.S. Government Printing Office, 1947.

Iacovelli, Debi. "Inside the Hurricane Center." *Weatherwise* (June–July 1994): 28–32.

"Insider Trading." *Business Week,* December 12, 1994, pp. 71–82.

Ippolito, Richard A. "Efficiency with Costly Information: A Study of Mutual Fund Performance, 1965–1984." *Quarterly Journal of Economics* (February 1989): 1–23.

Jacobs, Madeline. "Yesterday's Predictions." *Futurist* (February 1985): 42–45.

Jacoby, Jeff. "Riches Rain on Doctor Doom." *Boston Globe,* February 2, 1995, p. 13.

Jensen, Michael C. "Problems in Selection of Security Portfolios: The Performance of Mutual Funds in the Period 1945–1964." *Journal of Finance* 23(2) (1968): 389–415.

Jeremiah, David, with Carlson, C. C. *Escape the Coming Night: An Electrifying Tour of Our World as It Races Towards Its Final Days.* Dallas: Word, 1990.

Kadlec, Daniel. "Garzarelli Wears Celebrity Well." *USA Today,* February 2, 1994, p. 3B.

———. "Market Plunge Caught Strategists Off Guard." *USA Today,* April 7, 1994, p. 3B.

———. "World-Class Market Forecasts Questioned." *USA Today,* September 3, 1994, p. 3B.

Kahn, Herman, and Wiener, Anthony J. *The Year 2000: A Framework for Speculation on the Next Thirty Years.* New York: Macmillan, 1967.

Kaplan, Robert S., and Weil, Roman. "Kaplan and Weil Rejoinder." *Financial Analysts Journal* (September–October 1973): 14.

Kellert, Stephen H. *In the Wake of Chaos.* Chicago: University of Chicago Press, 1993.

Kelly, Kevin. "Cracking Wall Street." *Wired Online* (1993): article 2.07.

Kerr, Richard A. "The Lessons of Dr. Browning." *Science* (August 1991): 622.

———. "Upgrade of Storm Warnings Paying Off." *Science,* October 15, 1993, p. 331.

Keyfitz, Nathan. "On Future Population." *Journal of the American Statistical Association* (June 1972): 347–362.

————. "The Limits of Population Forecasting." *Population and Development Review* (December 1981): 579–593.

Keynes, John Maynard. *The Economic Consequences of the Peace.* New York: Harcourt, Brace and Howe, 1920.

Kleinknecht, Alfred. *Innovation Patterns in Crisis and Prosperity.* New York: St. Martin's Press, 1987.

Koretz, Gene. "A D+ for Dismal Scientists?" *Business Week,* September 25, 1995, p. 25.

Kriegel, Robert J. *If It Ain't Broke . . . Break It!* New York: Warner Books, 1991.

Kuran, Timur. "The Inevitability of Future Revolutionary Surprises." *American Journal of Sociology* (May 1995): 1528–1541.

Kuttner, Robert. "The Poverty of Economics." *Atlantic Monthly* (February 1985): 74–84.

Laderman, Jeffrey M. "But What Have You Done for Us Lately." *Business Week,* July 26, 1993, p. 71.

————. "What Made Elaine Shout 'Sell'." *Business Week,* August 12, 1996, p. 75.

Larson, Jan. "Burning Issues." *American Demographics* (November 1996): 43–47.

Lee, Albert. *Weather Wisdom: Facts and Folklore of Weather Forecasting.* New York: Congdon & Weed, 1976.

Lee, Cheng F. "Value Line Investment Survey Rank Changes and Beta Coefficients." *Financial Analysts Journal* (September–October 1987): 70–71.

Lemonick, Michael. "The Ice Age Cometh?" *Time,* January 31, 1994, pp. 79–81.

Levary, Reuven R., and Han, Dongchui. "Choosing a Technological Forecasting Method." *Industrial Management* (January–February): 14–18.

Lewinsohn, Richard. *Science, Prophecy and Prediction.* New York: Harper & Brothers, 1961.

Lewis, Kate Bohner. "Take a Bow Lee Iacocca." *Forbes,* November 21, 1994, p. 198.

Linden, Dana Weschler. "Dismal Days for the Dismal Science." *Forbes,* April 22, 1996, p. 65.

Lipset, Seymour Martin. "Futurology." *Across the Board* (March 1980): 17–26.

Little, Ian M. D., and Rayner, A. C. *Higgledy Piggledy Growth Again.* Oxford: Basil Blackwell, 1966.

Livezey, Robert E. "Variability of Skill of Long-Range Forecasts and Implications for Their Use and Value." *Bulletin of the American Meteorological Society* (March 1990): 300–309.

Lorie, James, and Hamilton, Mary. *The Stock Market—Theories and Evidence.* Homewood, Ill.: Richard D. Irwin, 1973.

Lynch, Peter. *One Up on Wall Street.* New York: Penguin Books, 1989.

Machiavelli, Niccolò. *The Prince.* New York: Bantam Books, 1981 (1st ed., 1513).

Maclaurin, Rupert W. *Invention in the Radio Industry.* New York: Macmillan, 1949.

Magnusson, Paul. "Need an Economic Forecast." *Business Week,* September 13, 1993, p. 38.

Maital, Shlomo. "Caution: Oracles at Work." *Across the Board.* (June 1993): 52–53.

Malkiel, Burton G. *A Random Walk Down Wall Street.* New York: Norton, 1990.

Malthus, Thomas Robert. *First Essay on Population.* London: Royal Economic Society, 1798.

March, James G. *A Primer on Decision Making.* New York: Free Press, 1994.

———. "Footnotes to Organizational Change." *Administrative Science Quarterly* (December 1981): 563–577.

Marcial, Gene G. *Secrets of the Street.* New York: McGraw-Hill, 1995.

"Market Plunge Caught Strategists Off Guard." *USA Today,* April 7, 1994, p. 3B.

Martin, Douglas. "Money and Metaphysics: New-Age Wall Street." *New York Times,* January 30, 1994, p. C-1.

Martin, James. *Future Developments in Telecommunications.* Englewood-Cliffs, N.J.: Prentice-Hall, 1977.

Martino, Joseph P. "Does the Kondratieff Wave Really Exist?" *Futurist* (February 1985): 23–25.

Marx, Karl, and Engels, Friedrich. *The Communist Manifesto.* London: Penguin Books, 1848. Republished in 1967.

McMaster, Michael D. *The Intelligence Advantage.* Boston: Butterworth-Heinemann, 1996.

McNees, Stephen. "An Assessment of the 'Official' Economic Forecasts." *New England Economic Review* (July–August 1995): 17–32.

———. "How Large Are Economic Forecast Errors?" *New England Economic Review* (July–August 1992): 25–33.

———. "The Uses and Abuses of 'Consensus' Forecasts." *Journal of Forecasting* (August 1991): 703–710.

McNees, Stephen K., and Ries, John. "The Track Record of Macroeconomic Forecasts." *New England Economic Review* (November–December 1983): p. 5–18.

McNeill, William H. *Plagues and Peoples.* New York: Anchor Press/Doubleday, 1976.

McPherson, James M. *Battle Cry of Freedom.* New York: Ballantine Books, 1988.

McWilliams, Gary. "The Farmers' Almanacs Start a Storm." *Business Week,* December 12, 1994, p. 48.

Meadows, Donella and Dennis, and Randers, Jorrgen. *Beyond the Limits.* Post Mills, Vt.: Chelsea Green Publishing Co., 1992.

———, Behrens III, William. *The Limits to Growth.* New York: Universe Books, 1970.

Militzer, Ken. "The Business Economist at Work: The Chief Economist at AT&T." *Business Economics* (January 1990): 42–46.

Miller, Annetta. "Putting Faith in Trends." *Newsweek,* June 15, 1987, pp. 46–47.

Mintzberg, Henry. *The Rise and Fall of Strategic Planning.* New York: Free Press, 1994.

Moore, Thomas. "Global Warming: A Boon for Humans and Other Animals." Internet article, March 20, 1995.

Morgan, W. Meade, and Curran, James W. "Acquired Immunodeficiency Syndrome: Current and Future Trends." *Public Health Reports* (September–October 1986): 459–464.

Morison, Samuel E. *The Oxford History of the American People.* New York: Oxford University Press, 1965.

Morris, Charles R. "It's Not the Economy, Stupid." *Atlantic Monthly* (July 1993): 49–62.

Naisbitt, John. *John Naisbitt's Trend Letter.* New York: Global Network, 1995.

———. *Megatrends.* New York: Warner Books,1982.

"Need an Economic Forecast: Maybe the I-Ching Can Help." *Economist* September, 13, 1993, p. 38.

Nayak, Rangantha, and Ketteringham, John M. *Break-Throughs.* New York: Rawson Associates, 1986.

Nelson, Charles R. "A Benchmark for the Accuracy of Econometric Forecasts of GNP." *Business Economics,* April 1, 1984, pp. 52–58.

Neumann, J. "Great Historical Events That Were Significantly Affected by the Weather." *Bulletin of the American Meteorological Society* (November 1975): 1167–1170.

Neumann, J., and Flohn, H. "Great Historical Events That Were Significantly Affected by the Weather: Part 8, Germany's War on the Soviet Union, 1941–1945." *Bulletin of the American Meteorological Society* (June 1987): 620.

"The New Breed of Strategic Planner." *Business Week,* September 17, 1984, pp. 62–66.

Nielsen, John. "5 Billion and Ticking." *Stanford* (March 1995): 44–51.

O'Hear, Anthony. *An Introduction to the Philosophy of Science.* Oxford: Oxford University Press, 1989.

Orwell, George. *1984.* San Diego: Harcourt Brace Jovanovich, 1949 (reprinted 1977).

Paddock, William and Paul. *Famine—1975! America's Decision: Who Will Survive?* Boston: Little, Brown, 1967.

Peters, Thomas, and Austin, Nancy. *A Passion for Excellence.* New York: Random House, 1985.

Peters, Thomas J., and Waterman, Jr., Robert H. *In Search of Excellence.* New York: Harper & Row, 1982.

Petersen, William. *Malthus.* Cambridge, Mass.: Harvard University Press, 1979.

Phelps, Charlotte. "Wives' Motives and Fertility." *Journal of Economic Behavior and Organization* 27 (1995): 49–67.

"Pick a Number," *Economist,* September, 13, 1992, p. 18.

Pindyck, Robert S., and Rubinfeld, Daniel L. *Econometric Models and Economic Forecasts.* New York: McGraw-Hill, 1976.

"Policy Statement." *Bulletin of the American Meteorological Society* (August 1991): 1275.

"Policy Statement: Hurricane Detection, Tracking, and Forecasting." *Bulletin of the American Meteorological Society* (July 1993):1377–1380.

"Policy Statement on Global Warming." *Bulletin of the American Meteorological Society*, January 1, 1991, pp. 57–59.

Popcorn, Faith. *The Popcorn Report: Faith Popcorn on the Future of Your Company, Your World, Your Life.* Garden City, N.Y.: Doubleday, 1991.

Popper, Karl R. *The Poverty of Historicism.* Boston: Beacon Press, 1957.

———. *The Open Universe: An Argument for Indeterminism.* Totowa, N.J.: Rowan and Littlefield, 1982.

Porter, Michael E. *Competitive Strategy; Techniques for Analyzing Industries and Competitors.* New York: Free Press, 1980.

Randi, James. *The Mask of Nostradamus.* New York: Charles Scribner's Sons, 1990.

Regenstein, Lewis. *How to Survive in America the Poisoned.* Washington, D.C.: Acropolis Books Ltd, 1982.

Richardson, Lewis F. *Weather Prediction by Numerical Process.* Cambridge: Cambridge University Press, 1922.

Robbins, William. "Midwest Quake Is Predicted; Talk Is Real." *New York Times,* August 20, 1990, p. 10.

———. "In Quake Zone, a Forecast Sets Off Tremors." *New York Times,* December 1, 1990, p. 11.

Rosenberg, Nathan. "Uncertainty and Technological Change." Paper presented at the Conference on Growth and Development, Stanford University, June 1994.

Ross, Philip E. "Show Me a Piece." *Forbes,* June 19, 1995, pp. 230–231.

Rowan, Roy. *The Intuitive Manager.* Boston: Little, Brown, 1986.

Rukeyser, William. "Pardon Me, But Is This Armageddon?" *Fortune,* February 6, 1995, pp. 84–85.

Rycraft, Michael. *The Cambridge Encyclopedia of Space.* Cambridge, U.K.: Cambridge University Press, 1990.

Salisbury, David. "His Beaker Runneth Over." *Stanford* (January–February 1997): 27–30.

Schlender, Brent. "Bill and Paul Talk." *Fortune,* October 2, 1995, pp. 75–86.

Schnaars, Steven P. *Megamistakes: Forecasting and the Myth of Rapid Technological Change.* New York: Free Press, 1989.

———. "Where Forecasters Go Wrong." *Across the Board* (December 1989): 38–45.

Senge, Peter M. *The Fifth Discipline; The Art and Practice of the Learning Organization.* New York: Currency Doubleday, 1990.

Serwer, Andrew. "Trend Surfing in the U.S.A." *Fortune,* April 15, 1965, p. 14.

Shalit, Ruth. "The Business of Faith." *New Republic,* April 18, 1994, pp. 23–29.

Sharf, Stephen. "Forget the Forecasters." *Ward's AutoWorld* (July 1989): 17.

Smith, Lee. "New Ideas from the Army." *Fortune,* September 19, 1994, pp. 203–206.

Smith, Stanley. "Tests of Forecast Accuracy and Bias for County Population Projections." *Journal of the American Statistical Association* (December 1987): 991–1003.

Smith, Stanley, and Sincich, Terry. "Forecasting State and Household Populations." *International Journal of Forecasting* 8 (1992): 495–508.

Sproul, Lee, and Kiesler, Sara. *Connections; New Ways of Working in the Networked Organization.* Cambridge, Mass: MIT Press, 1991.

Stacey, Ralph D. *Managing the Unknowable.* San Francisco: Jossey-Bass, 1992.

Stewart, Ian. *Does God Play Dice?* Cambridge, U.K.: Basil Blackwell, 1989.

Stewart, James B. "Calling the Crash: Pessimistic Predictions by Analyst at Shearson Make Her a Star." *Wall Street Journal,* October 28, 1987, p. 35.

Stickel, Scott E. "Reputation and Performance Among Security Analysts." *Journal of Finance* (December 1992): 1811–1836.

Stoto, Michael. "The Accuracy of Population Projections." *Journal of the American Statistical Association* (March 1983): 13–20.

Stross, Randall. *The Microsoft Way.* Reading, Mass.: Addison-Wesley, 1996.

Swidler, Steve, and Ketcher, David. "Economic Forecasts, Rationality, and the Processing of New Information over Time." *Journal of Money, Credit, and Banking* (February 1990): 65–76.

Thring, M. "A Robot in the House." In Nigel Calder, *The World in 1984.* Baltimore, Md.: Penguin Books, 1964.

Toffler, Alvin. *Future Shock.* New York: Random House, 1970.

Toffler, Alvin. *The Third Wave.* New York: Morrow, 1980.

Tough, Allan. "Intellectual Leaders in Futures Studies—A Study." *Futures* (May 1991): 436–438.

Townes, Charles H. "Quantum Electronics and Surprise in Development of Technology." *Science,* February 16, 1968, pp. 699–703.

Treen, Joe. "Search for Tomorrow." *People Weekly,* December 2, 1991, pp. 109–111.

Trotsky, Leon. *1909.* London: Penguin, 1971.

"Tucson or Bust." *Economist,* May 20, 1995, p. 29.

Uccelini, Louis W.; Kocin, Paul J.; Schneider, Russell S.; Stokols, Paul M.; and Dorr, Russell A. "Forecasting the 12–14 March 1993 Superstorm." *Bulletin of the American Meteorological Society* (February 1995): 183–199.

U.S. Congress. *The Congressional Budget Office: Responsibilities and Organization.* Washington, D.C.: U.S. Government Printing Office, 1976.

U.S. Department of Commerce. *Benefit-Cost Analysis for the Modernization and Associated Restructuring of the National Weather Service.* Washington, D.C.: Government Printing Office, 1992.

———. *Statistical Abstract of the United States.* Washington, D.C.: Government Printing Office, 1996.

U.S. Department of Health and Human Services. *HIV/AIDS Surveillance Report* (December 1994): 1–25.

U. S. House of Representatives, Committee on the Judiciary. *Impact of Illegal Immigration on Public Benefit Programs and to the American Labor Force.* Washington, D.C.: U.S. Government Printing Office, 1996.

Vaga, Tony. *Profiting from Chaos.* New York: McGraw-Hill, 1994.

Van Putten, Mark. "Values That Americans Hold Dearly." *National Wildlife* (December–January): 8.

"The Vision Thing." *Economist,* September 3, 1994, p. 67.

Von Hippel, Eric. *The Sources of Innovation.* Oxford: Oxford University Press, 1988.

Waldrop, Mitchell. *Complexity.* New York: Touchstone, 1992.

Watson Jr., Thomas J. "The Greatest Capitalist in History." *Fortune,* August 31, 1987, pp. 24–32.

Weaver, Warren. *Lady Luck: Theory of Probability.* Garden City, N.Y.: Anchor Books, 1963.

Weschler Linden, Dana. "Dismal Days for the Dismal Science." *Forbes,* April 22, 1996, p. 65.

"What Is a Meteorologist? A Professional Guideline." *Bulletin of the American Meteorological Society* (January 1991): 61.

Wheatley, Margaret. *Leadership and the New Science.* San Francisco: Berrett-Koehler Publishers, 1992.

White, Joseph B. "The Next Big Thing." *Wall Street Journal,* November 26, 1996, p. 1.

Whiteley, Richard C. *The Customer-Driven Company.* Reading, Mass.: Addison-Wesley Publishing, 1991.

"Who's Excellent Now?" *Business Week,* November 5, 1984, pp. 76–79.

Wildavsky, Aaron. *The Politics of the Budgetary Process.* 2d ed., Boston: Little, Brown, 1974.

Wolfe, David. "Why Marketing Executives Aren't Thinking Straight." *Advertising Age,* November 7, 1994, p. 34.

Womack, James P.; Jones, Daniel T.; and Roos, Daniel. *The Machine That Changed the World.* New York: Harper Perennial, 1990.

Wood, Richard A. *The Weather Almanac.* New York: Gale Research, 1996.

Woudenberg, Fred. "An Evaluation of Delphi." *Technological Forecasting and Social Change* (September 1991): 131–146.

Zarnowitz, Victor. "An Analysis of Annual and Multiperiod Quarterly Forecasts of Aggregate Income, Output, and Price Level." *Journal of Business* 52(1) (1979): 1–32.

Zarocostas, John. "Transport Sector Saves Millions with Weather Data, Experts Say." *Journal of Commerce,* October 17, 1994, p. 3B.

Index